THE HAIL MARY

THE HAIL MARY

A Verbal Icon of Mary

NICHOLAS AYO, C.S.C.

University of Notre Dame Press
Notre Dame   London

Library of Congress Cataloging-in-Publication Data

Ayo, Nicholas.
    The Hail Mary : a verbal icon of Mary / by Nicholas Ayo.
        p.   cm.
    Includes bibliographical references.
    ISBN 0-268-01101-X (alk. paper)
    1. Ave Maria.   2. Mary, Blessed Virgin, Saint—Cult.   3. Mary,
Blessed Virgin, Saint—Theology.   I. Title.
BX2175.A8A96   1994
242'.74—dc20   93-24743
                                                                                  CIP

∞ *The paper used in this publication meets the minimum requirements of*
the American National Standard for Information Sciences—Permanence
of Paper for Printed Library Materials, ANSI Z39.48-1984.

This book is dedicated to GENEVIEVE FRANCES COULON, my mother, and to HENRY NICHOLAS COULON and AGLAE GENEVIEVE RICHARD, my maternal grandparents whom I never knew, but from whom I received life and good faith.

CONTENTS

FOREWORD

This book treats the Ave Maria prayer as it is known today. In the scriptures of the New Testament, Mary's story is told in Greek. In the Middle Ages the praises of her life were sung in Latin. The Ave Maria was completed as we now know it in the late Middle Ages. What is known about this Marian prayer? What may be said about this text from the point of view of its language, shape, origin, development in history, biblical roots, church tradition, theology, the controversy surrounding it, and its rich mystery?

This book is a compendium study of the Ave Maria, a study historical and exegetical, critical and meditative. My hope is to say something about the fundamentals that pertain in an important way to an intelligent appreciation of the Hail Mary. Each line is examined word by word. Each phrase is analyzed in itself and in its relation to the other phrases. The Ave Maria has traditionally been divided into the evangelical tidings of Gabriel and of Elizabeth yoked together, and the Church prayer that addresses Mary as mother of God (*Theotokos*) and prays her to intercede for us poor sinners. These two groupings are studied both separately and in their interrelationship. The entire Hail Mary is situated in the context of Gospel faith. This overall review leads to the conclusion that these few words of Luke and of the Church community function as a summation of the understanding of Mary as the paradigm Christian. Using the resources of the church historian, the biblical exegete, the theological and literary critic, and the person of interior devotion and prayerful spirit, I try to write whatever might be said succinctly about the Ave Maria that would be helpful for an educated Christian of today. In short, this book is an omnibus study of a classic Christian prayer and a principal Marian devotion.

The Ave Maria will reward the study that I propose to give it. Most of the readers of this book will be familiar with the prayer, but might own they rarely have thought about it. We are called to love with all our soul, our heart, our body, and our *mind*. I want the reader to understand the Ave Maria, and not just to repeat its wonderful words without ever thinking about their roots. It is unlikely that those who pray the prayer and love its place in their spiritual life will have examined it so thoroughly. And yet, I propose to do just that and with the hope that the Hail Mary will thereby mean even more to all Christians, because it will be better appreciated when understood more deeply. The Jesus story and the Mary story are inevitably intertwined. The Easter story of the death and resurrection of Jesus Christ begins with the Christmas story of his conception and birth of the Virgin Mary. The birth and the death stories are the bookends of one life. The beginning of Mary's faith life in the Annunciation foretells her ending among the Christian disciples. We too await the fullness of the Holy Spirit in our lives, and we too hope to become what we already are—believers and disciples of Jesus Christ. What Mary became we too hope to be.

Most Catholic Christians are familiar with the Hail Mary from childhood. Whether in public devotion or in private piety, this ancient prayer has become a Christian psalm. The words might be changed as the words of any psalm might be, yet the Hail Mary has been prayed so often and for so long it has been canonized just as the psalms of old. Precisely because this prayer is so treasured in Christian tradition it deserves to be known with the same depth that we wish to know whatever and whomever we deeply love. With the hope that such a study endeavor will enrich the believer's appreciation of the Hail Mary I have written this book.

ACKNOWLEDGMENTS

The author would like to thank the many people who made this work possible. In particular I am grateful to the University of Notre Dame for assistance in ways innumerable in the accomplishment of this work. My gratitude to Our Lady's University begins in my undergraduate college education in the early 1950s and has continued off and on through the intervening years. In the work of translation in several languages I was assisted by Dino Cervigni, Daniel Sheerin, John Quinn, and Paul Beichner, C.S.C. William Facovec, S.M., at the Marian Library at the University of Dayton was especially helpful to me. Larry Cunningham of the Theology Department at Notre Dame and Phillip Sloan, Michael Crowe, Katherine Tillman, and Stephen Fallon of the Program of Liberal Studies encouraged me at times and in ways that are much appreciated. Edward O'Connor, C.S.C., and Robert Antonelli, C.S.C., have been of assistance with this or that problem. Among students at the University of Notre Dame I have been assisted by Ann Mariani, Hao Tran, and Marian Rukavina. To the unknown reader of the typescript in an early and miserable stage I owe an especial debt of gratitude. The criticism I then received changed the book so much for the better. And finally, I could not have finished this work without the generous help of the University of Notre Dame Press, and in particular I am grateful to John Ehmann and Margaret Gloster. Carole Roos has consistently improved my writing by her judicious suggestions of what to omit, how to rearrange, and her perspicacious editing of all the details of the text.

THE HAIL MARY

Hail Mary,
full of grace,
the Lord is with you.

Blessed are you among women,
and blessed is the fruit of your womb, Jesus.

Holy Mary,
mother of God,
pray for us sinners
now and at the hour of our death.
Amen.

A BRIEF OVERVIEW OF MARY

From the earliest commentaries about Mary, there arose two extreme positions about her role in Christian life. One might exaggerate the place of the mother of Jesus, or one might neglect its importance. The former group might argue that love excuses all excesses, and the latter might claim that after all she is just a woman and not a goddess. In the writing of Epiphanius (315–403), Bishop of Cyprus (Salamis), in the later part of the fourth century, one can already find the polarization of those who would maximize Mary and those who would minimize her. In his *Panarion*, generally known as the "Refutation of all Heresies" (*Haereses*), Epiphanius opposes both the Antidicomarianites (see Heresy 78), who reduced her role to an ordinary woman's and the Collyridians (see Heresy 79), who exaggerated her status in the Church. To the Antidicomarianites, who held Mary in no especial esteem and her life and death as no different from anyone else's, he writes: "If the Holy Virgin had died and was buried, her falling asleep would have been surrounded with honor; death would have found her pure, and her crown would have been a virginal one. Had she been martyred according to what is written: 'Thine own soul a sword shall pierce,' then would she shine gloriously among the martyrs, and her holy body would have been declared blessed; for by her, in truth, did light come to the world. Or it might be that she is still alive; for to God nothing is impossible, and he is able to do whatever he wills. As a matter of fact, there is no one who knows the end of Mary."[1] To the Collyridians, who were mostly women who practiced an exaggerated cult of Mary with overtones of the "magna mater" rituals of pagan antiquity, he writes: ". . . God came down from heaven, the Word clothed Himself with flesh from a holy Virgin, not, assuredly, that the Virgin should be adored, not to make

1

her god, not that we should offer sacrifice to her name, nor that, now after so many generations, women should once again be appointed priests. . . . Let Mary be held in honor, but let the Father, the Son, and the Holy Spirit be adored. Let no one adore Mary."[2]

In the recent Vatican Council, a well-debated vote was taken about the place of Mary in the council documents. Should a Mariological document by itself be draw up? Should the development of a fulsome position with regard to Mary, highlighted by the recent definition of the dogma of the Assumption in 1950, be pursued further? The council vote was very close, but Mary was given a place not to herself but within the document treating the Church. In short, the statements were given a context in which theology about Mary would be seen immediately as theology also about Mary within the Church, as part of the Church, and as situated within the larger concerns of the Church as the body of Christ. Subsequently, there was some lessening of Marian writings and popular devotion, but there is now a resurgence of both Catholic and Protestant interest in the Blessed Virgin Mary. Behind this developing comprehension of Mary there lies a renewed study of the scriptures in her regard, a stripping away of some preconceived and inaccurate readings of the infancy narratives in particular, and an appreciative discovery of Mary in the Gospels, who is seen anew as the paradigm of the disciple and believer, the woman of faith most of all, and Christian model for men and for women.

In the New Testament there are many theologies. The Christology of Luke emphasizes the Lordship of Jesus in his conception. The Christology of John suggests that the Word of God was from all eternity. Christianity is richer because we have four Gospel portraits of Jesus, each a true likeness, but with considerable differences in what features the writer wishes to underline or what objection to overcome. Paul's ecclesiology emphasizes freedom of spirit, whereas the pastoral epistles champion a structured hierarchical church order. The Christian community thought the canon of scripture should contain many viewpoints, provided the essentials of orthodoxy were maintained. The books in the New Testament passed the test of variety and orthodoxy. They leave us a rich heritage of ways to understand the mystery of Jesus Christ.

Similarly, there are at least two Mariologies, two ways of emphasizing the role of Mary in the mystery of Christ. High Mariology, or Mariology from above, emphasizes the privileges of Mary and her closeness to God. She is *Regina Coeli*, the queen of heaven. Parallels are drawn between the immaculate conception of Mary and the virginal conception of Jesus; the sinlessness of Mary and the sinlessness of Jesus; the dormition of Mary and the death and resurrection of Jesus; the assumption of Mary into heaven and the ascension of Jesus; the coronation of Mary and the seating of Jesus at the right hand of the Father. Low Mariology, or Mariology from below, emphasizes the humanity of Mary and her closeness to the human Jesus and to the disciples of Christ. She is one of them. Mary is within the Church. She is redeemed like one of us; she is in solidarity with all of humanity. She is *ancilla Domini*, servant-maiden of the Lord.

My approach in this book is mindful of the feminist and the ecumenical climate. It is aware of the shift in emphasis from a high Mariology to a low Mariology begun in *Lumen Gentium*, the Constitution on the Church, of Vatican II. Low Christology that emphasizes the humanity of Jesus has been explored in this century. A low ecclesiology that develops the ministry of all Christians in the Church is encouraged by several documents of Vatican II. Low theology, however, is not inevitably better than high; it is different. Low theologies may be fresher in our time and they may be more suitable to the Christian needs of the day. At some future date, the emphases and insights of this day will be found wanting and quite short of the fullness of truth. Other theologies will emerge with their own strengths and weaknesses. There may indeed be an overall development in this zig-zag course, but one ought never to believe that today's theology is the last word. A high Mariology may live to serve the faithful again, but it will be renewed and purified. Theologies do not die; they are transformed and then rediscovered.

A concern for a theology of Mary also arises because of a need on the part of all Christians to establish the truth. No Christian can afford to neglect the mother of Jesus. Who was this woman? What is Mary to be for the Christian? How are men and women to understand her, and in that wisdom pursue their own relationship to God? Mary is a blessed woman, who was at the heart of the intersection of the divine and the human in the incarnation of the Son of God. In her the mystery of life and death converge in the wonderful conception and in the transcendent resurrection of her Son. Around her the mysteries of human sexuality, of birth, of motherhood and parenting, of belief, and hope, and love are focused. Through the offspring of Mary the human race is delivered from the mortal burdens of human existence in this world, which for a time yet remains a vale of tears. The feminine in human nature and the feminine at the source of all life can be considered in her image. She suffers her innocent son put to death as so many other mothers have endured. She is only a young Jewish woman from a provincial town, and she is exalted above the angels and called mother of God. What is the truth about Mary, neither exaggerated nor diminished?

In the pursuit of understanding the Hail Mary, the emphasis belongs on scriptural interpretation. From Luke alone come the words that comprised the Angelus or angelic salutation of Gabriel and the words of Elizabeth, which when conjoined formed the Ave Maria as it was known for a thousand years. To begin with this Gospel may allow Christians of whatever persuasion to pray the Ave Maria insofar as it stems from Luke. The third evangelist taken without further elaboration provides a text of simple beauty. In Luke's narrative, moreover, we may recognize the intimation of what a later theology will develop.

We know that scripture comes out of early tradition, and that early tradition is what is embodied in scripture. Some Christians will be content to remain with the scripture prayer text. Others will want to begin with the scripture and go beyond it. They may do this for two reasons: (1) popular devotion, and (2) powerful theological, psychological, and symbolic motifs found in meditation upon the mystery of Mary and Jesus. An account of popular devotion to Mary would fill a small library. Some of this piety has been enlightened, without a split between the life experience and the needs of ordinary people and the insights of careful and devout theology. Some of this piety has fallen into excess or distortion and that regrettably. Even allowing for the correction of popular piety, at some point how one stands with regard to Church tradition and the development of doctrine will be an issue. One's own religious practice, taste, and history will influence which popular devotion will be embraced, even among the well-founded ones. Not everyone will be comfortable with the Hail Mary as their familiar prayer. Neverthless, my hope in this book remains so to explain the Ave Maria that the reader would find the words of John de Satge true of the present writing as well: "Understood in the way we have expounded, the Hail Mary is a prayer any evangelical should be happy to use."[3]

HISTORY OF THE AVE MARIA

The Ave Maria as we know it developed as a Christian prayer over hundreds of years. From scriptural quotation to liturgical antiphon and then to devotional prayer was a slow process. The first half, taken from the Gospel texts, emerged first. "Hail, [Mary] full of grace. The Lord is with you" (Lk 1:28) was joined with "Blessed are you among women. And blessed is the fruit of your womb [Jesus]" (Lk 1:42). This yoking of the words of Gabriel and the words of Elizabeth can be traced back in the East to the fourth or fifth century, and in the West to the seventh century or perhaps earlier. In the Vulgate (and its translations), the encomium of Mary "Blessed are you among women" (*benedicta tu in mulieribus*) is attributed to Gabriel in verse 28, immediately following "The Lord is with you." In verse 42, the Vulgate repeats this accolade, now spoken by Elizabeth, with a slight change noted in the Latin (*benedicta tu inter mulieres*). Verse 42 then continues with "And blessed is the fruit of your womb." Because of the use of the same phrasing, verse 28 was easily associated and joined to verse 42. The earlier *benedicta* is not found in all the Greek manuscripts of Luke, and there are those who think it is an interpolation derived from Elizabeth's greeting. The International Greek New Testament Project, a most recent critical edition (Oxford: Clarendon Press, 1984), considers authentic the *benedicta* in Gabriel's annunciation. Whatever the resolution of the text, Elizabeth's words would easily be seen as a completion of the tidings brought to Mary by Gabriel.

In the East, in the Syrian liturgy of St. James in Antioch and in the Coptic liturgy of St. Mark in Alexandria, the yoking of Gabriel's annunciation and Elizabeth's exaltation of Mary can be found.[4] A preserved Coptic ostracon (a clay tablet fragment with an inscription) from the sixth century also shows clearly the combination of texts: [5]

6

Hail Mary,
full of grace;
the Lord is with you,
the Holy Spirit too.
Your priests shall be robed in justice,
they that honor you shall rejoice and exult.
For David's sake, your servant, Lord,
save, Lord, your people, bless your chosen portion.

Hail to the glorious virgin,
Mary, full of grace.
The Lord is with you.
Blessed you are above all other women
and blessed is the fruit of your womb:
for him you conceived was Christ, the Son of God,
and he has redeemed our souls.

This Eastern Ave Maria is quite ancient. It conjoins the words of Gabriel and Elizabeth and adds a short phrase after the words "fruit of your womb": *because you have borne the Son of God, the savior of our souls.* In some texts of the Eastern liturgy, the name of Mary is added, and sometimes expanded to read "Mary, virgin mother of God" (*Maria, theotokos parthenos*). In the Egyptian liturgy of the Abyssinian Jacobites the angelic salutation to Mary is followed by a brief petition: "Pray and intercede for us with thy beloved Son that he forgive us our sins."[6] These liturgical texts may well have been in use in some form since the fourth century.

In the West the Ave Maria antiphon is found from the time of Gregory the Great in the early seventh century. The Offertory antiphon for the feast of the Annunciation and the Offertory antiphon for the Fourth Sunday in Advent present the salutations of Gabriel and Elizabeth combined.[7] The Ave Maria in the West, however, ended with the words "fruit of your womb" well into the Middle Ages. The second part of the Hail Mary as we know it developed in the late Middle Ages. It never enjoyed widespread use in the East. The devout repetition of this salutation of the angel Gabriel and the greeting of Elizabeth might be considered an implicit intercessory prayer to Mary. It was during this time

of increased liturgical devotion to Mary that the explicitly intercessory ending of the Ave Maria was developed.

The angelic salutation was also used in the early Middle
Ages as a non-verbal devotion to Mary. Gabriel's greeting of Mary
was imitated by a bodily bow, or genuflection, often performed
in front of an image or statue of the Virgin. The physical in-
volvement of the believer embodied a prayerful attitude of joyful
praise and perhaps tacitly invoked her intercession. In some circumstances the antiphon was accompanied by prostration, and
these often very numerous in the accomplishment of an ascetic
prayer discipline. "St Aybert, in the twelfth century, recited 150
Hail Mary's daily, 100 of them with genuflections, 50 of them with
prostrations."[8] The assignment of Aves as a penance (veniae) may
stem from this physically exacting form of repeating the angelic
annunciation to Mary.[9]

Extensive prayerful use of the Marian antiphon occurred
with the development of the Little Office of the Blessed Virgin
as early as the tenth century. This devotion was an abbreviated
version of the Common Office of the Blessed Virgin in the Divine
Office of the Church, and was often said by the choir monks as a
supplemental devotion to Our Lady. It could also appropriately
be recited in private. The Little Office of Our Lady (or the
Cursus) was championed in a special way by St. Peter Damien
in the eleventh century. Urban II at the synod of Clermont in
1095 designated the Little Office for special liturgical prayer on
Saturdays. The Ave Maria antiphon was used as the invitatory
for Matins and at the Magnificat for Vespers. It was also employed as the responsory and versical after the readings. In this
setting Gabriel's and Elizabeth's words were taken up in a choral
dialogue. When these texts were prayed alone, the two biblical
voices of the Ave Maria were again combined. The Little Office
itself became quite popular with both religious and lay persons.
It was later included in the Book of Hours, which was extensively
cultivated as a *vade mecum* prayer book for choir monk and lay
person alike.

Gradually an Ave Maria prayer developed that would be said
independently. Thurston writes "that some sort of Hail Mary was
generally known in and before the time of St. Bernard [twelfth

century] seems to me beyond dispute."[10] And Jean Laurenceau
concluded that "during the eleventh century, the Ave Maria began to be used as a formula of private devotion, especially in
monastic and clerical circles, familiar with the antiphons of the
votive office of the Virgin, and in ascetical circles and with the
pious laity (e.g., in Flanders) and there in the form of a repeated
prayer accompanied by penitential exercises. In these two con-
texts, it is remarkable that the Ave Maria prayer is placed in
relationship with the joy of Mary at the annunciation."[11]

Medieval devotion to the Blessed Virgin was both elaborate and widespread. From the early Middle Ages one can find
examples of preaching and commentary upon the Ave Maria.
St. Ildephonse of Toledo, St. Peter Damien, Abbot Baldwin of
Canterbury, John Waldeby, St. Matilda of Helfta, St. Bernard of
Clairvaux, St. Bonaventure, St. Albert the Great, and St. Thomas
Aquinas all write about the Ave Maria. These commentaries all
conclude with Elizabeth's words. If there were additional words,
they seem to have been diverse and eclectic. In formal recognition of the new role of the Ave Maria, Odon of Sully, Bishop
of Paris (1196–1208), in the diocesan statutes or canons of the
Synod of Paris (1198) insisted on the basic catechetical teaching
of the Lord's Prayer, the Creed, and the "salutation of the Blessed
Virgin." Many other synods in Europe, such as Trier in 1227,
Coventry in 1237, and Valencia in 1255, followed suit.[12]

Later Development

The second part of the Ave Maria evolved more slowly. From
the sixth century to the sixteenth there are various versions of a
prayer of petition added to the biblical words of Gabriel and
Elizabeth, which were orginally employed only as a liturgical
antiphon. Petitionary prayer to Mary characteristic of the second
part of the Ave Maria can be found in a fragmentary way very
early in the liturgical practice of the church of Alexandria. In
a subterranean sanctuary dating from third-century Alexandria
there is a fresco depicting the marriage at Cana with an inscription to "Holy Mary" (*Haghia Maria*).[13] The *Sub Tuum Praesidium*
is the oldest Marian prayer, cherished in the liturgy both of

the East and the West. It is remarkable because of its appeal to the intercession of Mary. The Greek text was discovered in the twentieth century on a fragment of papyrus estimated to date from the third century.[14]

> Sun tuum praesidium confugimus,
> Sancta Dei Genetrix; [Theotokos]
> Nostras deprecationes ne despicias in necessitatibus,
> Sed a periculis cunctis libera nos semper,
> Virgo gloriosa et benedicta.

> We seek refuge under your protection,
> Holy mother of God;
> Do not turn from our prayers in our need,
> But always deliver us from all danger,
> O glorious and blessed Virgin.

The Latin text is taken from the *Breviarium Romanum* (1972). The English translation is mine. A recently discovered Ethiopian hymn of the period 431–451 includes "pray for us" devotion to Mary.[15]

In the West the "Holy Mary [Saint Mary] pray for us" beginning of the second part of the Ave may well have its origin in the Litany of Saints, a prayer form that itself may go back to the seventh century. The Syrian Pope Sergius I (687–701) may have introduced to the West a flavor of the magnificent eastern Marian liturgies. Highly developed Marian litanies became very popular from the eleventh century on. The litany of Loreto is a prime example of such a litany devoted to the Blessed Virgin, and it shows some of the same exuberance found in the well-known and loved *Akathistos* hymn to Mary of the seventh century from Constantinople. Palmer concludes that the petitionary part of the Ave Maria indeed had its beginnings in the church of Alexandria in the fifth century.[16] "The 'Holy Mary, pray for us' became by successive amplifications the prayer one would make in the sixteenth century the 'second part' of the Ave Maria."[17] There is a legend that the Ave Maria was revealed to St. Ildephonsus of Toledo in the seventh century.[18] There is a weak tradition that the word *Jesus* (Jesus Christus. Amen), was added by Pope

Urban IV (1261–1264). There is not much evidence, however, for either attribution, although in the Middle Ages the account of Urban IV was widely believed.

In the East there is evidence of a sixth-century text, attributed to Severus, and probably designating the Patriarch of Antioch, which reads: "Holy Mary, Mother of God, pray for us sinners indeed. Amen."[19] In the West it is possible that the word "sinners" in the phrase "pray for us *sinners*" can be traced to St. Bernardine of Siena in the middle of the fifteenth century. The "now and at the hour of our death" may perhaps be traced to a thirteenth-century anonymous text in the East that asks the prayers of Mary at the "hour of our death because you are close to the good God and because we are sinners and poor. We pray that you help us always both while we live and at the departure of our soul from our body."[20] In the West the "now and at the hour of our death" would seem to go back at least to the fourteenth century. At the turn of the fifteenth century the Servites (the Servants of Mary), the Franciscans, and others used the Ave Maria in that form in their breviary prayer. The intercessory second part of the Ave Maria gradually replaced the bows and genuflection of medieval piety, and the Ave Maria became a verbal prayer of petition as we know it today. The second part of the Ave Maria was well developed in the form we know by the end of the fifteenth century. Savonarola's commentary on the Ave Maria printed a few years before his death in 1498 contains the text of the Hail Mary as we know it today, with the omission of only one word, *our*, in "now and at the hour of our death."

The final composition of the second part of the Ave Maria was universally established and combined with the familiar words of Gabriel and Elizabeth by the Dominican Pope Pius V in the reformed Breviary in 1568 under the aegis of the Council of Trent. The prayer was made officially part of the Divine Office, according to which both the Ave and the Pater were said silently before each "hour" began. In 1955, in the decree "Cum Nostra," Pius XII removed the Ave Maria from the official recitation of the Divine Office of the Church.[21] The Little Office of the Blessed Virgin, however, was made part of the public liturgy of the Church at the Second Vatican Council ("Constitution on the

Liturgy," Paragraph 98). The Ave Maria has also been prayed in the "Angelus" recited morning, noon, and evening in Catholic devotional practice since the thirteenth century or even earlier. The rosary of Ave Maria prayers has also been popular in Catholic circles since its peak development and propagation in the fifteenth century. Both of these devotions to Mary that employ the Ave Maria have received Church approbation and encouragement through the centuries. Paul VI's "Marialis Cultus" devotes a number of paragraphs to their vitalization (#40–55). The extended use of the Ave Maria, however, remains a topic too large to develop in this book.[22]

MARY IN SCRIPTURE

In the sacred scripture, most of what we know of Mary is found in the infancy narratives of Matthew and of Luke. In the opening two chapters of each Gospel the most references to the virgin Mary and the conception and birth of Jesus are located. In Luke's Gospel we find the most elaborate account of the mother of Jesus. The third evangelist's infancy narrative has been called the "Gospel of Mary." There are also a few references to her elsewhere in Matthew and Luke. Mark does not speak much of Mary. In John there are two well-known episodes involving Mary. Only in a small number of instances outside of the Gospels themselves is her memory recalled in the New Testament.[23]

Let us turn to the synoptic Gospels first, since there are parallel passages to consider in comparison. I will take Luke's Gospel as the outline for the exposition of Mary and add accounts from the other evangelists when appropriate. We will then consider John separately and the other books of the New Testament. The Old Testament does not contain anything indisputable about Mary, whose life was unknown to its authors. However, Matthew and Luke read the Old Testament in the light of Jesus. Some details in the story about Mary may also have their origin in the Hebrew scriptures. In her destiny the Old and the New Testaments meet. Her greeting to Elizabeth is the transition from the old dispensation to the new life of Jesus the Christ. The Old Testament analogue for Gabriel's tidings to Mary may possibly come from Zephaniah (3:14–17). The overshadowing of Mary by the Holy Spirit (Lk 1:35) has been seen as reminiscent of the cloud of glory that came over the ark of the covenant in Exodus (40:35). Similarly, the promises made to Mary of the future kingship of her son show some parallel with the promises made to David (2 Sm 7:12–16). Such literary derivations are not easily

13

proven, but the similarities often are suggestive of possible ways of reading the text. The annunciation to Mary (Lk 1:26–38) is found in Luke only. In Matthew the annunciation by the angel is to Joseph (Mt 1:18–25), and much of the infancy narrative tells his story. Matthew is quite explicit in his infancy narrative references to the Old Testament. He quotes a constellation of prophets, such as Isaiah "the virgin shall be with child" (7:14), Micah, "And, you, Bethlehem" (5:1), and Jeremiah, "Rachel weeping for her children" (31:15).

How shall we read the annunciation story in Luke from which the early version of the Hail Mary is composed? Does the evangelist present us with memoirs of Mary? Or does Luke tell us instead of an inner and ineffable experience of Mary, described in the pattern of similar birth announcements in the Old Testament literature?[24] Are the particulars of the annunciation a story that Luke composed to convey the essential meaning of the incarnation, however it may have actually happened in the historical life of Mary? Much of the recent scriptural investigation suggests that the infancy narratives in both Luke and Matthew do recount historical events but do not propose historical details in many instances. Rather, the evangelist constructs an amalgam of history and theology, of miracles and myth, of factual event and symbolic understanding. Raymond Brown writes: "We are not working with the hypothesis that he [Luke] is giving us substantially the memoirs of Mary. Rather, the possibility that he constructed his narrative in the light of Old Testament themes and stories will be stressed."[25]

Thucydides wrote a peculiar history wherein he composed speeches for historical characters. And yet his work is not fiction; it is more like a careful and conscientious historical novel. Where the facts are not entirely known, a dialogue or a speech is constructed, but based judiciously and truthfully on what must have been said and what corresponds to whatever was known to have happened. Among biblical scholars there would be widespread agreement that the annunciation to Mary is neither a purely historical account nor a completely theological construction. That the Lord God intervened in history is crucial to Christianity, whose core mystery is the actual and real resurrection of Jesus Christ. The resurrection appearances, however, remain a theologically edited account of the risen Jesus. The infancy narratives share this amalgam quality with the resurrection. Neither of these events—the beginning of the human life of Jesus and the close of the earthly sojourn—gives us history as biography with incontrovertible detail, and yet neither of them is reducible to only theological constructions, midrashic developments, or didactic devices. Although the infancy narratives in Matthew and Luke are not the memoirs of Mary, they may contain something of her recollections which were known to one of the evangelists. The Gospel account remains somehow for the believer a blend of biography and faith. Without trying entirely to resolve such complex and contested issues, I assume that Luke related a faith story, the exact historical details of which cannot be entirely recovered, and that "the angel's words to Mary dramatize vividly what the church has said about Jesus after the resurrection and about Jesus during his ministry after the baptism."[26] Lawrence Cunningham concludes that the story of Mary in the beginning of the life of Jesus is "not biographical fragments, but highly allusive and tautly rendered statements of theological belief reflecting the concerns and faith of the early Christian community."[27]

The reader experiences no difficulty reading the newspaper of today. Not everything in print is true, but there is some truth in the newspapers. However, one must read them with a nuanced perspective and a certain shrewd judgment. There is more truth in the obituary notices than in the advertisements. There is more factual history in the news stories than in the editorials. There is myth on the sports page, and highly symbolic language and ironic situations in the comics section. The contemporary reader learns easily to distinguish genres. Similarly, the reader of the Bible must become familiar with various kinds of biblical literature and their own peculiar rhetoric. Whether the angel Gabriel is real or a symbol the evangelist uses to tell us that Mary experienced an ineffable mystical experience, something wonderful and awesome did happen to her. In short and in sum, Jesus Christ who is Lord is her first-born son.

If one accepts the conclusion advanced by many scripture scholars today that the account in Luke does not give the memoirs of Mary, where then did Luke find some of his details? One assumes that Luke treats of what happened in history, but that the details of that happening are dressed in part in theological and literary strategies in order to bring out the meaning of these events. Thus, when Mary says "I am the handmaid of the Lord" (1:35), Luke may be borrowing the content of a later known and germane saying of Jesus: "My mother and my brothers are those who hear the word of God and act on it" (Lk 8:21). Mary is just such a person in Luke's estimation. Similarly, Elizabeth's greeting "blessed are you among women, and blessed is the fruit of your womb" (1:43) may echo the woman in the public ministry of Jesus who shouts "Blessed is the womb that carried you and the breasts at which you nursed" (11:27). Elizabeth's further praise of Mary, "Blessed are you who believed that what was spoken to you by the Lord would be fulfilled" (1:43) similarly picks up the words of Jesus to the woman in the crowd: "Rather, blessed are those who hear the word of God and observe it" (11:28). Old Testament sources for Elizabeth's greeting have also been suggested, such as Uzziah's words to Judith: "O, daughter, you are blessed by the Most High God above all women on earth" (Jdt 3:18). The visitation of Mary to Elizabeth is found only in Luke (1:39–45). Some readers have noted the similarity with David's dancing before the coming of the ark into Jerusalem (2 Sm 6:1–14). The Magnificat song of Mary (1:46–55) surely shows some derivation from the song of Hannah (1 Sm 2:1–10). Nonetheless, the connection between the Old Testament and the New presents many difficulties to the person trying to prove literary influence.

The birth of Jesus follows in the second chapter of Luke (2:1–20), as it does in the second chapter of Matthew. In Luke the Epiphany of Jesus is made to the shepherds, and in Matthew to the magi. Only in Matthew do we find the massacre of the holy innocents and the flight into Egypt, and only in Luke do we find the presentation of Jesus in the temple and the purification of Mary (2:21–40), as well as the later and final infancy narrative, when Jesus takes up the role of an adult male in the bar Mitzvah temple scene (2:41–52). Twice Luke mentions that Mary pondered in her heart the significance of all these events surrounding the birth of her son (2:19 and 2:51). The last reference, "his mother kept all these things in her heart" (2:51) probably refers to the entire breadth of the infancy narrative in chapters one and two. That conclusion would appropriately echo the earlier account of the shepherds: "And Mary kept all these things, reflecting on them in her heart" (2:19).

In the public ministry of Jesus, there are two episodes in the synoptic Gospels that touch significantly upon the mother of Jesus: (1) His family comes to visit him during his ministry away from Nazareth, and (2) Jesus himself pays a visit to his home town of Nazareth. In the first episode, Mark indicates that Jesus' family relatives thought he was "out of his mind" (3:21). When told that his mother and his brothers were outside asking for him, Jesus replies "Here are my mother and my brothers. [For] whoever does the will of God is my brother and sister and mother" (3:34b–35). Matthew tells the same incident (12:46–50), and so does Luke: "My mother and my brothers are those who hear the word of God and act on it" (8:21). Mark implies that the family of Jesus, and perhaps even Mary, did not comprehend what Jesus was doing and did not follow his mystery with sympathy. It is clear that Mary was not a follower of Jesus in his itinerant preaching. It is not known whether she was fearful about the public ministry of Jesus. She might well have had concern for him in his chosen vocation. Matthew and Luke allow for a reading of this episode that does not prejudice the family of Jesus and especially not his mother. Accordingly, what matters to Jesus is spiritual kinship or discipleship rather than blood relationship alone. The actual discipleship or faith of his family need not be at issue and may not even be known. Luke underlines this point. A woman in the crowd praises the mother of Jesus for having borne and nursed such a son (11:27). He replies to her that deliberate discipleship counts for more than familial relationship: "Rather, [even more] blessed are those who hear the word of God and observe it" (11:28).

In the second episode, Jesus visits his own home. He comes to Nazareth to preach. Mark in his account is again the most skeptical of the evangelists about the harmony between Jesus and his family (6:1–6a). Jesus complains: "A prophet is not without honor except in his native place and among his own kin and in his own house" (6:4). Matthew's account of Jesus' visit to Nazareth is somewhat softened (13:54–58). No mention is made of the unhonoring kin of Jesus: "A prophet is not without honor except in his native place and in his own house" (13:57). Luke's account (4:16–30) reduced the complaint of Jesus to even simpler terms that omit both kin and house: "Amen, I say to you, no prophet is accepted in his own native place" (4:24). From the other references to Mary as disciple and believer in Luke, it seems clear that he did not believe Jesus was finally rejected by his family, and in particular his mother, whatever might have been the perplexities along the way. Mary's presence in Luke's Acts of the Apostles leaves no doubt about such a final resolution: "When they entered the city they went to the upper room where they were staying, Peter and John and James and Andrew. . . . All these devoted themselves with one accord to prayer, together with some women, and Mary the mother of Jesus, and his brothers (1:13–14).

John's Gospel contains two important incidents that involve Mary as a central character in the life and death of Jesus. The wedding at Cana (2:1–12) places the mother of Jesus in a major role at the outset of the public ministry of Jesus. And the account of Mary and the beloved disciple at the foot of the cross of Jesus (19:25–27) locates her at a crucial place and time at the end of the life of her son. Although one cannot disprove that these events took place as described in detail, many scripture scholars do not think that either Marian episode relates in the details a historical event. John's Gospel is not without plenty of historical details in proper names and places, but the fourth evangelist primarily gives his community a theological account of Mary. She is the faithful disciple and the true believer: "Do whatever he tells you" (2:5). It is not biological kinship that makes for discipleship; it is not geographical or physical proximity that puts one in the presence of Jesus. It remains faith that places Mary, the paradigm disciple, at the foot of the cross. Those who come to believe in Jesus are *really present* in the events of his life, death, and resurrection. The long Christian history of a symbolic treatment of Mary as model of the Church and the new Eve may well receive some warrant here in John's account of her at Cana in the beginning and at the foot of the cross in the ending. She looms large in the mind and heart of the Johannine community with its highly developed theology. There are also several other verses in John (6:42, 7:1–10, 7:41–43, and 8:41) that speak of the origins of Jesus, and which may intend some reference to Mary his mother.

In summation, John's two major episodes with Mary and Jesus together in the public ministry are usually not read as literal history but as a theological and highly symbolical understanding of the mother of Jesus. If so, they do not tell exactly what happened, but they do tell the truth about Mary. The infancy narratives in Matthew and Luke are usually read as this kind of blend of history and kerygmatic elaboration of the faith of the early Church in the resurrected Jesus. If both Luke and John in their large-canvas treatments of Mary knew almost no detailed history of her, then those two family episodes in the synoptic Gospels that include her loom larger in our consideration. The family of Jesus coming to him in his ministry and Jesus going to his family in Nazareth contain crucial information about how Mary came to be understood in the Church. For John to have concluded in his Gospel episodes that Mary was the faithful disciple, and for Luke to conclude from the annunciation story to the Pentecost story that she was the prototype Christian believer demands that the Christian community for whom the evangelists wrote had come to see her relationship with Jesus as something more than a mother's stereotypical role. One might conclude that Mary was the first person introduced to the mystery of the incarnation, and that her subsequent life was caught up in the graced effort to comprehend and respond to God's ways: "Mary kept all these things, reflecting on them in her heart" (Lk 2:19, 51). One might well imagine that Jesus and Mary shared personal conversation about many things, and that indeed she became an intimate disciple, and if not altogether and at once, then surely after the resurrection experience.

Finally, the Book of Revelation, which has been traditionally ascribed to John (or the school of John) as author, gives an elaborate account in the twelfth chapter of "the woman and the dragon." Many readers have seen a figure of the virgin Mary in this text. One might draw insights pertinent to the mother of Jesus from this description of the woman who gives birth and is locked in mortal combat with the powers of evil in apocalyptic array. Often the text in Revelation is compared with the account in that advance "Good News" promising the enmity between the woman and the serpent (Gn 3:15). To claim, however, that either text surely and literally refers to Mary, the mother of Jesus, will fail to convince many readers and scholars of the Bible.

MARY IN THE APOCRYPHA

The Catholic Bible, which takes some of its canonical books from the Greek Septuagint, includes a number of books that the Hebrew scriptures exclude. These books, such as Ecclesiasticus, Judith, Maccabees, Sirach, and Wisdom, were either written in Greek or composed outside of Palestine, and for these and other reasons they were not included in the Hebrew Bible. The Protestant reformers followed that composition of the Old Testament. In non-Catholic editions of the Bible these disputed texts are usually included in an appendix known as the apocrypha. In Catholic editions of the Bible these books are called the deuterocanonical books and they are often conflated with the rest of the books of the Hebrew Bible.

The Apocrypha of New Testament times refer to various books of evangelical or prophetic tenor that have not been included in the canon of books that make up the New Testament today. Apocryphal works are often designated spurious works, but that meaning of the word is not primary in biblical studies. Over some centuries the Christian community sifted through many written works that might deserve inclusion in the community recognition of inspired holy scriptures. Some thirty apocryphal or uncanonical titles are known. There is a Gospel of Nicodemus, of Peter, of Thomas, and of Phillip. There is a Gospel according to the Hebrews, to the Ebionites, to the Egyptians, to the Nazaraeans, and to the Naassenes. One finds the Apocryphal Acts of the Apostles, the Acts of Pilate, of John, of Paul, of Thomas, and of Peter. Jewish apocalyptic literature includes the Ascension of Isaiah, the Apocalypse of James, and of Peter. These books are among the most accomplished of a large field of apocryphal writings. They were excluded from the sacred scripture because the Christian community over the years did not conclude that

21

the writing reflected adequately its own understanding of God and the incarnation of Jesus Christ.

The Proto-Gospel of St. James (*Protevangelium Jacobi*) contains artistic and theologically interesting apocryphal stories about the parents of Mary and her own childhood years. Her marriage with Joseph and the birth of Jesus are also treated in detail that has been well known through the centuries and the subject of many paintings and other artistic endeavors. Composed of many traditions compiled over many decades, this narrative of Mary is thought to date from the late second century, although it was not translated into Latin until the sixteenth century when William Postel did so. The Proto-Gospel of James was found in lectionaries in the Byzantine liturgy for many centuries, and the eastern church has long been devoted to its stories. In the Latin liturgy, the feasts of St. Joachim, St. Anne, the Birth of Mary, and the Presentation of Mary in the Temple have long been celebrated with annual feastdays. The Latin Pseudo-Matthew, composed pseudononymously probably in the sixth century, is a western version of James, along with parts of the Childhood Gospel of Thomas. The Gospel of the Nativity of Mary is a more tempered recension of Pseudo-Matthew. The Arabic Gospel offers a comprehensive account of the infancy and childhood of Jesus. The History of Joseph the Carpenter treats at length the death of Joseph, and the Transitus Mariae concerns itself with the end days of Mary. Other apocryphal works, such as the Ascension of Isaiah, the *Speculum Majus* of Vincent de Beauvais, the *Speculum Sanctorum* of Jacobus de Voragine contribute unverifiable details about Mary and Jesus.[28]

These accounts of the life of Mary are somewhat comparable to historical biographical novels, which add detail and elaboration from the author's creativity to fill out a historical record that is thin in this or that regard. Some of these texts are carried away with fanciful episodes that appealed to the popular piety of the day. Depending on the judgment of the author, the imaginative accounts might run from quite edifying to distasteful and distorted elaborations of the biblical accounts in the canonical scripture. In the Latin Pseudo-Matthew, the legend of the poignant reunion of Joachim and Anne, the traditional named

parents of Mary, at the Golden Gate leading into the city of
Jerusalem is a touching story of God's providential love, which
granted them a child when they had prayed perseveringly for new
life. In the Proto-Gospel of St. James, however, the account of the
midwife Salome, who examined Mary with her hand to see if she
was a virgin, is an indelicate picture, however well intentioned.
The scene is reminiscent of the unbelieving Thomas who was
invited to put his finger in the wounded side of Jesus (Jn 20).
The midwife's hand is burned because of her impiety, but it is
later healed by her picking up the child Jesus. Of these hagio-
graphic accounts there were many versions, of varying quality
and theological nuance.

We know almost nothing of the historical Mary from the
birth of Jesus to her own death. We know even less about the
childhood and marriage of Mary. That she had parents who
must have been holy people seems likely enough, but what were
their names and the story of their marriage does not allow of
any historical proof. Legends abounded, however, such as the
presentation of Mary in the Temple, perhaps derivative from
Luke's narration of the presentation of Jesus in the Temple.
Mary's vow of virginity, the staff of Joseph that brings forth a
dove, the annunciation to Mary delivered in an outdoor setting
by a fountain, the birth of Jesus in a grotto or cave are further
apocryphal details that stem largely from the Proto-Gospel of
St. James. Many of these legendary episodes in the life of Mary
have inspired scenes that Christian artists have depicted in their
work. The popular imagination of Christians blends without seam
scenes from Matthew and Luke with details from the apocrypha.

Like innumerable legends of the saints, one cannot prove
these wonderful tales to be historically true. However, one cannot
disprove them either. Often one must say simply that we do
not know. There is insufficient or no evidence. There could
be fragments of truth from an ancient oral tradition in some
legends about the saints and indeed about Mary. Recent exca-
vation in Bethlehem concludes that caves near the location of
the Basilica of the Nativity were lived in at the time of Jesus.
Whatever the factual account, the sacred legends always tell us
what people wanted of their holy ones. The apocryphal literature

that develops around a sainted person often reveals more of the author and of the faithful community that needed, demanded, and enjoyed such accounts. The often harsh circumstances of the believers' lives can be read between the lines, and the deep and constant yearning for the spiritual and for the holy appears as the ultimate content of these stories, which were told and cherished to sustain the hopes of the faithful in a God whose ways were ever gracious yet mysterious. In such accounts there may be little history, yet much wisdom.

OBJECTIONS AND PROBLEMS

Why should one reconsider a theology of Mary? Why not let a tradition that does not seemingly serve well psychological concerns, the ecumenical climate, and feminist issues of the day languish? Why has there been a renewal of contemplation of Mary? Let us look at the humanistic critique, the Protestant objection, and the feminist problem.

I

The humanistic objections to devotion to Mary begin with an overall suspicion that at least some of popular piety and devotion stems from non-Christian myth. Temples to the *Magna Mater*, the great mother, source of all life, dotted the landscape in the Mediterranean world of early Christianity. Artemis of Ephesus was the goddess whose fertility cult dominated the entire city and its silversmiths, who made their living from casting her image (Acts 19). In the Book of Revelation, the woman with the moon at her feet, who is often read as an image of Mary in heaven, dovetails with woman as feminine goddess reflecting the light of the sun and whose periodic fertility is measured by the lunar phases. The universe is her body. The Christian icons of madonna and child would have been familiar images portrayed in thousands of figurines of every size that supported the widespread devotion to the myth of the mother goddess Isis and Horus her son in the annual rebirth of Spring. Isis as the throne of Pharaoh and Mary as the seat of Wisdom and throne of God reflect a similar belief in female generation as the basic foundation of all power and virtue. The dove that hovers over Mary in Christian iconography hovered over the mother goddess long before. In pagan mythology birds were often a divine omen and sign of heaven's will. Thus the objection is brought that Marian devotion has roots in pagan psychology and early Mediterranean myths of the mother goddess and the fertility of cyclical life on earth.

Twentieth-century depth psychology transfers these observations from religion to the realm of the unconscious mind. Marian devotion is seen as a form of fascination with the feminine. At its best such piety is judged as a useful sublimation and even a soulful integration.[29] At its worst, it remains a neurotic frustration of adult sexual development.[30] The humanist objection amounts to this. What can Mary specifically add in the face of these powerful pagan myths already available to humanity, or in the face of actual women present to others, body and soul, here on earth? What place is left for Mary, unless she moves into the places already well taken? The objections, of course, are complicated by the defense that might be made. How else would God communicate with human beings except in their language, their psychology, their myths, what Boff calls "the radical yearning of our interior archeology"? In short, one might allow much of the objection and reply that "the myths only anticipate and point to the event of grace."[31]

An account of the psychological and symbolic motifs surrounding the story of Mary and Jesus would fill a small library. Depth psychologist Carl Jung thought that the assumption of Mary had an archetypal significance in bringing the feminine into God. Theologian Leonardo Boff speculates that the Holy Spirit was spiritualized in Mary in a hypostatic way, somewhat analogous to the union of the Son of God and the humanity of Jesus, or the human being brought into union with God in the beatific vision.[32] The exploration of the feminine in God, the eternal feminine in woman, and the role of Mary leads beyond the scriptures. Few people would deny the importance of the feminine in religion, but whether or not such application to Mary is Christian biblical theology or a blend of psychology with Christian sympathies remains a disputed issue. The question is not whether the feminine is enormously attractive to men (and women) in their religious quest, or that the feminine is locus for incredible beauty and human consolation. The question is whether the eternal feminine belongs rather more properly in God, who should also be imaged as female numinosity and glorious feminine fascination. To make Mary the female God-like figure may be finally unfair to God, and a distortion of who Miryam of Nazareth truly was in her own human role as the prototypical believer, for whom Jesus Christ her son was beloved in this life and the beloved for all eternity in the resurrection glory when all will be revealed to her and to the faithful disciples.

II

The Protestant objections to devotion to Mary begin with an overall suspicion that at least some of popular piety and devotion show signs of misunderstanding and exaggeration. There is an important place for Mary in Christian life, but her role should be delineated carefully. Some Catholics think that the church since Vatican II has reduced too severely the role of Mary in the liturgy. Protestant commentators often think the Catholic church did not go far enough. Catholics tend to allow a larger role for Mary, and Protestants a lesser one. Their objections are similar, however, and they differ mostly in degree.[33] Overall, the objection remains that Marian piety tends to be too emotional, too irrational, and too untheological. Popular piety generates a certain caution among the theologically well educated, who themselves, however, may be marginalizing the role of Mary. How could Luke possibly write to the early Church an account of its tradition with the inspired words of Elizabeth, "blessed are you among women," and of Mary, "all generations will call me blessed," unless there were already a basis in devotion to the mother of Jesus? The Protestant and Catholic ecumenical efforts have again brought the issue of Mary to mind. Catholics are today more sensitive to the abuses possible in maximizing Mary; Protestants are more aware of the loss to the integral Christian Gospel suffered in minimizing Mary.

The Protestant reformers argued that devotion to Mary must avoid idolatrous excesses and superstitious abuses, as did many Catholics such as Erasmus. To Luther praise and thanksgiving were to be given to Mary. Prayer of petition was problematic. Luther called for Marian prayer to be Christocentric, biblical, unexaggerated, and edifying.[34] Most Christians could agree in theory with that desideratum, though in practice where the lines were drawn might differ. In particular, objection is made that Mary is not the one mediator between God and human beings; Jesus Christ alone is the way to the Father. The Christ-event remains the one, total, and primary mediation between the human and the divine. Many Protestants find it disturbing that the feasts of Mary in the liturgy duplicate the feasts of Jesus. She appears to them all too easily as a "virtual incarnation of the Holy Ghost."[35]

The years between 1854, with the solemn definition by Pius IX of the Immaculate Conception of Mary, and 1950, with the solemn definition by Pius XII of the Assumption of Mary, have been called with justification the century of Mary. The papal definition of Marian doctrines, however, has seemed to many to surpass what is found in scripture and to have been determined without widespread collegial process in ecumenical council. Not that the substance of these doctrines is contested by most Christians, but rather the wisdom of defining them by the pope alone is questioned. More keenly than most Catholics, Protestants feel the objection of inadequate scriptural and ecclesial warrant for these definitions of doctrine. Overall, the Christian objection has been that Marian doctrine has claimed too much center stage.

III

The feminist objections to devotion to Mary begin with an overall suspicion that at least some of popular piety and devotion misunderstands the personal nature of womankind. Marian piety both undervalues the role of actual woman and overexalts the role of Mary of Nazareth. Feminists argue that biology is not destiny, and that women are persons called to lead adult lives active in many tasks. They are not only nor primarily to be biological mothers. The motherhood of Mary does not lead automatically to discipleship merely because of kinship. Human freedom transcends the body in its physicality, and hence Mary as believer and disciple is a more accurate category than Mary as mother. "Mother of God" is problematic as a title because "mother" misleads by claiming too little for actual women, and because "of God" misleads by claiming too much for one woman.

God as such does not take origin from Mary. It is Jesus who is Lord in his humanity that Mary mothers. Mary is exalted because she bears a son at the request of another, but for many women as witnessed throughout the centuries, that condition has been an imposition and an oppression. Virgin mother of God exalts Mary, putting her on a pedestal to be admired, but with no chance to be imitated by women called to be neither virgins nor mothers. The feminist debate wishes to return Mary to the sisterhood of man, and to give back to God all those feminine and divine characteristics bestowed with good intention, though mistakenly, upon Mary.

In the medieval commentary on the Ave Maria, Baldwin of Canterbury refers with devotion to Mary as "the mistress of the world in everything, the queen of heaven, of humankind and angels, the mother and daughter of God, the sister and spouse, the friend and companion."[36] Baldwin finds her "first after God, the love, the praise, and the splendor of human beings and of angels."[37] A more spare theology of Mary is seen today in John McKenzie, whose exacting and critical scriptural study of Mary in the Gospels concludes: "Faith in the Mary of traditional Christian devotion is faith in something which is not true."[38] The traditional Mariology claims the roots of its glorification of Mary can be found in the New Testament scripture. One must come to understand, however, the further implications of scriptural texts whose signification is undeveloped. The more limiting Mariology argues that no development can overcome the limited role that Mary is given in the scriptures. If a high Mariology wishes to be reading fairly out of the text, this low Mariology wishes to reject unfair reading into the text. It might be possible, however, to see something new in the text without unfairly reading into it. Let us try to put together a biographical story of Mary based on the Gospels read with contemporary concerns about the humanity of Mary uppermost in our focus. Elizabeth Johnson reasons that the Christian woman and disciple should be understood so as to affirm "a non-stereotypical understanding of the nature of woman, one which would recognize the values of autonomy, integrity of conscience, courage, correct use of power, the goodness of female sexuality, self-assertion, and the relation of motherhood and sisterhood."[39] Can the Gospel story of Mary be told in a way that supports this model of Christian womanhood? Can one attain a resymbolization of Mary that will empower women? Can one tell the Mary story with a different perspective, and yet not distort the scriptures in so doing?

Taking our clues from the Gospel stories of her as written one could compose this biography of Mary. She is an engaged but unwed young mother who chooses to keep her child. Her fiancé is informed that she believes she has a God-given vocation that she must follow regardless of his marital or career plans. Moreover, he must trust her expression of her sexual life as she presents it to him. Though betrothed to her, he must make room for her vocation as woman of God and mother of a unique son. In the Lucan account she is a young maiden who straightforwardly asks the angel Gabriel a theological question. With her own intellectual resources she decides how she will respond to God and to her husband. She is courageous in risking the fate of a woman caught in adultery, for which the penalty in the law was to be stoned until dead. While pregnant herself, she travels to her relative Elizabeth to assist her. Evident in an extraordinary way is "the simplicity of her being, the unexpected richness of her consciousness of poverty, her openness to God, and her availability to others."[40] She gives birth to her firstborn child in a questionable place without the presence of a midwife. She is a refugee woman on the road to Egypt with her newborn son. When the adolescent Jesus is separated from his parents, she disciplines him: "Son, why have you done this to us? Your father and I have been looking for you with great anxiety" (Lk 2:48). She knows a mother's pain when a son grows to claim his own way and leaves her behind. She tries at least once to bring him home. In Jesus' public life, according to John's Gospel, it is Mary who takes leadership and charge of the wedding embarrassment in Cana: "They have no wine" (Jn 2:3). At the foot of the cross his mother stands fearless with a few other woman, all the men having run away (Jn 19). Her son dies as the innocent victim of injustice and governmental violence. She is one of the mothers throughout the centuries who mourn their children torn unjustly from their midst. In the church council at Pentecost, Mary takes her place with the disciples awaiting the descent of the Holy Spirit and the empowering for mission in the Church that such grace will bring.

Here is a picture of no unreal nor timid woman. She represents the anawim, the poor, and the oppressed. Her nation is an occupied people; her race is a minority. She is an outsider from the countryside of Nazareth in Galilee. Her life as a woman without education or opportunity is limited. She stands as an example of the oppressed among the oppressed. She stands as an example of the woman who lacking human resources puts all her trust in God. This is the human Mary, the unexalted mother of Jesus, the woman of faith as she is presented briefly and without varnish in the simple yet profound Gospel accounts of her life.

Religion that fails to take the side of the poor and the oppressed fails to live the Gospel. Throughout the Bible, God is with the outcast and the victim of injustice. Liberation theologies, especially in Latin America, have found the Mary of the Magnificat a spokeswoman for the poor, the powerless, the oppressed, and the marginalized: "He has thrown down the rulers from their thrones but lifed up the lowly. The hungry he has filled with good things; the rich he has sent away empty" (Lk 1:52–53). Some feminists have found themes in Mary's life newly framed in such a way as to assist their efforts for the freedom of women. Other feminists have been unwilling to let a sister perish in an uncritical theology that they argue was imposed upon her, and which they would strive to correct with a better reading and understanding of scripture.

PART ONE

In the sixth month, the angel Gabriel was sent from God to a town of Galilee called Nazareth, to a virgin betrothed to a man named Joseph, of the house of David, and the virgin's name was Mary. And coming to her, he said, "Hail, favored one! The Lord is with you." But she was greatly troubled at what was said and pondered what sort of greeting this might be. Then the angel said to her, "Do not be afraid, Mary, for you have found favor with God. Behold, you will conceive in your womb and bear a son, and you shall name him Jesus. He will be great and will be called Son of the Most High, and the Lord God will give him the throne of David his father, and he will rule over the house of Jacob forever, and of his kingdom there will be no end." But Mary said to the angel, "How can this be, since I have no relations with a man?" And the angel said to her in reply, "The holy Spirit will come upon you, and the power of the Most High will overshadow you. Therefore the child to be born will be called holy, the Son of God. And behold, Elizabeth, your relative, has also conceived a son in her old age, and this is the sixth month for her who was called barren; for nothing will be impossible for God." Mary said, "Behold, I am the handmaid of the Lord. May it be done to me according to your word." Then the angel departed from her.

Luke 1:26–38.

All New Testament quotations are taken from the New American Bible, the revised edition of the New Testament (New York: Catholic Book Publishing Company, 1986).

HAIL MARY

The annunciation to Mary has been portrayed in poem and painting with enormous variety. The Proto-Gospel of James suggests that the annunciation took place at a fountain outdoors, and legend situates it in the early evening before dark. The archangel Gabriel[1] is sent by God to salute Mary of Nazareth in Galilee. Gabriel in Luke would readily be associated with Gabriel in the Book of Daniel (9:20–25), where this angel of the Lord announces the coming day of the Lord and the dawning of the messianic era.[2] Luke may imply that the angel Gabriel bowed to Mary. The incarnate Word of God would lift human nature above the angels. After the incarnation of Jesus, the angel of the Lord would not allow John to bow in deference (Rev 22:8–9). The *Ave* of the Latin has sometimes been turned around to spell *Eva*, with reference to Mary as the new Eve who is the lowly handmaid of the Lord and the mother of those born into eternal life. The entire annunciation scene is an icon of the infinite God's immensity accommodating itself to the small human dwelling of the body and soul of Mary. She will hold all Being as the fruit of her womb; she will nourish her creator with her own milk. She will support in her arms the Lord who sustains the whole world. Human imagination has been fascinated by Luke's portrait of Mary and the angel. That moment has been regarded by many as the turning point in the history of the world. Here and now begins a boundless ascent. The scene itself proclaims the visitation of God in the marvelous and unknown mystery of an infant who will save the world.

The annunciation to Mary differs from the parallel annunciation to Zachary in significant ways. Not only is Zachary an old man, and a priest of the temple, but he is also a public figure of the Old Testament. Mary appears in Luke's story supported

by only her commonplace name. The favor and grace given
to her remain totally gratuitous and unexpected. She does not
apparently see the angel but only hears the message, and in
her response there is nothing sensational. Her faith and her
loving assent to the ways of God are in the realm of the soul
and an affair of her inner life. And finally, Mary is not primarily the culmination of the chosen people as Zachary and
Elizabeth with John represent. Mary stands for the entire human family; she represents in her anonymity the salvation of
all peoples.[3]

The angel Gabriel's greeting begins with the Greek word
chaire. It has been translated for centuries as the customary greeting word before a conversation. Hail, hello, or greetings would
capture this salutation. More recently another reading of "Hail,
full of grace" (*chaire kecharitōmenē*) was argued.[4] "Rejoice, O
daughter of Zion" was the suggested reading. Using a concordance to the Septuagint Bible, evidence was marshalled that the
opening word that Luke uses in the annunciation to Mary presented not only initial greetings but also an invitation to rejoice
greatly. Argument was made that the use of *chaire* as a greeting almost always coincided with the Old Testament messianic
promises to the daughter of Zion. Jerusalem as the holy city
of Zion had come to be understood as the daughter of Zion,
that special part representing the whole of Israel. With elaborate
linguistic analysis, passages such as the following were offered
as the warrant for such an unaccustomed reading: "Rejoice and
exult with all your heart, O daughter of Jerusalem!...The King
of Israel, the Lord, is in your midst" (Zep 3:14–15), and "Rejoice greatly, O daughter of Zion!...Lo, your king comes to
you...humble and riding on an ass, on a colt the foal of an ass"
(Zec 9:9). Thus, Luke was thought to have intended to make
allusion to the messiah coming to save the daughter of Zion.
Consequently, the words of Gabriel are read: "Rejoice greatly,
O daughter of Zion. The Lord is with you." Max Thurian writes
that "Mary, the daughter of Zion, is the 'incarnation' of Israel."[5]
Thus, Mary is regarded as the female personification of Israel
and a figure of the Church.

Reading *chaire* as rejoice instead of as hail has been disputed. Jerome long ago did not translate the Septuagint in that fashion, and the recent Catholic-Lutheran task force on Mary in the New Testament did not find the evidence sufficient.[6] In opposition Brown offers this argument. The word "goodbye" has the etymological meaning of God be with you. It was originally an intercessory prayer wish spoken at a departure in a society centered on God. Some might own that they had not intended to say "God be with you" when they said "goodbye," but they would find such a sentiment corresponds to what is in their heart. Others might object that they intend no such reference to God, whom they do not here affirm, but mean only to wish the person well in their farewell.[7] The revisionist position presupposes a very special reading of the Septuagint by Luke, and that his readers would recognize complex allusions to it. The conservative position is reminiscent of the strict constructionist interpretation of the Constitution of the United States. Those who follow that reading claim that the text will support only so much. Further amplification may be needed, and even be just and true, but it cannot be concluded from the text as we have it. Similarly, there are those who would argue that to read "rejoice" where a simple greeting is all that the context supports is a form of eisegesis (reading into a text) rather than exegesis (reading out of a text). The Jerusalem Bible accepts "*Rejoice*, so highly favored!" whereas the New American Bible prefers "*Hail*, favored one!"

Perhaps there is a middle position that allows a critic to point out virtues in a text that the author was not consciously aware of and yet would be delighted to own as implicit once it has subsequently been pointed out. McHugh would try to reach a compromise between the two conflicting readings of the angelic salutation. "It cannot be proved merely by examining the text that Luke did have this symbol [daughter of Zion] in mind; equally, there is nothing in the text which tells against the idea, and it cannot be proved that Luke did not intend the symbol. But if anyone asked him outright, 'Do you mean that Mary is the Daughter of Zion foretold by the prophets?', he would have replied that this title summed up perfectly all that he meant to say."[8]

II

In the Gospel, Gabriel does not greet Mary by name, although Luke tells us that the angel was sent by God to a woman in Nazareth, "and the virgin's name was Mary" (1:27). The Hail Mary prayer inserts the name of Mary between the angel's initial greeting and the conferral of a special name for her, *full of grace* or *highly favored one.* Thus, "Hail, *Mary,* full of grace."

Names in the Bible often carry an inner meaning that illuminates the vocation of the person who bears the name. Abram is given a new name when he is called by God to leave his home and to follow into a new land that the Lord will show him; he will be Abraham. Sarai becomes Sarah, "mother of nations" (Gn 17:15–16). Jacob will be Israel. Simon will be Peter. The converted Saul is given the new name of Paul. When a new name is not given, the original name often carries some special import. As the Roman aphorism goes: *nomen est omen,* that is, one's name is a prediction.

When we turn to the name by which we know the mother of Jesus, there is not much agreement about its etymological roots. Moreover, the name seems to be not at all special. Mary of Nazareth was to all appearances an everyday young maiden of a provincial town with nothing of heritage, education, or wealth to distinguish her. Luke only says "and the virgin's name was Mary." No attention is drawn to Mary precisely because nothing more is said of her, her family background, or her personality. Her name is commonplace. All else comes from her inner and unseen faith and love, and ultimately from God's grace. In John's Gospel when Judas goes out from the supper to betray Jesus, the evangelist gives only a brief yet pregnant description: "And it was night." So Luke says of the coming of the eternal light into the world only: "And the virgin's name was Mary."

The name Mary in Hebrew is *Miryam* or *Miriam,* which is pronounced and sometimes spelled *Maryam* or *Maryah.* In Greek and Latin the name is Maria, also written *Mariam* or *Maryam.* The sister of Moses was named Miriam, and her triumphant canticle (Ex 15:21) at the crossing of the Egyptian sea suggests a comparison with Miriam of Nazareth in the outpouring of her joy in the Magnificat (Lk 1:46–55). The meaning and etymology of the name Miriam has not been agreed upon. A large number of theories circulate. One earlier theory suggested "well loved" or "beloved of God," following this logic. Miriam is composed of an abbreviated word for Yahweh, *Yam* in some form, which in turn may have been connected to the Egyptian word *Ra,* which also belonged to divinity.[9] The root MYR in Egyptian meant beloved. The Egyptian word *meri* meant to like or to love. One author claims "One can see in the Eyptian Museum in Turin, the tomb of Meri (merit) or Mary the noble wife of a government official who lived in the fourteenth century B.C."[10] Miriam meant therefore "the beloved of Yahweh." A second ancient theory supported by St. Jerome thought that Miriam in Syrian and in Aramaic means Lady (compare *Mar*anatha or Come, *Lord*). Peter Chrysologus proposed *bona domina* or good lady as a likely meaning. Daniel-Rops concluded that Miriam "no longer meant 'the beloved of the Lord' " as it did for Miriam of the Exodus. [11] Miriam meant something more like a good-woman or everywoman. Thomas Aquinas thought the name Maria meant "enlightened."[12] In the Middle Ages both Bernard and Bonaventure read the name of Mary to mean illuminating star, and in particular, star of the sea or *stella maris*. Cruden's *Concordance of the King James Bible* lists the following meanings for *Miriam*: exalted, bitterness of the sea, myrrh of the sea, lady or mistress of the sea. The *American Heritage Dictionary* indicates that the Hebrew word *Miryam* means rebellion in the sense of hope of change. Richard Klaver argues that Maria or Miriam means beloved if the derivation is Egyptian. If the derivation is Hebrew, however, then the name Mary means either rebellion from the word *Marah,* or well-nourished (or beautiful) from the word *Mara.*[13] Probably the most philologically accurate theory is explained by Joseph Fitzmyer, who argues in his commentary on Luke that the name MRYM is from a Semetic root and means summit or height.[14] It would not be implausible to conclude that the name Mary means "exalted." That conclusion is now widely shared among scholars.[15]

Even were the etymology of the name of Mary surely discernible and agreed upon, there would be this further question. Does the name in this instance guarantee any insight into the person? Might Mary be named without regard for a meaning that embodied her mission in life? Andrew Key writes that children in the Old Testament literature were given proper names under a number of rubrics: (1) the real or supposed meaning of the name (Gn 32:28); (2) what the mother or father might have said when the child was born (Gn 30:18); (3) some physical trait that suggests a name (Gn 25:25); (4) some symbolic event associated with the birth (Hos 1:9); (5) the place where, or an event when, the child was born (Gn 32:30).[16] With Mary, however, as far as we know we have none of the above exceptional circumstances to appeal to. Her name is apparently ordinary. No other female name in the New Testament is so common. We read of Mary of Bethany, the sister of Martha, who anointed the Lord's feet (Jn 12:3). Mary of Magdala is the first witness to the resurrection in John's account (Jn 20). Mary, the mother of James and Joses (Mk 15:40, 47), and Mary, the wife of Clopas (Jn 19:25) are placed at the crucifixion of Jesus by the evangelists. In Acts we read of a Mary who is the mother of Mark (12:12). In short, the name Mary is an ordinary and prevalent female name at the time of the birth of Jesus, and nothing is told us about his mother or her antecedents before the annunciation except this one spare pronouncement: "And the virgin's name was Mary." A non-etymological connection, however, might be suggested. Just as Miriam, the sister of Moses, was present and active in the salvation of the Israelites, so too a new Miryam, the mother of Jesus, is present and active in the salvation of the new Israel.[17]

The Ave Maria prayer initially inserts the virgin's name in the greeting: "Hail, Mary." The second part of the Ave repeats the name: "Holy Mary." In both instances, the line would stand without the proper name: Hail, full of grace, and Holy mother of God. Evidently the people who prayed to the mother of Jesus cherished invoking the name of this maiden mother of their Lord. Although we may not know what her name exactly means, and although her name was undistinguished in her lifetime, that name on the lips of the believer has become wonderful. In the garden of the resurrection when Mary Magdalene fails to know Jesus, whom she thinks is the gardener, he calls her to recognition simply by her name: "Mary!" And she replies instantly to that familiarity: "Rabbouni" (Jn 20:16). Love has its own language.

St. Anthony of Padua spoke of the name of Mary as "joy to my heart, honey to my mouth, a sweet melody to my ear."[18] Whatever the name means, however common its use in Israel, the name Mary has brought enormous joy to those who have repeated it oft in prayer.

FULL OF GRACE

Gabriel and Mary dialogue in the annunciation. Elizabeth and Mary converse in the visitation. At the annunciation Mary is proclaimed "full of grace" or highly favored to give birth to the Son of the Most High; at the visitation she is proclaimed blessed among women for the fruit of her womb is Jesus. How does one connect the celebration of such a motherhood to the spiritual endowment that is implied in "full of grace"? How does one keep from understanding "full of grace" in a way that exceeds Luke's praise? How does one do full justice to the implications of the unique intimacy with the Son of God that his mother enjoys? In short, one wishes to say neither too much nor too little about Mary.

The archangel does not greet her by the name Mary, but Gabriel does give her a new name. In Greek her biblical name is *kecharitōmenē*, which has been translated into English either as "full of grace" or as "highly favored one."[19] *Maria Graciada* or Mary Graced or Blessed (Virgin) Mary becomes a proper name for the mother of Jesus, just as Jesus the Anointed One or Jesus Christ becomes a proper name. However, *kecharitōmenē* would seem to address not so much Mary's overall spiritual condition, but rather her great favor and privilege in the angel's tidings of her predestined role as mother of the Son of the Most High. The lines that follow, "Do not be afraid . . . you have found favor with God . . . you will conceive in your womb," should be read as commentary on the initial greeting and name bestowed upon her: "Hail, full of grace," graced and favored to bear the "Son of the Most High" into the world. Obviously, the motherhood of Mary and whatever else one might wish to say or not to say about her are related. Nevertheless, those further considerations should be worked out mindful of the limited focus of the immediate text in Luke's annunciation story.

Differences in interpretation of the angel's salutation begin with the first words. *Chaire kecharitōmenē*, Hail, full of grace, has been read in two ways. Jerome in the Vulgate translated the Greek *chaire* as the Latin *ave* (hail), and the Greek *kecharitōmenē* as the Latin phrase *gratiae plena* (full of grace). The latter phrase has its merits as a translation because a plentitude is suggested by the Greek word and by the very Christ event. The theological understanding that has followed upon it, however, has created problems of exaggeration, which are especially felt by Protestants. Full of grace should mean that Mary has received a great favor from God in being the woman chosen for such an intimate relationship with Jesus as his mother over so many years. Full of grace does not mean that the grace of Mary is beyond measure, nor does the Greek text of Luke entitle the reader to conclude Mary is full of grace that is hers to bestow. In his comprehensive study of the infancy narratives, Raymond Brown concludes that Gabriel's greeting is a "relatively stereotyped salutation" and that "'full of grace' is too strong" a translation. The grace or favor that Mary received is precisely her selection as mother of the Word of God.[20] Because of such confusion, real or perceived, about the graces given to Mary, and because of the further interpretation by some commentators that Mary is presented in Luke as grace-giving because grace-abounding, some English translations have avoided the word "grace." An Anglo-Saxon translation of the Ave Maria reads "mid gyfe gefylled," which means "filled with a gift." The King James, which did not follow the Vulgate, renders the Greek: "Hail, thou that art highly favored." And the Revised Standard version reads: "Hail, O favored one." The New English Bible builds on that tradition: "Greetings, most favored one!" Both of the Bibles in liturgical use in Catholic worship avoid the word "grace": "Rejoice, so highly favored!" in the Jerusalem Bible; and "Hail, favored one!" in the New American Bible.[21]

Charis (gift or favor) is a frequently used word in the New Testament. Charity (giving love) and eucharist (thanks-giving) are derivative words. To for*give* (thoroughly give) in the Gospel is sometimes rendered with another related Greek word, *charizomai* (see Lk 7:42). The root of the word *kecharitōmenē* is also related to the word *charis*, from which we take the English word "charism," a gift or special talent. There is an implication in the Greek text that the favored status, the gifted condition, is fulsome and ample. The same word is used in Ephesians and its connection with abundant grace is manifest: "for the praise of the glory of his grace that he granted us in the beloved" (Eph 1:16). Hence Jerome translated it, *full* of grace, and several contemporary translations say "*highly* favored one." Called to be the mother of God, Mary was given special favor. Blessing and grace in this context can be interchanged. Before meals one is invited "to say a blessing" or "to say a grace." Mary was especially blessed; Mary was especially graced. How special and exactly how so has been the subject of much conversation over the centuries. If she is held blessed beyond all degree and filled with grace beyond measure so that the Christian can never say enough about her privileges and her union with God, that is surely a conclusion to be formulated precisely and carefully by theological consideration and church teaching, and not by appealing to Luke's *kecharitōmenē* to carry all of that weight.

"Full of grace," the name or title that Gabriel gives Mary, has occasioned controversy. It is not just that the Latin of Jerome does not yield a perfect translation. "Full of grace" has been understood in at least two ways: (1) Mary is full of grace *because* she is about to be the mother of God and God could do nothing less than prepare her for this role with every grace possible, and (2) Mary is full of grace *in that* she has been chosen to be the mother of God, simple Galilean woman of faith that she remains. One can see how the implications might differ. The first position leads to a high Mariology and the exaltation of her boundless virtues. The second position leads to a low Mariology and the celebration of her solidarity with the human in all its situational limitations.

It is also possible to understand Mary's graced condition not so much as (1) an overall preparation for the role of mother of God, or as (2) the validation of her vocation to the motherhood of God, but (3) as the overshadowing of the Holy Ghost. The consequent indwelling of the Spirit assures Mary a fullness of grace. Accordingly, Mary is full of grace because the Holy Spirit overshadows her, just as Jesus is full of grace at his baptism when the Holy Spirit descends upon him. In the eucharist the gifts of bread and wine become graced when the Spirit is called down upon them so that they may become the body and blood of Jesus Christ. Mary is especially espoused of the Holy Spirit, and therefore she is holy and full of grace. In the annunciation we do celebrate the *overshadowing* of Mary by the Holy Spirit, whose creative sovereignty not only brings about the conception of Jesus, but whose holiness re-creates the body and soul of Mary. If John the Baptist leaps in the womb of his mother at the approach of Jesus in the womb of Mary, how much more would Mary be lifted up with the coming of the Son of God. Mary conceives by the overshadowing of the Holy Spirit, a sovereign descent of the creative power of God into the world, reminiscent of the Spirit hovering over the chaos in the beginning. The same Spirit of God descends upon Jesus in baptism (Lk 3:22), shines upon him in the transfiguration on Tabor (Lk 9:34), and comes upon the apostles and by implication upon Mary (Acts 1:14) in tongues of fire and a rushing wind on Pentecost day. In the end, it will be manifest in her body and soul all that God's Spirit has wrought in her earthly life with its own human freedom from its first beginnings until its final end.

Leonardo Boff suggests that Mary is so intensely the bride of the Holy Spirit, and the overshadowing of her is so graced, that she is taken up into the Holy Spirit. Boff argues that the Holy Spirit is made spirit in Mary in an analogous way with the Word of God made flesh in Jesus. "Mary is assumed by the Holy Spirit, and thus elevated to the level of God." Mary is not very God, for the Holy Spirit did not become incarnate. But the Holy Spirit did become spiritualized in Mary, and she is full of the Holy Spirit who dwells perfectly in her as the Spirit dwells in the blessed in heaven. Boff wants to say of her what he would say of any Christian drawn fully into the life of the Trinity in the beatific vision. Her virtues in this life were the work of the Holy Spirit's perfect indwelling. "Mary, in her totality, becomes the tabernacle and temple of the Holy Spirit."[22] What is predicated of the one can be predicated of the other. Not many readers, however, will wish to go nearly this far with him.

If Leonardo Boff represents a high mark in the development of a doctrine of Mary, one can also cite a low mark. Stephen Benko argues in his study of the role of Mary that attention in the New Testament is not drawn to her at all. Only Luke gives a significant account of Mary, and Benko argues that the third evangelist does so only to establish the origin of Jesus who is from God and to establish that his birth was more important than the birth of John the Baptist. Mary serves to enhance the identity of Jesus and to establish the followers of Jesus over the followers of the Baptist. "It does not appear that the New Testament is sufficiently concerned about Mary to see in her the symbol of anything. . . . If for any reason—ecumenical, homiletic, or rhetorical—one wanted to assign a representative role to Mary there is only one role that she could have on the basis of the unanimous witness of the Scripture and early Christian tradition: She is there the figure of the synagogue."[23] And Benko understands the synagogue as a symbol of the Old Testament, of the Law, of the flesh that does not harken to the Spirit, and finally of unbelief in Jesus Christ. To read in one sitting Leonardo Boff and Stephen Benko, both capable theologians, writing about Mary in Christian faith is to be astonished at how such polar opposite conclusions about her might be reached.

Does a consideration of the *indwelling* of the Holy Spirit in the virgin Mary take the text beyond Luke? If Mary is already proclaimed "full of grace" or "highly favored" and if the Holy Spirit will overshadow her so that what is born of her will be called the Son of the Most High, would it not be implicit that in her dwells the Holy Spirit? To continue down this road is to explore the perfections of Mary, both in her origin and in her human history. It is a road that the Ave Maria prayer does not compel one to walk. One can leave the mystery of Mary contained in its fullness in just those words, whatever they may truly and completely mean: full of grace. The maiden that Gabriel promises will conceive by the Holy Spirit is somehow graced, somehow free of sinfulness, and somehow fit for the descent of the Spirit, who gives not only God's presence but the reception so that God's presence is not missed in the one who is to receive it. The Spirit brings the receptivity for the gift as well as the substance of the gift. And thus it is that we can say in truth that all is grace, even our freedom, which is God's gift without in the least damaging our own integrity. Nothing is more ours than what God totally gives to us. That is the very nature of creation, when the Spirit hovered over the waters in the beginning. There was nothing, and all that would be would owe its everything to God, and yet the creation was not God, and the creation was good, and the creation was itself.

We claim here nothing for Mary that we do not hold as the vocation of the Christian. The Ave Maria is a paradigmatic Christian prayer, recited by believers innumerable times because it speaks to what they deeply are called to be. Our claim is not that Luke's Gospel itself will deliver all of what is being claimed for Mary in the fullness of the Catholic tradition. Christian life suggests that grace is everything, and we owe all that we are in our salvation to the work of the Holy Spirit. In this sense Mary embodies that fullness of grace that is claimed for everyone in the end. Her origins reflect this reality with no lag in time in this world. Her heavenly assumption suggests no lag time in the world to come. Working backwards in time Catholic doctrine of Mary reached faith in her Immaculate Conception. If she was called to such high vocation, she was prepared by God to fulfill it. Working forward in time Catholic doctrine of Mary reached faith in her assumption into heaven. If she fulfilled such a high vocation, she was honored by God to preserve it. If the wages of sin are death, the wages of "full of grace" are life. From a more sober point of view, there need be nothing to suggest that Mary was spared anything human. She knew doubt and temptation; she knew fear and darkness. If Jesus really suffered, surely the humanity of Mary was no less called to do so. In summary, Mary, full of grace, should be understood as the fullest unfolding of the Christian life which all the faithful hope to share.

After all of the exploration of the words of Gabriel, and the examination of an alternate reading of the first words of the angelic annunciation to Mary, what can we conclude? The Ave Maria prayer enjoys an initial wording that can hardly be changed. "Hail, Mary, full of grace" has been a part of the tradition too long to be subject to a rewording because of further

biblical precision in reading the Gospel text. And yet, one need
not apologize for the English wording based literally as it is on
Jerome's Latin translation. The hailing of Mary can be presumed
to be accomplished with great joy, and hence the word need not
exclude the invitation to be happy and to rejoice greatly. Full
of grace is not a condition at all removed from being highly
favored. Rejoice, highly favored one and hail to you who are full
with grace need not be seen as worlds apart. Grace and favor are
related, and the superlative is suggested by either wording.

Those who wish to expand the privileges of Mary are anxious
to defend "full of grace" as the biblical warrant for such a developed theology. Those who argue that the Lucan text refers to
full of grace for the task of being mother of Jesus wish to defend
the integrity of the Bible. They may indeed be in sympathy with
a high Mariology, but they do not think it is just to the scriptural
text to extract such further and expanded meaning from it.
Thus the conception of Mary could be celebrated as a special
providential moment of grace for the woman chosen from the
first moments of her life to be mother of Jesus who is Lord,
but the explanation should not exceed its biblical warrant by a
further elaboration.[24] The two positions, however, are not that far
apart in substance. Even if one grants that Mary's fullness of grace
is directed to her vocation as mother, that vocation need not be
limited to a biological role for a dependent infant. Parenting
continues throughout a lifetime, though its manifestations differ
appropriately according to the age of the offspring. Moreover,
mothering or fathering is a developmental task. Parents raise
children, but children help raise their parents as well. Children
teach their mother or father how to be generous, because they
make demands of them and call them forth. Children form
their parents and make them grow up by assuming their new
responsibility for dependent life. Teachers are taught by those
they teach. Those who give to the poor are also enriched by
them. Mary was favored to raise Jesus, and thus to be raised by
him, raised as a person of responsibility and charity, and raised
up in grace by him who was also Lord God.

Unless you become as a little child you cannot enter the
kingdom of heaven, where the first will be last and the last first.

Whoever would save their life must lose it. The mothering of Jesus is not just specialized grace for a limited task. The mothering of Jesus will be decisive grace. It will make all the difference in Mary's life. She will be full of grace because she will now live her life in a constant situation of grace with Jesus Christ. The fullness of grace is guaranteed to her by Gabriel's annunciation of her vocation. The infant that is baptized receives a corresponding infallible promise of Christian grace. Being raised as a Christian will make all the difference in that child's life. Baptism into Christian community is decisive grace, and all other graces will be included in it. Similarly, Mary is mother of Jesus, and Mary is full of grace throughout her life. The two realities imply each other, support each other, and are not opposed to each other.

Not all believers, Catholic or Protestant, will want to urge a triumphal role for Mary, and they may wish to claim her as disciple and one of us more than as exalted beyond us. Especially they do not wish to read "full of grace" so as to cast her in the role of mediator of all graces, because Jesus alone is mediator. In the incarnation of Jesus we lack nothing further to join us with God. But the theological arguments here are long and complex. Suffice it to say that the Ave Maria prayer should be said with assurance, greeting Mary with profound joy for she is indeed full of grace as God favored her greatly. To enter spontaneously generously into this holy and ancient prayer we need not wait to untangle all of our theological differences. We wish to speak to the mother of our Lord Jesus, and to recall that she is blessed because she bore the savior of the world, first in her heart and then in her womb,[25] and forever after in her faithful living. And we are blessed greatly because of her and because of him whom she bore, our Lord and our God. We would imitate the words of Luke about Mary who "kept all these things, reflecting on them in her heart" (2:19).

THE LORD IS WITH YOU

"The Lord is with you," which concludes verse twenty-eight of Luke, does not have a verb in the Greek nor in the Latin translation. It could be translated the Lord *is* with you, or the Lord *will be* with you, or even in the optative mood, (may) the Lord *be* with you. Such a prayer-like greeting of Mary on the part of Gabriel would not be out of place. However, the context of Gabriel's speech seems to favor a declarative mood, since the angel continues with a commentary that Mary has already found the grace of God: "Do not be afraid, Mary, for you have found favor with God" (1:30). The future tense might in some way be supported by the narrative, "you *will* conceive in your womb and bear a son" (1:31), but the overall context reveals that the action of God is already accomplished, and lacks nothing in the present moment but the faith response of Mary. "The Lord *is* with you" would seem to capture the whole context of the annunciation in Luke.[26]

Gabriel's words would bring assurance to Mary. Insofar as "the Lord is with you" is read as a simple greeting, customary and found as such in the Old Testament, Mary would be put at some ease.[27] The German greeting, "Grüss Gott," would offer a contemporary example of such a religious salutation. Moreover, in the context of the joyful angelic annunciation, the greeting would furthermore be understood as an indication of God's concern and an implicit promise of assistance.[28] All the resources of God will be at the disposal of the woman chosen to be the mother of Jesus the Christ. "The Lord is with you" echoes throughout the Bible in similar circumstances of mission. When God gives a difficult religious vocation to someone in Israel, God is with them. "The Lord is with you" declares that God who wills the end also wills the means. What God has begun, God will finish: "Behold, I

50

am with you." The divine mission is impossible in human terms, but "nothing will be impossible for God" (Lk 1:37). "Blessed are you who believed that what was spoken to you by the Lord would be fulfilled" (Lk 1:45).

There is no definite article in the Greek or Latin, and the usual English translation employs the definite pronoun: *the* Lord is with you. Elizabeth says "how does this happen to me, that the mother of *my* Lord should come to me?" It has been argued that the line "the Lord is with you" belongs more logically to Elizabeth, and that it was relocated by the evangelist to the end of Gabriel's words. The argument follows this logic. "The Lord is with you" is a common enough greeting. We use it in liturgy even to this day when the president of the assembly wishes to greet the people of God. Gabriel has already greeted Mary with the Hail, full of grace. She would be troubled by that greeting, but not by "the Lord is with you," which was a customary greeting. The angel goes on to reassure her that she should not be afraid, because she has found favor or grace with God. Thus, "the Lord is with you" might not be congruent and in some ways interferes with the flow of the dialogue. It is possible that the line belonged with Elizabeth, and for whatever reason the evangelist moved it to the end of Gabriel's words. Recall that in the Vulgate, the "blessed are you among women" was given to Gabriel as well as to Elizabeth from whom it may have been borrowed by the evangelist or by later scribes. If "the Lord is with you" belonged to Elizabeth, the logic would be improved. She would thus greet Mary with the common salutation: "The Lord is with you. Most blessed are you among women and blessed is the fruit of your womb. And how does this happen that the mother of my Lord should come to me?"[29] In any event Elizabeth does speak of the Lord as *my* Lord (Jn 20:13). And Thomas says of the risen Lord: "*My* Lord and *my* God!" (Jn 20:28).

Over a period of time, the Christian community began to refer to *our* Lord Jesus Christ, who taught us to call upon *our* Father. It is curious that until some hundred years ago, the Hail Mary prayer in English was worded: "*Our* Lord is with you." Cardinal Wiseman writes:

In the *Ave Maria,* Catholics have always, till lately, been accustomed to say "*Our,* Lord is with thee"; as it is in that version [the Rheims], and as it was always used in England, even before that translation was made. But, in conformity with the change of text, we have observed of late a tendency to introduce into the prayer a similar variation, and to say "*The* Lord is with thee:" a change which we strongly depreciate, as stiff, cantish, destructive of the unction which the prayer breathes, and of that union which the pronoun inspires between the reciter and Her who is addressed. . . . It has never been the custom of the Catholic Church to say, "*The* Redeemer, *the* savior, *the* Lord, *the* Virgin"; "Redemptor *noster,* Dominus *noster,*" and so "*our* Savior, *our* Lord, *our* Lady," are the terms sanctioned; and, therefore, consecrated by Catholic usage since the time of the Fathers. . . . If, therefore, it be considered too great a departure from accuracy in translation to restore the pronoun in the text of our version, let us at least preserve it in our instructions, and still more in our formularies of prayer.[30]

Nonetheless, the customary translation today of *the* Lord corresponds well with the usage of this phrase throughout the Old Testament, and it is likely that this usage was paramount in the mind of the evangelist. Even though Luke writes of Mary with the resurrection faith of the early church in *Our* Lord Jesus Christ, it would be an anachronism to give such words to Gabriel's greeting. There is nothing to prevent, however, the Christian community composing its prayers which are based on scripture with whatever wording it sees fit.

The *Lord* who is with Mary could be read in two ways. "Lord" translates the Latin *Dominus* and the Greek *Kyrios.* Contemporary scripture scholars commonly hold that the reference is to Adonai, the common word pronounced aloud in deference when Yahweh Sabaoth is intended. Thus, the Lord, the transcendent and mysterious God of the history of salvation in Israel, is with Mary.[31] Some readers hold that the reference is to the incarnate Word of God soon to dwell within the mother Mary. The Lord will be with you in bearing this child or, in effect, the Lord is now with you. Emmanuel, or God with us, has taken up an abode in the maiden Mary. Thus what is meant by the Lord is with Mary is more than the presence of the creator, the assistance of providence, the saving action of God, and the sanctifying presence of the Holy Spirit. God does all these things throughout the history of salvation, but the enfleshment of the Son of God is a unique and ineffable presence within Mary. From the point of view of the resurrection community that treasures the annunciation to Mary in the Gospel of Luke, it is true that the Lord Jesus Christ was known to them. Nonetheless, the question remains how does Luke use the phrase in the mouth of Gabriel? If the line "the Lord is with you" were given to Elizabeth, and at the time of its utterance Mary was indeed carrying the Son of the Most High, it would be more plausible to read the line as a reference to the indwelling of God. John who is quickened in the womb by the approach of Mary bearing Jesus might be an argument in favor of such a reading. But Luke gives the line to Gabriel at the annunciation, and the more conservative reading would maintain that the line refers to the many times in the Old Testament that a difficult mission is given and God's presence is promised as the guarantor of the success of the endeavor undertaken in God's name and by God's initiative. One will walk with God, who will be of unfailing assistance. As Matthew puts it at the end of his Gospel: "And behold, I am with you always" (28:20).

The divine assistance promised in the phrase "the Lord is with you" can be traced throughout the Bible.[32] I have chosen a number of texts, not because they are the only ones, but because they are representative and the exact choice of words fits my purpose. The promise to Abraham, father of faith, is passed on to Isaac: "Fear not, for I am with you and will bless you and multiply your descendants for my servant Abraham's sake" (Gn 26:24).[33] When Jacob stops on his journey to rest for the night and dreams of a ladder that reaches to heaven, he hears a voice promising: "I am with you and will keep you wherever you go . . . for I will not leave you until I have done that of which I have spoken to you" (Gn 28:15). When Moses at the burning bush fears being sent to the pharaoh and laments "who am I?" that I should be the one, "I am who am" reassures him: "But I will be with you" (Ex 3:11–12). As successor to Moses and chosen to lead Israel into the promised land Joshua is assured: "You shall bring the children of Israel into the land . . . I will be with you" (Dt 31:23). And, "as I was with Moses, so I will be with you" (Jos 1:5; see also 1:9 and 3:7). To Gideon in doubt about leading Israel into battle the angel of the Lord appeared to him and said: "The Lord is with you" (Jgs 6:12; see also 6:16). When Samuel anoints Saul with "the Spirit of the Lord," he says to him: "Do whatever your hand finds to do, for God is with you" (1 Sm 10:6–7). Jeremiah fears being the prophet of the Lord and would decline the invitation because "I am only a youth." But he is told by the the Lord: "I am with you to deliver you" (Jer 1:6, 8). When Israel would doubt its providential care, Isaiah reports that the Lord says: "Fear not, for I am with you" (Is 41:10; see also 43:5). When his enemies surround him, Jesus tells them: "The one who sent me is with me. He has not left me alone, because I always do what is pleasing to him" (Jn 8:29). And finally, in the Book of Revelation as the new Jerusalem is descending from on high, a voice proclaims: "Behold, God's dwelling is with the human race . . . and God himself will always be with them" (21:3).

It is almost certain that Luke did not intend that "the Lord be with you" depict Mary as the pregnant mother of the Son of the Most High. The Lord surely would come to be with Mary and to dwell in her womb, and the post-resurrection church understood the incarnation in the light of their faith that Jesus is Lord. Nonetheless, in the annunciation account such a reading of that line is to jump ahead of the story. In the recitation of the Ave Maria prayer, however, surely overtones of the many meanings of "the Lord is with you," including the incarnate presence and also mystical union with God, will amplify the believer's devotion. One always is well advised to begin with what Luke said; one need not conclude nothing further can be said.

The reading which promises the companionship and protection of the Almighty Lord of history fits well the Christology of Luke. He does not have a prominent notion of a pre-existent Word of God that at a point in time becomes flesh. Rather, Luke sees the son of Mary taken up into God. Luke's understanding of Mary would be more ecclesiological than Christological. "The Lord is with you" speaks more of the protection of God for God's chosen ones that it does of the actual presence of God in Mary.

Mary is seen as the faithful disciple who must walk all her life in trust that God is indeed with her in this mystery that only now begins gradually to unfold within her. It is John who evolved a Christology of the Son of God who from all eternity is with the Father, and who in a moment of time becomes incarnate in the virgin Mary. In that reading Mary is seen as the throne of God drawn into God's mystery from the beginning. This is not a question of the substance of either reading being wrong as much as it is a question of which reading fits the context of Luke's work.

It might be possible to combine both readings of our text. The appeal would be to the larger picture of the annunciation. Whether one reads "the Lord be with you" as a reference to the divine assistance to Israel or as a reference to the divine presence in the incarnate Jesus Christ, there remains an annunciation to Mary that she is the chosen one of God. She is the Bride of the Lord. Both the ecclesiological reading that holds her as the faithful servant of God and the christological reading that holds her as the temple of God have this in common. The Spirit of God overshadows this woman, and the work of the Spirit in her life will be magnificent. The immortal and boundless God touches the life of this mortal woman. "The Lord is with you" might be read simply as the One is with the Many. The Creator is with the creation. The Lord God of history has indeed visited his people in a unique moment wherein eternity touches time. The fullness of the assistance of the past in the sacred history of the people of God here reaches a pledge of further assistance culminating in the very presence of the Most High, the Word of God enfleshed in the womb of the virgin Mary. In the beginning, the Lord made out of nothing the world of all things incomprehensibly existing outside of God who is everything. Never could this world exist without God, who sustains all things. The Lord God must be with us always. In the re-creation, in that moment of history known to God alone, the Lord made out of a virginal beginning a new world of beings mysteriously inside God who is everything. The Lord is with Mary both as creation and as incarnation, for in her the two realities are conjoined. The divine assistance culminates in the divine presence. The word of God that spoke in silence "in the beginning" of the world, a world that may have exploded into being, is here spoken in silence to a maiden whose soft whisper is a human response prepared by the presence of God through the history of the world, and in particular, throughout the sacred and saving history of Israel.

Finally, the annunciation has been understood as an engagement by God of the virgin Mary. She is to be the spouse of God. Spouse is to be understood as a special love of God reaching out to this particular person given the unique vocation to be mother of the Son of God. "The Lord is with you" now means the Lord loves and desires you. The Lord is with you becomes the Lord would espouse you. Especially if Mary is construed in the annunciation as the daughter of Zion, a figure of the people of God and of the Church, the imagery of the bride of God resonates with many passages in scripture.[34] In such a theology, Gabriel announces a mystical betrothal. The divine assistance has become the divine encounter. Promise has become fulfillment, and time has become eternity. The One is not just the assistance and guarantor of the Many, the One seeks to become ineffably at one with the Many. The enfleshment of Jesus is the definitive and irrevocable marriage of God and humankind. In the incarnation of Jesus, the One and the Many will be transcended and wonderfully united. God and creation will be as one. The coronation of Mary is the crown expression of our faith in just how close our God has drawn to us in the self-gift of God's only Son.[35]

BLESSED ARE YOU AMONG WOMEN

During those days Mary set out and traveled to the hill country in haste to a town of Judah, where she entered the house of Zechariah and greeted Elizabeth. When Elizabeth heard Mary's greeting, the infant leaped in her womb, and Elizabeth, filled with the holy Spirit, cried out in a loud voice and said, "Most blessed are you among women, and blessed is the fruit of your womb. And how does this happen to me, that the mother of my Lord should come to me? For at the moment the sound of your greeting reached my ears, the infant in my womb leaped for joy. Blessed are you who believed that what was spoken to you by the Lord would be fulfilled."

Luke 1:39–40

We turn now to the visitation itself (Lk 1:39–56), and to the words of Elizabeth that are included in the Ave Maria (Lk 1:42). When Mary and Elizabeth meet in an embrace, the Old Testament encounters the New Testament. John the Baptist, the last and greatest of the prophets recognizes even in the womb the coming of the one greater than he. The visitation is the passing of the baton from the spent runner to one who runs the last lap, who will race for the end time. The visitation is transition. The annunciations to Zachary and to Mary represent a complete contrast, the old and the young, the public and temple role of the old man, and the private and ordinary role of the young woman. Elizabeth and Mary continue that scene. Elizabeth is the Old Testament touching on the New; Mary is the Old drawn into the light of the New Testament. The new covenant greets the old and receives a blessing from it. The leaping with joy of John yet unborn in Elizabeth and both of them being filled with the Holy Spirit by the greeting of Mary has made the visitation reminiscent of the coming of the Ark of the Covenant into Jerusalem. David danced with unrestrained joy around the Ark, which remained some three months in the city (2 Sm 6:1–14).

The visitation scene is a mini-Pentecost, the early outpouring of the Holy Spirit in the New Testament. Accordingly, Mary in the annunciation is the first catechumen, who hears the Good News preached to her about the savior, and then becomes the first disciple when she received that news to heart and assents to receive her Lord: "Behold, I am the handmaid of the Lord. May it be done to me according to your word" (1:38). Her visit to Elizabeth follows her own evangelization and reception of the Holy Spirit. Mary is the first apostle, sent out on a mission to bring Christ to others. She is a vessel of grace; she brings Jesus Christ to others. Urged on by the charity in her heart, she hastens into the hill country.

When we give a blessing to someone or something, we speak well of it. We acknowledge that the object of our blessing takes its origin from God and is oriented to God. The word "bless" comes from a Latin word, *bene-dicere*, which has two roots: to *say* and to say *well*. In Greek, *eulogēmenē* shows the same derivation. To well say something or someone is to bless them. Thus, when Elizabeth blesses Mary, she says well of her by claiming that she would be well spoken of among womankind. They would recognize her worth. "Well spoken among women are you" would translate "blessed are you among women."

When we give a blessing at meals, or say grace, we speak well of the food before us. We acknowledge that it is good, necessary to our physical life, and prepared attractively. But more than that, we acknowledge that it is a gift. We say of our food something very good; it is given to us. Not only do we acknowledge the human freedom that finally cannot be constrained of the farmer, the provider, the cook in the kitchen, and the one who serves the meal, but we recognize that we are indeed served with a great love. That love seasons our food, and it nourishes not only our body but also our soul. People, gathered as a family around the table and who partake of the love of those who provided and prepared and served the meal, know very well that their soul is fed most of all. Accordingly, we say a blessing for our table or give thanks for our food to God because we know that ultimately our life and this meal which preserves it come from the loving hand of God. God's feeding us food reminds us that God feeds our life in all its dimensions, heart and soul, and that all the time. Thus, a blessing which says well of what is blessed ends as a thanksgiving, since what is most telling is that what we bless is a gift. Moreover, everything is gift from God. All is grace. Nothing is to be taken for granted. "What do you possess that you have not received?" (1 Cor 4:7). Eucharist means thanksgiving, and it is a meal in which a long grace is said over the bread and the wine. The blessing cup is consecrated by telling the story of what God has done and saying well of God in his love for us. We are God's gift. We are gifts to each other, and life is God's gift. In the preface of the eucharistic prayer we are reminded over and over again to "give thanks always and everywhere." This gratefulness is no exaggeration. The whole of life is gift from God about whom we cannot say well enough, because whatever we say well of is always God's gift. Blessing becomes thanksgiving. Human life is gratitude; Christian life is eucharist.

From the Old Testament one can see how blessings were given and how the words of Elizabeth to Mary at the visitation would be read as a culmination. In Genesis Melchisedech blesses Abraham: "Blessed be Abram by God Most High, maker of heaven and earth; and blessed be God Most High, who has delivered your enemies into your hand!" (14:19–20). In Deuteronomy Moses relates to the people all the blessings that will flow from keeping the covenant with God: "And if you obey the voice of the Lord your God. . . . Blessed shall you be in the city, and blessed shall you be in the field. Blessed shall be the fruit of your body, and the fruit of your ground" (28:1–4). Uzziah says to Judith: "O daughter, you are blessed by the Most High God above all women on earth; and blessed be the Lord God, who created the heavens and the earth, who has guided you to strike the head of the leader of our enemies" (Jth 13:18). To give birth to the messiah would deserve the highest blessing, for all blessings were providential preparation for this blessed event.

Elizabeth filled with the Holy Spirit at the greeting of Mary cries out in a loud voice, "Most blessed are you among women, and blessed is the fruit of your womb." It has been suggested that Luke may have taken Elizabeth's words spoken in a loud voice from a hymn in use in the early church liturgy, which praised the mother of Jesus.[36] A similar origin for the Magnificat of Mary has been put forth. Luke used a verb (*anephōnēsen*) for crying out with a *loud voice* that is typically used to introduce sacred song. Nonetheless, the conclusion that songs to Mary are pre-gospel is not held widely. However, some form of devotion to Mary would seem to underlie the visitation canticles of Elizabeth and Mary herself. Elizabeth in effect gives us a commentary on Gabriel's annunciation. Mary who is so favored and graced is indeed blessed among women, and her son as well. She is blessed because of her son, whom Gabriel announced as the Son of the Most High. Blessed is the mother and blessed is the child. Following our earlier conclusion that Mary is favored and graced because of her role as mother, so Elizabeth's twin blessings should be read in a subordinate way. Blessed is the mother because blessed is the child. Overall, blessed is God. And Mary joins this chorus of thanksgiving to God in her own hymn of praise: "he has looked upon his handmaid's lowliness; behold, from now on all ages will call me blessed" (Lk 1:48).

Elizabeth speaks of Mary as most blessed among women. The text does not suggest that Mary is blessed *beyond* all women, but rather very blessed *among* women. Similarly, Elizabeth's words proclaim Mary *most* or very blessed among women; they do not claim Mary is *the most* blessed woman who ever lived, though later generations would reach such a conclusion. One might ask: should Luke's text be read as blessed among women because she is a woman? In effect, should one read blessed are you as a human being, but since you happen to be a woman, blessed are you among women? Or, should it be read, blessed are you precisely in your pregnant womanhood? Should one read blessed are you among women who bear children, because of your son? The implication is that Mary is well spoken among women of childbearing years, and precisely because her child is the Lord: "And how does this happen to me, that the mother of my Lord should come to me?"

Later in Luke's Gospel a woman will bless Mary precisely for her maternal role. "Blessed is the womb that carried you and the breasts at which you nursed" (11:27). The point at issue is important because objection has been made that Mary should be extolled as a person of faith, who happens to be a woman, rather than as only a biological mother of a child. One might respond that motherhood need not be understood as only a biological episode or merely a temporary and accidental role. Relationships formed by family ties might be seen as person-enhancing. Freely embraced, the family is a mini-church. There is a response to this issue in Luke following upon the praise of the maternity of Mary: "[Jesus] replied 'Rather, blessed are those who hear the word of God and observe it' " (11:28).

In Luke, Mary stands with the women in the Bible who seem unfulfilled, but for whom God provides life where no life was expected. She embodies the content of the Magnificat; the lowly God raises up. This reversal is a forerunner of the paschal mystery, when God will raise up from the dead those who have loved God. Both Mary and Elizabeth are taken from unfruitful women to become the bearers of life where it was humanly impossible to expect it. Both are in social positions that are powerless, and both women emerge courageous. New life comes through these women in their visitation from above. They are surprised by God. In the poverty of unfulfilled hope the poor are made rich. The barren are quickened with new life. In the visitation of Mary and Elizabeth, there embrace the two women, each carrying her male child, but dependent only on God. Their lives are not centered on their husbands but on their Lord and God. God is praised for doing the impossible. God who created from nothing can re-create from the poverty and mortality of this life. The virgin conceives; the old is made fruitful. Thus Mary and Elizabeth already anticipate the paschal mystery. They knew lowliness and life's limitations; they knew the coming of the Spirit, the creation of new life, and the raising up of their hope. The mystery of the resurrection begins with the annunciation, for both mysteries are entirely the work of the sovereign Lord God.

In the genealogy of Jesus in Matthew, a long line of male progenitors is given from whom his descent was taken. A man might have several wives, and hence the descent of a child was traced through the father. In addition to the male forbears, four women are included in this lineage of Jesus. Mary is put among women, moreover, whose lives were a scandal. Her own predicament, pregnant and not living with her husband, is an alleged scandal. Joseph is minded to divorce her. She could be stoned to death for her apparent adultery (Dt 22:23). What do these four "shady ladies" have in common with the mother of Jesus? Why were they included at all?[37] Were they sinners whom God used in a providential way? Their lives were surely touched by irregularity. Were they all unwed as Mary was unwed, and yet the child of their body became a link in the life that was passed on to Jesus of Nazareth? Tamar seduces Judah by a ruse to give her a child, when Judah was obliged to give his son to her as husband. Rahab was a prostitute who was spared by Joshua in the fall of Jericho because she sheltered his scouting party in time of discovery. Ruth is alone in a foreign land without a male protector and must trust her life to Boaz. Bathsheba is the innocent wife of another man, and Solomon is born from her and King David. What all these women seem to have in common is danger and lack of defense for themselves or their child. Such was Mary's situation, and the implication is that her motherhood required great trust in the providential ways of God. She was not only fruitful in body; she was faithful in soul. The Good News was thus first preached in Galilee of the Gentiles. God is with the outcast; God sides with the abused woman and with the endangered or unwanted child. Those who lose their life will find it. With God death is not victor, but life. Those who enter the mystery of the cross, enter the paschal mystery of the resurrection to eternal life.

The women of the Old Testament are usually associated with bodily fruitfulness, but not always. Mary's story of the birth of a child in circumstances when a child is impossible ("I have no relations with a man") does parallel the story of the matriarchs of the past who were too old to bear a child or who were unexplainably barren. Consider Sarah with Isaac, Rachel with Joseph, Hanna with Samuel, and the parents of Samson (Jgs 13). But there are other great women in the Old Testament whose faith and courage is sung, and whose blessedness comes more because they took an active role and not because they bore a child. Judith cuts off the head of Holofernes and saves her people. Esther risks entering the presence of Xerxes and thus intercedes for and saves her people.[38] Abigail takes the initiative and feeds David's band of soldiers and her whole household is spared. Deborah is a heroic leader. Susannah perseveres in the truth despite slander. Ruth is faithful to her commitment. And Mary of Nazareth "kept all these things, reflecting on them in her heart" (Lk 2:19 and 2:51). While the motherhood of Mary is the beginning of her role in salvation history, the faith of the mother of Jesus preceded the life of her child and perdured after his death. She is found among the women with the disciples who believed and awaited the coming of the Holy Spirit in Pentecost (Acts 1:14). "Blessed are you among women."

The historical criticism of the Bible may seem to leave the Christian community bereft of the comforting stories of the infancy of Jesus with his mother Mary. That lovely Christmas story in all its richness is not lost, of course, but the story as a biographical memoir seems unlikely. We do not know the events in detail, though we know the events happened. And yet, the memoirs of Mary, even if we had them in some detail, might not tell us as much about her soul as the twice-repeated disclosure that we do have: "And Mary kept all these things, reflecting on them in her heart" (Lk 2:19). That Mary pondered in faith and love the ways of God tells us more about her than any number of particulars in her memoirs. We do have a glimpse into her soul and what the events *meant* to her: "And his mother kept all these things in her heart" (Lk 2:51).[39] Mary stands at the beginning of Christian faith. To her is the Word of God made flesh first announced. She is to Christian belief what Abraham is to Jewish faith—the first of many called by God to walk in the way that God would show them. What Abraham is to the synagogue, Mary is to the Church.

Elizabeth adds a blessing for Mary that goes beyond her role as mother of Jesus. She praises her for her faith and trust in God, which implies the entire mystery of God in Jesus. "Blessed are you who believed [unlike Elizabeth's husband Zachary] that what was spoken to you by the Lord would be fulfilled (Lk 1:45).[40]

When Thomas would put his hand into the side of Jesus before he would allow himself to believe in the resurrection, Jesus says to him: "Blessed are those who have not seen and have believed" (Jn 20:29). We are blessed because Mary believed; we are blessed because Jesus rose from the dead; we are blessed because we have not seen but have believed.

AND BLESSED IS THE
FRUIT OF YOUR WOMB

Elizabeth blesses Mary among women and then blesses Jesus, the child of Mary. Similar two-part blessings have been noted in the Old Testament, for example: "Blessed be Abram . . . and blessed be God (Gn 14:19–20). Mary who is blessed among women is the maiden flower which bears the blessed fruit. "Blessed is the branch and blessed the stem which bore such holy fruit." The blessed virgin is further blessed as a mother. The woman is blessed in the child. Gabriel's promise is fulfilled in Elizabeth's sight. God's assistance to Mary becomes God's presence in Jesus. The child is the origin and end of Mary's graces. And blessed indeed is that woman "who believed that what was spoken . . . by the Lord would be fulfilled." If Luke did not have the memoirs of Mary to work with nor the exact words of Elizabeth, it has been suggested that he may have taken the words of the unknown woman who praises Mary, "Blessed is the womb that carried you" (11:27a), and given them to Elizabeth. Similarly, the response of Jesus to that woman, "Rather, blessed are those who hear the word of God and observe it" was given to Elizabeth for her concluding remarks to Mary: "Blessed are you who believed that what was spoken to you by the Lord would be fulfilled."

Luke uses an unusual construction in the words given to Gabriel to announce to Mary. "Behold, you will *conceive in your womb* and bear a son." There is redundancy in this phrase, which emphasizes the body of Mary as the locus for this unique communion of the divine and the human. Elizabeth calls blessed the fruit of Mary's womb and twice mentions that her unborn child leapt for joy at the sound of the voice of Mary (1:41 and 1:44). In the presentation of Jesus in the temple, Luke quotes the law of the firstborn: "Every male that opens the womb shall be consecrated to the Lord" (2:23 quoting Ex 13:2).

Elizabeth praises Mary's child with words that are not customary to our ears but which resonate with Old Testament allusion. The Hebrew phrase, "fruit of the womb," manifests a desideratum that went back to the patriarchs of Israel. When Jacob is dying, he leaves his sons with this blessing: "by the God of your father who will help you, by God almighty who will bless you with blessings of heaven above, blessings of the deep that couches beneath, blessings of the breasts and the womb" (Gn 49:25). The fruit of the womb and the more general expression fruit of the body appear in a number of places in the Bible.[41] "For thou didst form my inward parts, thou didst knit me together in my mother's womb. I praise thee, for thou art fearful and wonderful" (Ps 139:13–14). If a child is the fruit of a woman's body, the child is also the fruit of God's Spirit. Adam and Eve gathered in the death-dealing fruit of Satan's promise, "you will be like God." In the biblical tradition Mary brings forth the life-giving fruit, "the Son of the Most High." Patristic texts often point out that Mary first conceived in her heart and then in her womb. Faith preceded enfleshment. One must first hear the word, then conceive it. Mary is the mother of the living God, and in some way the ultimate fulfillment of Eve, mother of all the living. There was a legend that the tree of life in the Garden of Eden once grew on the place where the tree of the cross of Jesus was planted, and at the foot of which Adam and Eve were buried. The fruit of the tree of the cross truly is everlasting life. Hence the fruit of Mary's womb is not just any child, but the life of the world.

By definition, a fruit is an ovary of a plant that carries seeds capable of reproducing the plant. A woman is born with the seeds of endless life within her, because in principle one woman has in the fruit of her womb the potential for a boundless number of descendants expanding by geometrical progression. It is that mystery of life that Elizabeth grasps in her traditional blessing of Mary's offspring. By implication she recognizes that Jesus is the ultimate Lord of life who will bring the whole human race to everlasting life with God. From a spiritual point of view "we are all his maternal relations, his mother's people."[42] Baldwin of

Canterbury writes: "Who is this fruit but the holy one of Israel, and who is this seed but that of Abraham, the sprout of the Lord, the flower rising from the root of Jesse, and the fruit of life whom we have received?"[43]

In the East the "*compassionate* Buddha" is the over-arching title for the transcendent as touching upon this world. In Hebrew the word for compassion, as in compassionate love, is a word related to the root word for a woman's womb. "Can a woman forget her sucking child, that she should have no compassion on the son of her womb? Even these may forget, yet I will not forget you" (Is 49:15). In Eastern Christianity Mary is referred to as *Uroborus* or the *womb of God*.[44] Mary is seen as the ark of the new covenant, the temple of the Spirit, the veiled tent, the enclosed garden, the golden tabernacle, the holy grail, the Shekinah cloud of the glory of God in which the sovereign Spirit is enwrapped. In the mystery of the incarnation Mary contains him who fills the whole universe; she nurses him who feeds everybody; she supports him who upholds everything.

Gerard Manley Hopkins writes of Jesus at his conception: "warm-laid grave of a womb-life grey."[45] Human beings are born to die. To be born is already to have begun to expend a limited number of days that stretch before the certain grave. The womb is from whence we came; the tomb is to whence we surely go. The greyness of the womb and its inchoate life is like the darkness of the tomb and its incipient dissolution. The virgin womb of Mary where no life had ever lain is reflected in the tomb of Jesus, newly hewn from the rock, where no body had ever lain. Virgin womb of Mary in all its implication leads to Mary immaculata (conceived without sin); virgin tomb in all its implication leads to Mary assumpta (assumed bodily into heaven).

Virginity is of God. It is the infinite God who is virgin, having no one outside God, needing no one but God, who is sovereign in creation. "All things came to be through him, and without him nothing came to be" (Jn 1:3). The infinite God is virgin by essence; the creator God is virgin made fruitful in a wonderful way. Many children are brought forth where nothing had been before. "We have an ontological virginity that can only be espoused by God."[46] That virgin creation of the world is echoed in the conception of Jesus in the virgin Mary, from whose nothingness we have all received. Max Thurian writes: "The whole church is also living in this consecrated submissiveness, contemplative poverty and this eschatological newness, symbolized by Mary's virginity."[47] The virgin providence of the world is echoed in the sovereign resurrection from the empty tomb of Jesus, from whose sovereignty we have all received.

After Jesus was born of Mary, her body provided his food. In her body and from her blood he grew in life and limb. From her blood turned into milk he was fed as an infant at her breast. Her body was food. Her bones were a tree from which hung the fruit of paradise. In an analogous way the body of Jesus is food for the disciples. From his body hung on the cross they are born into the life of the Spirit. From blood issuing from his spear-wounded breast they are fed. They are bathed with water from his side and nourished with the blood of his heart in the paschal mystery of Calvary. His body becomes food, the bread of life. In the sacrament of the eucharist, Christians eat his body and drink his blood.

Mary is given into the care of John as they both stand at the foot of the cross, underneath the lanced side of Jesus from which "blood and water flowed out" (Jn 19:34). In John's account the Church is born from this wounded side of Jesus just as Eve was taken from Adam's side when he was cast by God into a deep sleep. Then his bone was fashioned into hers. The Christian is born from the womb of God, which is the Spirit of God. "No one can enter the kingdom of God without being born of water and Spirit" (Jn 3:4). The baptismal font is the womb of the Church, mother of the living, the indwelling of the Spirit.

In pagan mythology Athene is born from the head of Zeus. Ancient wisdom was feminine, but not born of woman. Jesus, however, is born of woman. He is a real human body contained in a real human body. Flesh from flesh, the fruit of her womb. The human body is not an idol to be adored as the only life we mortals have. Nor is the flesh in this life a cornucopia of delights, for tomorrow we die. The flesh is not our enemy, to be overcome with violence and abuse. The human body does not belong to others to use or abuse, to exploit or oppress, to torture or to kill. Jesus is of the body, and the body is of God. Nonetheless, the body must finally be surpassed. The body must not, however, be jettisoned in its wounded condition, but rather transfigured, wounds and all. Then the transformation of the flesh glorified by God will shine out forever. Then will the body be flower and fruit, unsurpassable beauty from the hand of God.

Among her many titles Mary is called "mystical rose." The beauty of the rose is legendary. Its petals enfold a hidden core, an implicate mystery, a subtle fragrance. Its crimson color has reminded the beholder of the red blood of the human body. The rose is a lover's token: "My love is like a red, red rose." A delicate flower, it takes its rise from the dark and heavy earth. Tightly closed in the bud, the rose reveals itself in gradual bloom, its petals yet curtaining and concealing its hidden seed. It falls full blown in death and drops away. In the medieval cathedral, the rose window faced west with its falling light. Its many stained glass panes captured the complex petal structure of the circular rose. One window and many petals. One creator and many creatures. One Love and many loves. Dante's paradise is imagined as a white heavenly rose that contains all those persons created by the infinite One, and finally enfolded in imperishable rapture before the face of God. Mary is the mystical rose. From her vulnerable body in this life there bloomed a rose "from tender blossom sprung," whose beauty was unsurpassable, the body of the Lord. The madonna with the child in her arms, the baby whose eyes were the color of her own and whose bones were fashioned from her, has been an icon of inexhaustible poignancy for the religious imagination. The mystery of the incarnation is depicted at once in the madonna and child.

JESUS

The first part of the Hail Mary prayer ends with the name of Jesus: "blessed is the fruit of your womb, *Jesus.*" Elizabeth does not use the name of Jesus in the Lucan text, although the name Jesus comes from the Gospel account. In the annunciation of the angel, Mary is instructed: "you shall name him Jesus" (Lk 1:31; see also Mt 1:21). The Ave Maria in the form it was said in much of the Middle Ages ended without the name of Jesus. For example, Aquinas in his commentary on the Ave Maria concludes with the words: "blessed is the fruit of your womb."[48]

If prayer is a conversation with God, one would not be surprised to find a proper name to address. If human beings love to repeat the names of the persons they love, one is not surprised that the name of Mary appears twice and the name of Jesus concludes the scriptural portion of the Ave Maria. On some accounts the addition of the name of Jesus to the Ave Maria was at the initiative of Pope Urban IV (1261–1264). I have not seen any certain confirmation for this attribution.

The etymology of the name Jesus is not as disputed as the name of Mary. The name of Jesus comes from two roots: the short form of the word for the mysterious and unnamed God of Moses and the people of Israel, the YAH of allelu-*ia*, and the root word for save. "Yehoshua" thus signifies YAH saves. In English we say Joshua. The formal address of Jesus would have been Rabbi Jeshua ben Joseph (Rabbi Joshua son of Joseph). Jesus is a shortened form of Joshua. The name suggests clearly the God who saves, or the savior.

In the name of Jesus the disciples work wonders (see Mk 16:17; Acts 3:6 and 16:18). Peter testifies: "There is no salvation through anyone else, nor is there any other name under heaven given to the human race by which we are to be saved' (Acts 4:12).

Paul urges that "at the name of Jesus every knee should bend, of those in heaven and on earth, and every tongue confess that Jesus Christ is Lord, to the glory of the Father" (Phil 2:10–11). In times past God spoke through many prophets and with many words. In the fullness of time God sent his only son, the one Word of God, the final, total, and last Word of God, Jesus Christ who is Lord. The Ave Maria concludes the first and scriptural part of the prayer with that simple Word of God, Jesus.

PART TWO

The second part of the Ave Maria is a church prayer of few words. The Good News remains that the God of salvation gives both the gift and its reception within us. One without the other is not salvation. The Holy Spirit is given to humanity so that we might not miss the gift of God in Jesus Christ. Mary whose life is touched by the Spirit from its beginnings does not fail to receive the gift that is Jesus Christ. "Us sinners" have unredeemed hearts to the extent we have failed to receive the gift the Holy Spirit provides for us. All of our life is a preparation both for the now and for the hour of our death. Those times shall come to coincide. No wonder that we pray to stand in the eternal moment with her who held him both as a baby body in the womb and as a dead body by the tomb. Holy Mary, mother of God, pray for us sinners, now and at the hour of our death. Amen.

HOLY MARY

Holy Mary echoes the lines of Elizabeth in the Ave Maria prayer. She who is blessed among women is *holy* Mary. The Blessed Virgin Mary is Holy Mother Mary. She who is blessed is the mother of Jesus who is Lord. Therefore she is called *holy* Mary, mother of God. How blessed she was among women and how blessed the fruit of her womb was not fully known by Elizabeth. The second part of the Ave Maria picks up the echo of these lines and carries them to a further contemplation. She is more than blessed, she is holy. Her child is more than blessed, he is the Lord God. Therefore she is *holy* Mary, the "mother of my Lord," the mother of God.

If someone or something is called holy, it is because of a relationship with God who is all-holy. Vessels which are set aside for temple worship are holy because they are consecrated for a sacred purpose in God's house and service. The holy is always set apart from the profane and the quotidian. Holiness is related to wholeness and completeness, for the closer one draws to God the more one is enriched with the fullness of being. People of exemplary moral conduct are holy because they are close to God who is without sin. Holiness of character reveals godliness. Those with holy office are blessed and consecrated to service and intimacy with God. The holy is a chosen and adorned vessel of election.

Mary was made holy in her call to serve God as the mother of the Son of God made human. Mary grew in holiness as she lived side by side with her son Jesus, who "advanced in wisdom and age and favor before God and man" (Lk 2:52). Mary's character was holy because her free response to God was total, responsive, and full of faith. As Aquinas says: (1) she heard, "the Holy Spirit will overshadow" and so forth; (2) she consented through faith,

"Behold the handmaid of the Lord" and so forth; (3) she kept the Word and carried it in her womb; (4) she brought the Word forth, "she brought forth her first-born son"; (5) she nourished the Word and nursed it.[1] Her holiness did not stem from being a virgin woman, nor was she virgin because it was the condition of being holy. Her virginity is not valued primarily as a bodily condition, but more as a condition of soul. Her virgin soul over-shadowed her virgin body. As a total person she belonged to God. In her being God re-created the world anew through Jesus Christ. She was the handmaid of the Lord, and not of anyone else, male or female. She was a believer in God, a disciple of Christ, a woman of communal faith. Her magnanimous self was close to God and we rightly address her in body and soul as *holy* Mary.

We have considered above that holiness in Mary comes from her dedication to God and from her own generous and personal goodness before God. There is also a holiness in her that comes from her association with the Son of God. In the Byzantine liturgy at the communion rite, the priest says: "Holy things for holy people." In receiving the eucharist Christians are made holy by their intimacy with the holy one in the eucharistic bread. As the mother of Jesus Mary is drawn closer to God. Aquinas writes that the Blessed Virgin as mother of God enjoys "a certain infinite dignity from the infinite good which is God."[2] Gabriel says to Mary: "Therefore the child to be born will be called holy, the Son of God." Paul writes: "If the root is holy, so are the branches" (Rom 11:16). A theologian might well conclude as Boff does: "Mary is holy because she would hold the Holy in her womb."[3] A bad tree does not bear good fruit. Mary's holiness is revealed by the holiness of the fruit of her womb. "By their fruits you will know them. Do people pick grapes from thorn bushes, or figs from thistles? Just so, every good tree bears good fruit, and a rotten tree bears bad fruit" (Mt 7:16–17). Her own personal holiness and her God-given role converge without loss to either her freedom or God's sovereignty.

In Greek, the invocation of Mary is rendered: *Haghia* (not earthly) Maria[4] or *holy* Mary. In Latin, the word "holy" is writ-ten *Sancta* Maria. The Ave Maria prayer makes no problematical claim to her holiness. It says simply holy Mary or Saint Mary. The litany of the saints in Latin would use exactly the same words. Sancta Maria would find an echo in Sancta Lucia or Sancta Cecilia. The litany of saints begins: (1) Holy Mary, pray for us; (2) Mother of God, pray for us. The martyrs and the confessors of faith that came to be sainted were those whose lives in this world were recognized to be holy and given to God. At their death, they were taken up into the saints in heaven; they belonged to the communion of saints. Their lives did not cease; they were alive in God and in the body of Christ. The communion of saints was the Church in triumph, the Church before the face of God. The believer yet living in this earthly life might call upon the saints in heaven. Saint Mary, Blessed Mary, Mary whom is in heaven, Mary who is before God, pray for us. The Ave Maria is a prayer of petition to the mother of Jesus, who the Christian community holds as one of the saints, indeed the premiere in the Kingdom of God. The earliest extant prayer to Mary, from the third century, begins: "Under your patronage, O *holy* mother of God."[5]

One may well wish to hear or not to hear overtones of a more radical claim for Mary as sinless and Mary as mediatrix, but nothing so elaborate is given in the Ave Maria. It claims only to address Mary as one of the saints in heaven. The person who prays the Ave Maria may hold in mind a further theology with regard to Mary, or they may hold nothing further than the words and their simple forthright content. Regardless of one's theology, surely every Christian can say "Holy Mary." Peter writes to the Christian community: "as he who called you is holy, be holy your-selves in every aspect of your conduct, for it is written, 'Be holy because I [am] holy'" (1 Pt 1:15–16). Surely, Mary of Nazareth, as known in scripture and in the tradition, was considered a holy woman, to whom one might address a prayer. Generations of Christians throughout centuries of prayer both liturgical and personal have been delighted and privileged to do so.

MOTHER OF GOD

In the Ave Maria, the Latin *mater Dei* is translated mother of God. The Litany of Loreto gives many titles to Mary, and the second part of the Ave Maria might have employed any one of them as a title in a prayer addressed to Holy Mary. For example, "Holy Mary, *help of Christians*, pray for us" might have served well. In the New Testament, Mary is referred to as mother some twenty times, and no other title approaches this frequency. The scriptures do not refer to her as mother of God, however, but as mother of Jesus, or "mother of my Lord." Dante Alighieri, whose *Divina Commedia* exalts Mary, speaks of her as "Vergine Madre, figlia del tuo figlio," that is "Virgin Mother, daughter of your son." Perhaps his phrase captures more poetically the wonder and mystery of the Blessed Virgin Mary. The second part of the Ave Maria, however, includes only one title, and that title a simple one, most ancient and solemn: *mother of God*.

The reason for the preeminence of the title "mother of God" can be traced to both a historical conciliar definition and to its theological insight. Following upon the councils of Nicaea (325), which defined Jesus as consubstantial (*homoousion*) with the Father, and of Constantinople (381), which defined the Holy Spirit as equally to be adored with the Father and the Son, the third ecumenical Council at Ephesus (431) entitled Mary *Theotokos*, literally the "bearer of God," which was colloquially understood as "mother of God," especially in the Latin church. As a theological term *Theotokos* was previously found in the Greek patristic writers such as Origen, Cyril of Jerusalem, and Gregory of Nyssa. The Council of Constantinople had already spoken of Jesus as "born of the virgin Mary," although it should be noted that the earlier Council of Nicaea did not include reference to Mary in its creed. Gradually the Christian community came to fathom the mystery that Jesus was Lord God, and that therefore Mary must be the mother of the Lord God. If she were not, then either Jesus who is Lord was not born of a human mother, or the son of Mary was not the Lord.

The Council went beyond the scriptures to say something about Mary in order to preserve what was said in the scriptures about Jesus, but only by implication about Mary. The Greek term *Theotokos* functioned much like the Greek word *homoousion*. It was argued that *homoousion* (consubstantial) was a necessary non-scriptural word to be included in the doctrine of faith precisely in order to defend the orthodox scriptural meaning of Jesus as Son of God, consubstantial with the Father and not just a demigod creation of the Father. Subsequently, *Theotokos* was seen as necessary to protect *homoousion*. *Homoousion*, which was coined to overcome the Arian denial of the divinity of Jesus, leads to *Theotokos*, coined to overcome the denial that Mary bore the one *person* of Jesus, both God and man. Mary did not bear a human person, and God provide the divine person. Mary is mother of the *one person*, Jesus who is Lord-God. Of his human nature, she is mother; she is not mother of his divine *nature*. In the one person of Jesus the two natures are united and yet not commingled in the one person. *Homoousion* and *Theotokos* become the two great password defenders of the orthodox understanding of the incarnation: Jesus is both fully God and fully human. He is one person with a divine nature and a human nature. Jesus is Lord. Jesus is Son of God. Mary bore him; Mary is his mother. Therefore she is mother of God. Mother of *God* corresponded to and was correlative with Jesus is *Lord*. Both entitlements were seen to rise and fall together.

Thus Mary as *Theotokos* was the rejection of the demi-divinity Jesus of Arius and the unfleshed Christ of the Docetists and Gnostics. Mary as *Theotokos* is the validation of the orthodox understanding of the incarnation. Jesus was Lord God from the moment of his conception by Mary, and not just from the descent of the Spirit of God upon him in his baptism. Against the Arians, Mary is mother of *God*, and against the Gnostics, she is *mother* of God. Jesus *Kyrios* (Jesus is Lord) is convertible with allegiance to Mary *Theotokos*. Such a strategy may not have been the only way to defend the mystery of the incarnation in all its complex wonder and glory, but it does reflect the actual history of Christianity. Even the reformers stood within that tradition. The Lutheran Formula of Concord in 1577 affirmed Mary as mother of God (*mater Dei*).

Theo-tokos is translated into Latin by either of two terms: *Dei Genitrix* or *Deipara*. Both terms suggest that the Greek defines Mary as the one who bears God into this world. She generates Jesus who is Lord-God in the flesh; she is *Dei-Genitrix*.[6] *She gives birth or parturition; she is Dei-para.*[7] The Council of Ephesus did not precisely call Mary "mother of God."[8] In Greek there is an expression *Theometeros*, which literally means mother of God. The Latin translation of *Theotokos* does not use the words of the Ave Maria, *mater Dei*, or in English, mother of God. Maloney more precisely translates *Theotokos* as "birth-giver of God."[9]

This doctrine of Mary might also be captured by the term *Christotokos* or "birth-giver of Christ," if adequately understood. Nestorius promoted a low Mariology when he held that Mary was *Christotokos*. She was the mother of Jesus of Nazareth. This was true enough, just as it was true to say Jesus was human. Nestorius wished especially to defend the humanity of Jesus. Mary was therefore the mother of the human Jesus. While the Council of Ephesus rejected *Christotokos,* the Council of Chalcedon (451) just twenty years later dealt with the essential understanding of that term. It is Christian doctrine that Mary is mother of one person, Jesus Christ the Lord, both man and God. She was the mother of this one person and this person was Son of God. Therefore Mary gave birth to the Son of God in the flesh and is called mother of God. The Council of Chalcedon would formulate the role of Mary: "ex Maria virgine Dei genitrice secundum human-itatem" or "from the virgin Mary, genitrix of God, according to his humanity."[10] Mary gave birth to the Son of God in his human nature. But Mary is not the mother of God in any causal or sovereign sense. The person of the Son of God existed from all eternity in the bosom of the Father. It is this person who took flesh of the virgin Mary, but Mary is not the mother of his divine nature.

The history of the Council of Ephesus shows how difficult it is to reconcile two different ways of looking at the scriptures. Some of those who supported *Christotokos* were opposed to Mary as *Theotokos* because they were opposed to Jesus as Lord-God. But not all of the supporters of the school of Antioch were in such error. Nestorius was not. *Theotokos* carried the day in Ephesus, but some of its success was due to theological, political, and personal motives in the on-going conflict between the biblical theology of Alexandria and that of Antioch. Cyril of Alexandria followed a high Christology in proposing Jesus as Lord and Mary as *Theotokos*. The Gospel of John proposed a similar ontological understanding of the Word of God made flesh. *Christotokos*, however, need not be the expression of an unorthodox Christology. It speaks of a low Christology, which need not deny the divinity of Jesus while emphasizing his humanity. The synoptic Gospels knew Jesus as Lord, but it was the result of knowing him as a man sent from God. A Christology of pre-existence was not necessary to faith in Jesus as Lord. It was a question the synoptic evangelists did not pose. Antioch read the scriptures more as literal story; Alexandria read the scriptures with a symbolic and metaphysical sophistication. Antioch and Alexandria collided in conflict over how to understand the mother of Jesus as mother of the Lord. To this day that tension remains in the Christian community between those who read the scripture texts about Mary from a more historical and evangelical viewpoint and those who read them from a more symbolical and theological one.

However *Theotokos* might be translated, it is clear that this unique relationship with Jesus and with the Son of God is what has made a theology of Mary a peculiar enterprise. Because she is present at the crossroads of the human and the divine, of time and of eternity, many implications about Mary were elaborated. If such an exalted end was willed by God for the purpose of Mary's life, then adequate means to that end must have been provided her. Who wills the end wills the means. Her vocation as *Theotokos* included her beginnings and reached to her endings. Of the *Theotokos* Cardinal Newman writes succinctly, "It is the issue of her sanctity; it is the origin of her greatness."[11] John Damascene writes: "Just the name, Theotokos, Mother of

God, sums up the whole mystery of salvation."[12] Vollert loosely quoting Abbe Blondiau writes: "At the base of the entire edifice of Marian theology, veritable cornerstone on which it rests and which assures its cohesion and solidity, is this truth, contained in Scripture, affirmed by tradition, and defined at Ephesus: Mary is the Mother of God."[13] The theology of Mary claimed her to be immaculate in order to fulfill her vocation as *Theotokos*. Once that was accomplished in her, the theology of Mary extrapolated to her assumption into heaven because of her unique privilege before God as *Theotokos*. From her sanctity comes the incarnation, and from that Christ-event stems her coronation. Such has been much of the classical Marian theology of past centuries.

The central issue, however, is the incarnation of Jesus. Who and what Jesus is drives the concern about Mary. It would be wrong to see Mary as the primary issue, even if a valuable devotion to Mary arose out of the consideration of her privileged role in the incarnation. Information about Mary was peripheral, except insofar as it became the rhetoric through which the incarnation was understood. Mary in Matthew and Luke provides a language and vocabulary that the theological defense of the incarnation adopted. If we could rest assured that Jesus is Lord, it would not be necessary to insist that Mary is mother of God. Not that one would want to deny that conclusion, but it would not be so stressed unless the underlying issue was the defense of Jesus Christ incarnate.

In a similar way, the empty tomb provides the language and rhetoric of the explanation of the resurrection. The empty tomb, however, is not the proof of the resurrection. By itself it only proves that something extraordinary happened. The resurrection is finally an event of faith, even though that faith has been yoked to the particulars of the empty tomb. Similarly, the virginity of Mary has become the language in which the divinity of Jesus is argued. And yet, the virgin conception does not prove Jesus is God, but only that he is a miraculous child. John's Gospel establishes the divinity of Jesus by appealing to the pre-existence of the Word of God rather than by an appeal to the virginity of Mary. The belief in the divinity of Jesus and the fullness of the incarnation comes finally from faith, and not from the belief in a virgin birth. Mary as *Theotokos, Dei Genitrix, Deipara,* bearer of God, or mother of God is simply shorthand for that enormous leap of faith that brings the Christian to cling to the living and infinite God: Jesus is Lord! This point is well made in the Vatican II document of Ecumenism, *Unitatis Redintegratio.* Mary is described as "God's most holy mother so that, in accord with the Scriptures, Christ may be truly and properly acknowledged as Son of God and Son of Man" (#15).

We have seen that the word *Theotokos,* which functioned as the touchstone of the Council of Ephesus, is not perfectly translated by "mother of God." When one hears the word "God," most people understand the Father Almighty. Mary is not the mother of the Father, nor of the divine nature of God. Mary is not the mother goddess, nor the queen mother of the infinite One. She is mother of the Son of God made flesh. *Theo*tokos speaks of God; Theo*tokos* speaks of man born of a woman. *Theotokos* speaks, in sum, of the God-man and Mary who bore him. "Mother of God" was an imprecise translation which became more and more established, especially in the West. Because it could be understood to claim too much, since Mary is not the cause of God as a human mother causes a child, the term has occasioned some contention. "Bearer of God" also carries some ambiguity, for it should not be read to mean that Mary was only a conduit for the bearing of God into the world and thus not a real mother in every way. Since the second part of the Hail Mary prayer as composed in the fifteenth century uses the term "mother of God," some hesitation to embrace unreservedly the piety of this classic Marian prayer obtains to this day.

In the patristic writings and the spiritual writings of the Middle Ages it was not exceptional to read of Jesus as mother. Jesus was mother because Jesus was food and nurture. At his birth he was laid in a manger, the crib where food was placed for farm animals. The disciples at Emmaus recognize Jesus in the breaking of the bread. His body was to be eaten and his blood to be drunk. The eucharist was food, the body and blood of the Lord: "Unless you eat the flesh of the Son of Man and drink his blood, you do not have life within you" (Jn 6:53). Just as a woman gives milk to the hungry child, so the nurturing man on the cross pours out his life from the wound in his side. His blood in the eucharist is now the life of those who drink, and his body broken on the cross is now broken as bread to be eaten from the altar. Just as women give birth with blood and water, so the Church is born from the wounded side of Jesus on the cross. Corpus Christi (the body of Christ) is a feast that was urged by many of the women mystics of the Middle Ages, whose writings are filled with the insight that a woman's body is food as the Lord's body is food. Woman is life-giving, not just as biological mother, but also as victim whose sufferings were food just as the sufferings of Christ became the eucharistic bread of the last supper and the Calvary sacrifice. From such bodies given up as bread to be broken, one might expect a new birth of spiritual life: "Both Christ and woman were food in so far as they were bodies."[14]

The phrase "mother of God" might be enhanced by such an explanation of the body as food, provided it does not reduce the body to a lower function of mere physical support but exalts the body to a higher function of giving life to the soul. Jesus as the bread of heaven and Mary as the mother of God, where mother means life-giving care, show a point of comparison. Both mother and son nurture God in other human beings. Their bodies bring salvation. The priest consecrating the eucharist,[15] the faithful receiving the consecrated bread, and the body of Mary as matrix of life would be analogous examples of bringing to earth the body of the Lord. The Word was made flesh in Mary of Nazareth, and the Word is ever made flesh in the mystery of the eucharistic bread given as food.

Mary was considered mother of God in the biological understanding of that time. The woman was the earth womb in which the seed grew, and from which the seed would assume its nutrition and finally its substance. She was mother earth. Jesus had no human father. Nothing was known of the role of a human mother whose egg contributes half the chromosomal composition of her child.[16] This diminished understanding of human motherhood is wrongly applied to Mary in her relationship with God. Whatever fullness a mother is known to have Mary had. Properly understood her role is not subservient but exalted. *Mater*, the Latin word for mother, is related to the Latin word *materia*, which is translated into English as matter. Mary is the "*mater*-ia of God." From her will be born the savior, Christ the Lord. In her will be conjoined heaven and earth, the One and the Many, the infinite and finite, the divine and the human, the eternal and the temporal. She is the matter of God's creation. She is the mother of God within whom the Lord will take flesh. The incarnate Jesus will be both human and divine, created and uncreated, the Many in the time of creation and the One in the eternity of the creator. Mary is *mater Dei*, the mother of God, the matter of God. She represents the world that is the womb of the creative Spirit of God. She is the Many that is the temple of the One. She creates the body of God as the matter composes the special creation of God. To be matter, to be *mater*, to be body, to be mother, to be alive, to be created, to exist: these are analogous terms. All of them are sacred and exalted references to the creation of this world.

Mother of God might thus be seen as a title not only about the body of Mary and the body of Jesus, but a claim upon her relationship with the mystery of God. She is the mystery of creation within which the uncreated took matter and flesh in the embodiment of the only Son of God, one in being with the Father Almighty. In her, time and eternity overlap, the One and the Many are reconciled, and the whole creation is saved because "God so loved the word he gave his only begotten son" (Jn 3:17). Mother of God is the epitome of being human. Mother of God is acceptance of the human body and its life-giving destiny. In the image of the madonna with the child the whole universe is held in the hands of the baby in her arms. In the mother of God with the child in her arms, the Many holds the One that holds the Many. In Mary eternity rests in time and her child is called Son of God. Mother of God thus contains infinite mystery. It is a title that should never be distorted; Mary is not God. It is, however, a title that should never be minimized. Mary is not just a human body, not just biological progenitress. She is a whole human being, whose personal freedom is always before God as a delight. In her and in all of us, the body is not an obstacle to

God, but the very stuff of which God made the world, the *materia Dei*, the mother of God, and with whom God made a body for his only Son, Jesus Christ our Lord.

Will such an exalted Marian theology serve today? Does it collapse because its presuppositions are not seen any longer as defensible? One objection is that the language of *Theotokos* stems from "androcentric presuppositions."[17] The early conciliar formulation presupposed that God is related to the human as the male who gives is to the female who receives. In truth both men and women exist to receive God. Thus Mary should be seen as a type of humanity. Receptivity, however, may mistakenly appear to make the creature only a servant of the creator. We believe, nonetheless, that God intended to create a world with its own life and its own independence. Human beings are not just adjunct to God; they enjoy a God-given separation. That separation is not ultimately one of radical independence from God, but it does demand its own creaturehood and identity. Humanity is not related to God as women were related to patriarchy. The mystery of the One and the Many allows creation to exist truly in itself, while all the time maintaining that the infinite God encompasses the creation. Similarly, women are not ancillary to men; the human female is not just receptive to the active human male. Virgin, wife, and mother are attributes that Mary has been glorified by, but they need to be understood in a way that does not make her, nor women in general, human beings who are defined by a role in relation to men or to male imagery rather than in relation to their own personhood before God. Can the "mother of God" be given a life more of her own? Can the motherhood of Mary take its justification from her faith and devotion as disciple? She is not mother and disciple, but *mother as disciple.* In all events of her life she listens to God. Thus in her discipleship Mary should be seen as the prototypical Christian, who whether male or female, is devoted to the spiritual life that makes up the Church, the body of Christ.

The critique of the traditional role of Mary has been far-reaching. The tradition states: blessed is Mary because blessed is the fruit of her womb. In other words, holy is Mary because she is the mother of God. The objection is not just that Mary is unique and so exalted she cannot fuction as a model for contemporary Christian women, but that Mary has been the victim of a patriarchial theology that elevates her while correlatively demoting actual historical women. "Our tainted nature's solitary boast"[18] isolates Mary and excludes others, not because it must do so but because in practice whomever we enthrone we distance from ourselves. She is "alone of all her sex."[19] "Mother of God" is a problem because the reference to God seems in effect to claim too much for Mary and the reference to mother seems to claim too little for womankind. Everyone loses, even God, since Mary seems to coopt the tenderness and nurture proper to the Holy Spirit as well as the receptivity and readiness of men and women to hear the word of God and conceive new life. I say "seems" because the evaluation of these matters varies. Not everyone, by any means, has difficulty. Many people, however, do struggle with how to address Mary. In short, for many Christians triumphal Mariology is not only not helpful, it is an obstacle.

The Litany of Loreto contains a large number of titles for Mary. Many of them contain hidden poetical and mystical overtones. Nonetheless, most of the titles of Mary, old and new, pale beside the most traditional and emphasized ones: virgin, bride, and mother. Mary is madonna. Mary is virgin, bride, mother; she is quintessential woman. All these titles refer to her body. The critique of women challenges Mariology precisely in this regard. Woman is uncritically defined, not in and of herself as person, but in regard to her biological role. Virgin, bride, and mother are presented as roles she plays for men. Perhaps they need not always be so construed, but all too often Mary has been portrayed in such a "patriarchal pattern of male fantasies."[20] Elizabeth Johnson objects rightly to Mariology as a "male projection of idealized femininity."[21] Mary is the perfect virgin, the perfect spouse, and the perfect mother of the perfect son. Actual women then come to resemble Eve, remembered as the mother of sin in the world. The First Epistle to Timothy provides a questionable critique: "She must be quiet. For Adam was formed first, then Eve. Further, Adam was not deceived, but the woman was deceived and transgressed. But she will be saved through motherhood, provided women persevere in faith and love and holiness, with self-control" (2:12–15). Actual women come to resemble the temptress Eve, or the sinful Magdalene of popular biblical construction. Insofar as Mary is lifted on a pedestal they are cast down. Most objectionable of all, women continue to be seen only in relationship to men. In Virginia Woolf's succinct assessment, women do not have "a room of their own." They are not valued enough for themselves. Man is the icon of Christ; man acts. Woman is the icon of the Church; she reacts. Men do. Women are done unto. Fathers create a household; women are sheltered. Husbands marry; women are married. God the Father creates; mother earth accepts. Christ is redeemer; women receive the forgiveness of their sins. The priest is another Christ, and women are ministered the sacraments of the church.

All too often women find women portrayed in theological commentary from a male point of view. Thus, Mary is seen as too physical; men seem unduly concerned with her both as a virgin and as a mother. In the former state she appears to be asexual and consequently women's sexuality is demeaned by implication. In the latter she is too subservient, and women as biological mothers are held to be the norm for all women. In short, the objection claims that Mary and her sisters are portrayed in too much Marian theology as passive people, uninvolved with mature decision, pure and detached, with a humility that is not courage but a lack of ego-strength. Accordingly, women should be timid and sweet, silent and self-sacrificing. Consider the shortcoming in the image of Mary as mother of Jesus, mother of God, mother of us all, the ever-ready and always self-giving mother who is always available to the needs of others but who has no life of her own to give them. Her reality is not centered in herself, but in relationship always to others, and those others are usually men with endless claims and demands.

What is being objected to in the feminist critique is not a woman's care for others. The human person is defined as some-one with relationships. The Blessed Trinity is defined as subsistent relationships. To want to be so independent as to belong to no one in any way is to want to be no longer creature but to be a caricature of a self-sufficient God. God is not alone and unrelated in the three divine persons of the Trinity. The objection is not to Mary as virgin, bride, and mother, if these roles are rightly understood so that Mary as woman, and women in general, are enabled as persons. Their fulfillment as individuals should be enhanced by any gender-specific service of the common good. Elizabeth Johnson writes: "To sum up: being responsive to the inspiration of the Spirit, being virginal, and caring for the needs of one's children are not bad things—in fact they are quite excellent values in themselves. But when in the tradition about Mary they are set within an androcentric framework, so that the ideal of woman becomes the passively obedient handmaiden, the a-sexual virgin, and the domestically all-absorbed mother, then the tradition implicitly and explicitly supports the truncation of woman's fulfillment and is vigorously contested in the interest of a greater wholeness."[22] In short, the line in Luke reads "behold I am the handmaid of the Lord"; it does not read behold I am the handmaid of anyone at all. Women wish to serve freely and not to be taken for granted as servants. "I no longer call you slaves. . . . I have called you friends" (Jn 15:15). Therefore one can say that Mary "is not only the realization of the ideal woman. She is the realization of the ideal human being."[23]

The hesitation of some feminists with the theological statement, "mother of God," which has been central to a theology of Mary, might be overcome if a rehabilitation of the stereotypical concept both of mother and of God were undertaken. If motherhood did not connote biological determinism or psychological oppression by assuming every woman should be mother by the claim of men, then the freedom of choosing to accept the vocation of mother might emerge. If Godhead were not portrayed as justice without mercy, or punishment without pity, then we might not need to direct the feminine qualities of God upon Mary. Human motherhood might be restored to Mary and the divine woman restored to God, who remains everything feminine as well as masculine. Mary might be given back to her sisters and brothers as a genuine woman with the struggle to be herself in a world that made all too many demands of servitude upon the oppressed. And God might be restored to all human beings as the prodigal loving Father, full of tenderness and with maternal compassionate solicitude for the uncared for and the helpless.

Although Jesus in his physical needs was attended by the Gospel women who followed him, he himself had no property, no wife, no children. His life was ultimately supported by his Father in heaven. When Jesus said "call no one on earth your father" (Mt 23:9), he was undercutting a patriarchy whose ownership and control were oppressive to women and all of the poor and marginalized people in society.

Motherhood seems not to contribute to human wholeness when it is seen as only relational in a biological way. Woman as nature; biology as destiny. These are the slogans that feminists reject. Personal wholeness calls for friendship among equals. The woman whose life is exhausted meeting the needs and demands of others, especially if she has not fully and freely chosen to meet them is oppressed.[24] Mary as simply the mother of Jesus or the mother of God does not provide automatically any further responsible and growthful relationship with him as an adult. If such a relationship between a mother and child does develop, it goes beyond the physiological bond. It includes the faith and love that founds any and all mature adult human relationships. Mere motherhood does not establish such personal bonds. The surrogate mother or the absentee mother, who gave birth but does not relate to the child over a period of time, does not embody motherhood. What makes motherhood rich for a woman is the further possibilities of personhood. Thus Mary as mother of Jesus is transcended by Mary as friend of Jesus, as believer, as faithful disciple, as a woman committed to the same salvation of the world as her adult son, not essentially because he is her son, but because she freely chooses to believe in him before God and to love God's ways in his and her life. Accordingly women wish to be disciple, friend, and apostle and not only or just merely virgin, wife, and mother. Women wish to have a relationship not just from and with a man in their life (read God, father, husband, priest) but they wish to relate to anyone as a human being and a person. Augustine writes "More blessed was Mary in receiving Christ's faith, than in conceiving Christ's flesh."[25] Mary was "more happy to be a disciple of Christ than to be the mother of Christ. Therefore Mary was blessed because, before she gave birth, she carried the teacher in her womb."[26] Such insights do not demean Mary as mother of God, but they do offer a commentary upon the full challenge and dignity of the life of a woman who is also a mother. Not mother and disciple but *mother as disciple.*

Not only would a resymbolization of "mother" in the title "mother of God" be good for women, it would liberate men as well. They are not made free when they live in the assumption that they are to be served. All freedom comes from serving, not because one must, but because one chooses to do so. If the concept "mother" can be rethought to free both women and men to be more whole and responsible as persons, it will be possible to restore our image of God as well. A God who needs to be placated or cajoled by a pleading and winsome woman intercessor does not look like a God who is abundantly and even prodigally generous. Such a God looks more like a man, a man who is imprisoned by his own lack of generosity and sensitivity. Chaucer describes Mary as "true pity's well." God wields patri-archal justice and power but they are surrendered to a woman's plea for pity and mercy. To grant woman a fuller wholeness would also restore to God those womanly and feminine characteristics that belong to the Holy Spirit, but which have been displaced upon woman, because God has been imaged as a man. In sum, Jesus Christ is the one and complete mediator. The Son of God made flesh is accessible to human beings over whom he wept. He is close to them without further intermediary. The Holy Spirit of Jesus is the feminine face of God who is intimate, tender, caring, intuitive, and comforting. When our understanding of the soul and its relationship with the Spirit is not ample and true, then no one is free, neither women nor men nor God herself.

When Jesus is victim on the cross, he says this about his life: "No one takes it from me, but I lay it down on my own" (Jn 10:18). He is willing to give his life; he accepts his role as sacrifice. There is pain and oppression in his last days that he could escape, but he chooses not to. He stays in Jerusalem, because his hour has come. He seeks in the garden that this chalice might pass, but not his will but his Father's. Similarly, women do not wish to cease ap-preciating the kind of magnanimity involved in being holy virgin, faithful spouse, and self-giving mother. But they cannot make this

kind of gift in any other way than freely. Otherwise, someone is
taking their life. Mary's acceptance in the annunciation, "May it
be done unto me" (Lk 1:38), must not be seen as the fearful and
timid "whatever you say" of a woman whose life is being taken
from her in a demand for her sacrifice so that others may live. It
must be seen as the mature free decision of a woman who chooses
to live in a certain way. No one must take her life away; she must
lay it down freely. And if she wishes, she must be able not to lay
it down at all, or to do so later, or to act as she finds it within her
to do on her own. Mary is the mother of her Lord, the creature
who carries her creator, the woman who gives her breast to the
hungry child whose life is infinity. That motherhood is much
beyond biology. That motherhood is somehow life giving to the
soul. That motherhood is somehow a question of first conceiving
Jesus in her heart and then in her womb. This woman must be a
mother of faith and not just a mother of nature. She is disciple
and believer. She is a human person hearing the word of God
and keeping it through the darkness of this life. Not mother only,
not mother and disciple, but *mother as disciple*.

With this kind of amplitude, rehabilitation of traditional
Marian categories would be possible. Mary is virgin, not because
unmarried women are compelled to be, but because she chooses
to hold her entire self for commitment to a God-given vocation
that will be fully life-giving at a time in the future. Mary gives birth
as a virgin because she would give new life with a clear witness
that it comes from nowhere but from God. Mary is ever a virgin
because her commitment to a vocation from God is not temporary, but includes all of her self and thus all of her lifetime.[27]
Mary as mother is in relationship not only with her child but
also with her God. John McHugh writes: "her motherhood of
Jesus was entirely dependent on her faith, and God gave her that
immeasurable faith in order that she might be the mother of
Jesus."[28] Faith of heart is related to Mary's motherhood as the
soul is related to the body. She gives life not only by physical
support, but by instructing the waiters at the wedding at Cana
that they must "do whatever he [Jesus] tells them." To do the
will of God is to live, to give life, to be not thirsty, to marry in
joy. The wedding at Cana is thus more of a story of the true

disciple who lives by faith and love than the story of a miracle or the proof of intercessory prayer. Mary directs others to God, as Mary Magdalene directed the apostles to the resurrection by her self-witness to having seen the Lord. At the foot of the cross, Mary is mother to the beloved disciple, who is the model of the Christian. From the wounded side of Jesus come forth blood and water, those graces that would be embodied in fire and wind in the Pentecost descent of the Holy Spirit in Luke's upper room. In both of these accounts, the mother of Jesus is there with the disciples, the Church, the body of Christ.

PRAY FOR US SINNERS

The Ave Maria prayer petitions the mother of God with
these words: "Pray for us sinners." Intercessory prayer in the
second part of the Hail Mary is directed to Mary briefly and
simply. There are not many words. Nothing specific is requested;
pray for us suffices. Pray for us-sinners, or for us, who are sinners.
Below we will explore whether the word "sinners" carried any
particular significance in a prayer whose words are so sparing,
and which was so carefully constructed from Gospel texts in its
first part. The issue before us immediately is the explanation of
this petition in the Ave Maria, which may also provide a modest
defense of its inclusion.

Even before talking of the specific words "pray for us sinners" we should consider some prior issues that often keep
people uncomfortable about prayer in general. Is prayer even
possible? Does God listen? Does God care? Does prayer make any
difference to a providence of infinite wisdom and power? Does
God need praise or want thanks? Prayer itself is an overwhelming
mystery. How one understands the mystery of God reveals how
one employs prayer in daily life. Petitionary prayer is even more
of a mystery, for surely God does not need to be asked for
blessings which God knows we need and which God is lavishly
generous to give. Intercessory prayer is yet more problematical,
for now we petition God not directly but through and together
with the prayer of someone else not God. Let us explore briefly
the mystery of prayer in general, of petitionary prayer, and of
intercessory prayer in particular. If believers have difficulty with
any one of these three facets of the mystery of God, they will not
pray the Ave Maria with ease.

What understanding can we offer for prayer itself? How
does God listen? How does God care? Why should an infinite

God pay any attenion to a minuscule human creature on planet earth in the immense immeasurable universe? Newman speaks of a contemporary "generation which emphatically denies the power of prayer in toto, which determines that fatal laws govern the universe, that there cannot be any direct communication between earth and heaven."[29] The Old Testament is an early and strong witness to the conversation with God that is prayer. There can be no true prayer unless God is listening and the believer's assurance of that is God's intervention in Israel's history. God directed Abraham, revealed the divinity to Moses, and inspired the prophets. Just to talk to someone is already to include them implicitly in one's regard. People we ignore we do not even talk to. That God not only listens but also cares finally rests upon the mystery of the messiah. The conversation between Yahweh and Israel was both tender and threatening. The final outcome was not yet achieved. In Jesus Christ Christians believe that God has spoken one final, complete, irrevocable, and love-filled word, who is God's own Word, God's own only Son, the Lord who is with us. Prayer is possible because "God so loved the world that he gave his only begotten Son, so that everyone who believed in him might not perish, but might have eternal life" (Jn 3:16). Whatever the difficulties of prayer, however enormous the very conception of prayer that a creature should hold spiritual intercourse with its creator, nonetheless we believe in prayer because Jesus taught us to pray: "Our Father in heaven . . . give us today our daily bread" (Mt 6:9, 11).

If the mystery of prayer can be accepted in such a faith and if one enters that mystery by daring to speak to that silence who never answers with a sound, one is ready to ask a further question. Suppose one can lift up mind and heart to God. Can one pray for someone or something? Prayer as worship and contemplation may be possible, but is petitionary prayer defensible? Can the eternal God be moved? Does God wait to be asked? Does prayer for this or that outcome make any difference to the event? In short, does God ever intervene? These are all valid questions that we must consider.

Both the Ave Maria and the Pater Noster begin with declarative prayer. They both make declaration and then give praise before raising a petition to God. In addressing the Father, we pray "hallowed be your name, your kingdom come." In addressing Mary we repeat Gabriel's and Elizabeth's greeting of praise: "full of grace" and "blessed are you among women." Prayer of praise of God and thanksgiving to God are readily understood. Prayer of petition then follows. We hope such prayer is not just wishful thinking or its efficacy an illusion. The Our Father petitions in the second half of the prayer for daily bread and forgiveness of sins. The Hail Mary petitions in the second half of the prayer with only a general intercession, "pray for us sinners."

At first glance petitionary prayer would not seem to be possible. If God is supreme, knows all things, and holds all events in an infinitely wise and good providence, what need is there for human suggestion and what room for human initiative? Surely prayer of petition is unnecessary even if humanly reassuring. God foresees all things; God is not stingy and does not need to be coaxed to give good things to the world and to God's beloved children. The problem of petitionary prayer is similar to the problem of creation. Neither mystery seems possible by human logic. If God is everything, how can something be anything? How can the finite even exist in the presence of the infinite? What room is there for something more? The One and the Many is the mystery of the infinite God who created from nothing beings who are not God and yet who cannot be apart from God. God is always around and within creation, and yet creation is not the creator. Similarly, the providence of God reaches to all events, both cosmic ones and those human initiatives dependent upon human independence. God is Lord of all causes, and human freedom is also within God's provident care, without compromising the integrity of the human will in any way. God is doing all things, and yet human beings are free to live their own lives. God makes freedom work from within what God has created, without in the least undermining its integrity. Prayer of petition is part of this mystery of the One and the Many, the Providence of God and human history, the whole world which rests securely in God's hands and our anxious prayers for this and that which also depends on our care and concern. Note how Jesus himself prayed at his baptism (Lk 3:21), before choosing the apostles (Lk

6:12), on Mt. Tabor (Lk 9:28–36), in the Garden of Gethsemani (Lk 22:39–46), and at other times and places.

Prayer of petition follows easily upon the paradigmatic prayer that Jesus left his disciples. "Give us today our daily bread" in the Lord's Prayer is a very specific petition, and for something that would seem at first blush to be ordinarily well within our resources to provide for ourselves. Yet, given an infinite God upon whom all being depends, we ought also to pray for our next breath. Our prayer ought not be anxious, but it should be realistic. Nothing is just a *mere* given. All of existence and life, including our next breath, is a freely bestowed given from God. That the sun rise is not automatic; God makes the sun rise, howsoever many intermediate causes may intervene. Ultimately, we can peacefully and hopefully pray for all things and at all times as St. Paul urges, for every bit of existence and every event in human history lies within God. God is not one more agent among many in the world. God is not one cause among many in the history of the world; the world's history is ineffably within God. Our freedom unfolds because God gives us space and time each moment with an on-going creative glance filled with the love of the Mother and the Father almighty. To this God we as believers pray always and everywhere, and not just when we seem to be at the end of our own resources. We pray for the day to dawn and not just for the rain to fall. We pray to draw our next breath and not just to overcome fatal disease. All things, our daily bread included, are God's gifts to us. We pray for them; we are thankful for them. We see the whole world as resting within the wonderful and mysterious life of the infinite God. And yet, we exist and we are free to pray. We ask not so much to change the hand of God in our lives as to see the hand of God. We ask not so much for God's remedial intervention in history as a recognition that God is acting in our behalf always and everywhere and from the beginning. "One thing have I asked of the Lord, that will I seek after; that I may dwell in the house of the Lord all the days of my life, to behold the beauty of the Lord and to inquire in his temple" (Ps 27:4).

The Christian community on the day of the commemoration of the death of the Lord on the cross prays extensively and solemnly for all the peoples of the world. On Good Friday the Church was born in blood and water that poured forth from the pierced side of Jesus on the Cross (Jn 19:34). Petitionary prayer on that day is constitutive of the Church. Jesus died for all, and the salvation that he would bring by sharing the everlasting life of God with us mortal creatures is a gift ever to seek and ask for. The Church never tires of petition. The prayers of the faithful at daily eucharist range over all the joys and sorrows of the world, and particularly those we feel close at hand. The prayer of the Christian follows the story of the mother of Jesus at the wedding at Cana. She points out in genuine concern: "They have no wine." She does not demand a particular answer to this implicit request. Hers is to pray for need. In like way we pray for daily bread. For the specific outcome we leave all in the provident hands of the Lord: "Do whatever he tells you." In short, have faith; trust in the power of prayer; believe in the Lord of the whole world. In Luke's discourse on prayer he writes: "Will not God then secure the rights of his chosen ones who call out to him day and night? Will he be slow to answer them? I tell you, he will see to it that justice is done for them speedily. But when the Son of Man comes, will he find faith on earth?" (18:7–8). Presumed in all petitionary prayer, of course, is the hope that human beings will do actively all they can and should to help themselves and one another, and that human activity enabled by God is a principal part of God's response to prayer.

II

Christians have always believed in the power of prayer. The community of disciples after the resurrection gathered in the upper room to pray together as they awaited the coming of the Holy Spirit and the birth of the Church. "All these devoted themselves with one accord to prayer, together with some women and Mary the mother of Jesus, and his brothers" (Acts 1:14). In the bidding prayers of the faithful before the offertory of the eucharist, that church tradition of praying for the needs of the community perdures even to this day. The Christian community has always prayed to the Father in the words that Jesus gave to his disciples when they asked him how to pray. The Lord's Prayer sums up and collects all of our requests. Petitionary prayer to God also comprehends the example of Christ who frequently went off to pray by himself all night to his Father. Jesus taught his disciples his own prayer-life and clearly wished to include them in his own prayer to the Father: "I pray . . . that they may all be one, as you, Father, are in me and I in you, that they also may be in us" (Jn 17:21).

Christians have not always agreed, however, on intercessory prayer addressed not directly to God, but indirectly through those holy men and women in the Christian community who are living, and in particular those who have died. The Protestant reformers were reluctant to pray for the souls departed or to pray to the saints in heaven because their theology of prayer could account for no such practice. In addition, abuses in popular devotion to the saints abounded at that time. Bogus miracles and unworthy petitions scandalized conscientious believers. Moreover, saints provide a mediation that is not necessary. The Christian prays to Jesus Christ, or to the Father through Jesus Christ our Lord. Jesus is the one and all sufficient mediator with God. The dead are with God, and beyond needing the help of prayer here below or offering their assistance to the living. It is God who provides for the needs of God's people in this life and in the next. The communion of saints in prayer refers to the living, who can and do pray to the Lord for one another. Within the Church on earth there can be a solidarity in charity and in prayer. One can ask the living for prayers, and the church membership typically prays together for the needs of the community in which it lives. Paul writes: "He [Jesus Christ] rescued us from such great danger of death, and he will continue to rescue us; in him we have put our hope [that] he will also rescue us again, as you help us with prayer, so that thanks may be given by many on our behalf for the gift granted us through the prayer of many" (2 Cor 1:10–11). The communion of saints, however, does not extend in intercessory prayer to the saints who have died. Such is the opposition argument.

The Catholic practice of intercessory prayer, however, has always included prayer to the saints in heaven, who can pray for us, just as the living can now pray for us and our needs. The saints in heaven are only physically dead; they live in the Lord in eternal life. The poet Robert Southwell writes: "Not where I breathe do I live, but where I love."[30] Presence is a spiritual reality. Love relationships are forever; they transcend our mortal bodies. In the mystical body of Christ we share one divine and omnipresent Holy Spirit who prays in us all, whether living or dead. Our prayers can affect the saints. In particular this theology of prayer makes room for the prayer for the souls in purgatory, who need to be helped. Correspondingly, the prayers of the saints in heaven can affect us, just as we hope that people in this life who pray for us in our troubles and in our needs assist us. Prayer is one communal voice, the living and the dead, raised to the one God for the entire community. The communion of saints includes those separated not only in space, but also in time. It embraces not only those far away from us but also those who lived before us. The seventh chapter of the Vatican II Constitution on the Church (*Lumen Gentium*) is entitled "The Eschatological Nature of the Pilgrim Church and its Union with the Church in Heaven." Petitionary prayer to the saints and in particular to Mary the mother of Jesus falls within such a perspective. Because we stand in only one place and at one time, our prayer must be defined. We cannot think specifically of everyone and everything, but we can unite our particular prayers with this universal prayer of the body of the whole Christ who sits at the right hand of the Father.

The concept of intercession and intercessory prayer may have originated in the early church from familiarity with the system of patronage in Roman society. Then as now one was tempted to say that what matters is not what you know but whom you know. Patrons were powerful lobbyists near the throne, or themselves capable of bestowing considerable wealth or favor upon their protegees. A patron was an advocate who could intercede or a benefactor who could intervene. The word "patron" itself comes from the Latin *pater*, and the father in the Roman household held the decision-making power of the family. To the father one must appeal as to a patron who provides. The mother of the family could appeal as no one else to the father and master of the whole family. Patron saints became in the Christian community intermediaries, spiritual intercessors who would help bring one's petition before the throne of God, the almighty Father in heaven. The cult of saints rose in part to guarantee mercy and justice in this world for all who come before the throne of a human patron established in the world above and capable therefore of protecting all of his or her intercessors. Prayer to Mary the mother of Jesus and queen of saints would not have been difficult.

Just as some patrons were more rich in the goods of this world than others, and some were better positioned to gain the ear of the high and mighty, so among the saints the Christian community counted holiness of soul as the wealth that gave rank and favor before God. Jesus himself said: "whoever has my commandments and observes them is the one who loves me. And whoever loves me will be loved by my Father" (Jn 14:21). In the Old Testament, it is Moses, the man of God, whose upheld and outstretched arms over the battlefield ensure success for the Israelites. Judith is besought: "So pray for us, since you are a devout woman and the Lord will send us rain to fill our cisterns and we will no longer be faint" (Jdt 8:31). In the New Testament, the Greek-speaking Jews who wish to see Jesus ask Phillip to arrange an audience with his master. In the multiplication of the loaves and fishes, it is the disciples who intercede for the hungry crowd. It is the mother of Jesus who points out the predicament of the bride and groom at Cana, and who presents their need: "They have no wine" (Jn 2:3).

Intercessory prayer in the Christian community may well have been stimulated by the plight of the martyrs and petitionary prayer in their behalf. One cannot stand by idly at the torture and execution of those one loves. Something has to be done. If we cannot rescue them from the hands of their tormentors, we can pray for them to the God who can strengthen and console them. We can pray for them to God who can re-create their broken bodies to be transfigured in the eternal kingdom of God. Newman says of the early church prior to the recognition of Constantine: "Christians could not correspond; they could not combine; but they could pray for one another."[31] Particularly in times of persecution, one could pray for those fellow Christians whose ordeal and crisis of faith were imminent. One prayed for their perseverance in the faith and for their true life.

Quite naturally this practice of praying *for* the martyrs in their sufferings grew into prayer *to* the martyrs for the living in their present sufferings. The martyrs lived on in heaven and were considered on-going members of their original human community though now dwelling in eternity. The Church was readily seen as this kind of communion of saints. Time and eternity touched in prayer. Christians prayed to their martyred saints in heaven for the faith and courage to imitate them. In the early church the eucharist was celebrated on the tomb of the martyrs in the catacombs of Rome. Altar stones were reliquaries of the martyr and confessor of the faith. Prayer to the saints became prayer to confess the faith with the way one lived and the way one died. The root sin was disbelief. The "test" from which one prayed in the Lord's Prayer to be delivered was apostasy. Baptism of water brought initial faith; baptism of blood confirmed a final faith. One prayed for the persecuted Christians that God might sustain their faith to the bitter end. One prayed to the sainted martyrs (the Church triumphant) that they might join the general prayer to God to sustain the faith of the living (the Church militant) now and at the hour of our death. "Their [the martyrs'] intimacy with God was the *sine qua non* of their ability to intercede for and, so, to protect their fellow mortals."[32] In the Acts of the Apostles Stephen in his martyrdom prays for his persecutors, just as Jesus did. On the road to Damascus, Paul, who assisted in the martyrdom of Stephen, becomes the beneficiary of Stephen's prayers. In the ending in heaven, the communion of all the saints will rejoice in the communion of life that they gave and received by including one another in their prayers to God to whom we all were taught to pray: *Our* Father. . . . Give *us* this day our daily bread . . . and do not subject us to the final test, but deliver us from the evil one" (Mt 6:10–13).

If there can be intercessory prayer addressed to the saintly dead as well as to the holy living, then prayer to Mary as one of the saints with whom we are in communion must be well considered. The second and petitionary part of the Ave Maria may have grown out of the Litany of the Saints, where "Holy Mary" is the customary lead invocation. She is first among the saints. Luke's Gospel has been read as containing a presentation of Mary as the original Christian. To her is first given the Good News in the annunciation, which she is the first to accept with her *fiat*, and the first to share with another in the visitation. John's Gospel also portrays Mary as the premiere Christian, the central figure in the beginning of the public life of Jesus at Cana, and at his side along with the beloved disciple at its end on Calvary hill. Would not Christians pray to Mary, the most "possessed by God's Spirit of Love,"[33] if they were to pray to any of the saints? Would not the faithful pray to Mary especially at the "hour of our death"?

Comparison has been made between Abraham as father of faith in the Old Testament, whom God called into a land of promise, and Mary as mother of faith in the New Testament, whom the Spirit called into a new life. Just as the descendants of Abraham's seed were numerous like the sands of the seashore, so the disciples of Mary's son would constitute the great Church of God's people. Just as Lazarus lay in the bosom of Abraham when he died and went to God, so the Christian soul would take rest in the arms of Mary who carried the savior of humankind. To pray to Mary would be thus to pray for spiritual birth in the Church. Nonetheless, Mary is not the savior, although she intercedes for her children through her role as mother of the Church, the mystical body of Christ. We read in *Lumen Gentium*: "This maternity of Mary in the order of grace began with the consent which she gave in faith at the Annunciation and which she sustained without wavering beneath the cross, and lasts until the eternal fulfilment of all the elect."[34] Cardinal Newman writes: "I consider it impossible then, for those who believe the Church to be one vast body in heaven and on earth, in which every holy creature of God has his place, of which prayer is the life, when once they recognize the sanctity and dignity of the Blessed Virgin, not to perceive immediately, that her office above is one of perpetual intercession for the faithful militant, and that our very relation to her must be that of clients to a patron, and that, in the eternal enmity which exists between the woman and the serpent, while the serpent's strength lies in being the Tempter, the weapon of the second Eve and Mother of God is prayer."[35]

Intercessory prayer fervently directed to the mother of Jesus, however, is open to misunderstanding. Mary is called mother of God, but it is unfortunate when that title is understood to mean that she is like a mother God. Mary is never a substitute for God. Prayer to Mary is not prayer for her to fulfill the role of God as giver of all good gifts. There is only one human mediator, who is Jesus Christ our Lord. We need no one else. He is very close to all of us, always approachable, and ever truly tender in our regard.[36] The role of Mary with regard to Jesus Christ her son is well modeled in the position that the "Constitution on the Church" in Vatican II gave to the mother of Jesus. There the doctrine of Mary was given a relative place within the theology of Jesus Christ, and her role was conceived within the body of the Church. Chapter VIII of *Lumen Gentium* is entitled: "The Blessed Virgin Mary, Mother of God, in the Mystery of Christ and the Church." Her inclusion within that context was a deliberate embodiment of a theology that sees Mary ever in relationship to her Son and always in solidarity with the Church of which she is a member. In divine providence she is part of the history of salvation and the ultimate answer to all prayers which is contained in the salvation of the whole world. And yet, she is not God. She is not the unique mediator and intercessor with the Father that Jesus Christ remains alone by virtue of his humanity. It may be more Christian to say "to Mary through Christ" than "to Christ through Mary."

The relationship of Mary to Jesus Christ raises all kinds of objections. No one wishes to make Mary a goddess, without the limitations of the creature and the wear and tear of this life and its human condition. Catholics would not have Mary take the place of Christ before the Father, "delighting to play before the children of men." Protestants in particular resist suggesting her as mediatrix of all graces, thereby overshadowing the role of Jesus Christ. And yet, no one, no critic of whatever persuasion, whether feminist, Protestant, or Catholic, wishes not to honor and esteem the mother of God. She is not just one of the communion of saints; she is closest to Jesus the Saint himself.

She is not just in the tradition; it is out of her life that the tradition was born, as the Christian revelation emerged from the ancient Jewish covenant. She is Mary of Nazareth, the mystery of a particular historical woman brought into the infinite eternal mystery of the Blessed Trinity. "Behold from now on will all ages call me blessed" (Lk 1:48).

Similarly, Mary is not a substitute for the Holy Spirit in our lives. She who was so close to the Holy Spirit must not be confused with the Holy Spirit. She is the grace of the Spirit and not its origin. To Jesus through Mary ought never be read as a denial that it is the Holy Spirit that ultimately brings us to know and love Jesus. The tender mercies of Mary do not exceed the infinite delicacy and graciousness of the Holy Spirit who breathes where She will. God is both father and mother. God is both justice and mercy. Isaiah writes of the Lord God: "Can a woman forget her suckling child, that she should have no compassion on the son of her womb? Even these may forget, yet I will not forget you. Behold, I have graven you on the palms of my hands" (49:15–16). God as mother is superabundantly creative, life-giving, nourishing, nurturing, fruitful, accessible, sympathetic, careful, compassionate— our life, our sweetness, and our hope. Jesus weeps over Jerusalem as a mother who has lost her children: "Jerusalem, Jerusalem, you who kill the prophets and stone those sent to you, how many times I yearned to gather your children together as a hen gathers her brood under her wings, but you were unwilling!" (Lk 13:34). Indeed, one could rewrite the well-known text in Acts to read: "In her we live and move and have our being" (17:28). To give the maternal qualities of God back to the Holy Spirit is not to deprive Mary, but rather to give her back to humanity as the woman who embodies the sisterhood of man. She is not God; she is one of us. She is not woman only; she is man in the human family. She is not the feminine face of God in an exaltation that makes her little less than a goddess. Mary is the human face of God in a woman who is altogether one of us.

Finally, it would also be possible to see the Ave Maria as not just prayer *to* Mary or intercession *of* Mary, but a more complex prayer. The first half of the Ave Maria is not primarily petitionary prayer at all. It presents in the dramatic words of the evangelist the annunciation and visitation scenes from Luke's Gospel. The overshadowing of the Holy Spirit, the personal embodiment of the Word of the Lord, and the mission to others to share what one has received present the core evangel of all Christianity. In that sense the Ave Maria is a prayer not only *to* Mary but first of all and primarily *with* Mary, whose life we seek to imitate in its devotion to the Lord. After all, prayer is a relationship. We need to listen as well as to speak. We therefore pray *with* as well as pray *to* the communion of saints. Along with them we enter the mystery of God. Our prayer acknowledges and expresses our common destiny and life together in the one and infinite God. Alla Bozarth-Campbell writes of a childhood misapprehension of the Ave Maria. She heard and thus said: "play with us sinners."[37] With adult reflection she concluded that her childhood error contains a hidden wisdom. Prayer is indeed divine play. God delights in human beings. Of the creation of the world Wisdom says: "and I was daily his delight, rejoicing before him always, rejoicing in his inhabited world and delighting in the sons of men" (Prv 8:30–31).

In the eastern Orthodox rite, Christian prayer surrounding Mary the mother of God and ever blessed Virgin is taken yet one further step. Often in Marian piety "East has led the way for the West—in devotion, in doctrine, in art."[38] The eastern church prays to and with Mary, but they also pray *for* Mary.[39] From a logical point of view that would seem to be an idle prayer, since Mary before the face of God needs no assistance to enjoy that glory. Yet, from the point of view of eternity, where there is no past and no future, the free decision of Mary, her *fiat* to God (let it be to me according to your word), is a moment in time that is always present to every generation in the Church. "With the Lord one day is like a thousand years and a thousand years like one day" (2 Pt 3:8). After all, God is not in time. God belongs to eternity. God made time itself, and time was begun by God and time will be ended by God. Thus there was a time when there was no time. Eternity overwhelms time. Time was created from out of nothing. With God it is always now, always today, only this day, the eternal day, the one day of God. Augustine writes of God: "your years are one day, and your day is not day after day but this day [today]."[40] In his letter to Lady Proba, Augustine comments about the life of eternity: "There, the days do not come and go in succession, and the beginning of one day does not mean the end of another, all days are one, simultaneously and without end, and life lived out in these days has itself no end."[41]

Christians believe that we now spiritually encounter Jesus Christ in the paschal mystery of the passion and resurrection, just as his contemporaries would have. Insofar as we also today must make a decision of faith in this regard, so we might think that each generation encounters Mary in the moment of her eternal consent to God. Because we also wish to consent to God along with her, why cannot we pray for her and she pray for us? Since that moment of grace in her life is a moment of time in touch with eternity, and since grace is always given in the community of God's people, and since we are united in the solidarity of charity that allows whatever any one of us does for the good to enhance the life of all of the rest of us, then we can intercede *for* Mary. Her decision is in some ways ours, and ours in some way was part of hers. All of the saving moments of grace are part of the one providence of God, and though there are many freedoms exercised in the many historical moments of time and place, nonetheless it is only one efficacious grace in eternity which encompasses us all in the one saving Word, Jesus Christ, who is Lord. We commemorate the annunciation to Mary just as we commemorate the last supper of Jesus. The mystery of salvation is re-presented and we are invited to stand neither before nor after the Christ-event, but truly and simply with the Christ-event. Mary holds a unique and irreplaceable role in the Christ-event, and hence we pray *to* her in intercession, *with* her in imitation, and even *for* her in remembrance of her with whom we share an eternal solidarity.[42] Do this in memory of me. The faithful memory of Mary ever remains a part of the memory of the Church.

III

"Pray for us *sinners*." Why *sinners*? Sin is a failure to muster a living faith. We have no other true enemy but such sin. We need no other boon than heartfelt belief. In a *carmen votivum* (votive song) written during a visit to the shrine of Our Lady of Walsingham in England, Erasmus, the scholar-friend of Thomas More, wrote this ode:

> Hail, Jesus' Virgin-Mother ever Blest,
> Alone of women Mother eke and Maid,
> Others to thee their several offerings make;
> This one brings gold, that silver, while a third
> Bears to thy shrine his gift of costly gems.
> For these, each craves his boon—one strength of
>   limb—
> One wealth—one, through his spouse's fruitfulness,
> The hope a father's pleasing name to bear—
> One Nestor's eld would equal. I, poor bard,
> Rich in goodwill, but poor in all beside,
> Bring thee my verse—nought have I else to bring—
> And beg, in quital of this worthless gift,
> That greatest meed—a heart that feareth God,
> and free for aye from sin's foul tyranny.
>
> Erasmus, his vow[43]

Petitionary prayer often asks for worldly gain, and the prayer may include what amounts to a bribe. Neither the favor asked nor the way it is asked reflects a deep and living faith in God as righteous savior unto eternal life. Notice that Erasmus does not ask for any of the specific kinds of favors that Marian popular piety generated. Nor does he come with worldly goods in hand to offer in exchange. Like Solomon, he asks for only one gift: fear of God or wisdom in the conduct of one's soul before God. One's whole way of life must embody true piety. Erasmus was a vigorous critic of the abuses of Marian piety that contributed to the Protestant reformation. Favor was bought. A century after his visit to Walsingham, the shrine was torn down by the Puritan reformer Oliver Cromwell. The excesses of Marian piety and of Puritan zeal both give witness to the sinfulness of the human condition. Erasmus knew that all human votive offerings were worthless to manipulate God or the Blessed Mary. Prayer was rather a submission to God. The only prayer that is guaranteed to be heard is the one that Erasmus utters: free me from sin and give me a heart attuned to God's ways.

Jesus tells Martha that "There is need of only one thing" (Lk 10:42), and that Mary has chosen the better part in listening intently to the word of God. To be free of sin so that we can be joined in a holy union of will with God is to be granted all favors and given all requests. Whatever good we think we may need to enhance our life or whatever evil we must avoid, the only lasting good is the possession of God, and the only genuine obstacle to that communion is our own sinfulness. Hence to be free of sin is to know God. Faith is to believe with trust in God; sin is not to believe in God but to believe that I have only myself to achieve the good life. "Pray for us sinners" thus is a universal request made to Mary. Pray that we be delivered from sin, so that we may know and love God, in faith in this life but then face to face. Sin is fed from unbelief. Mary is the first woman to hear the Good News; she is the premiere Christian in Luke's account; she is a woman of great faith. Mary is freely devoted to God body and soul. Unlike Eve she does not mistake her happiness; she allows God to be God and she dwells within that mystery. Free of sin and of unbelief she is full of that grace that confesses the one true God. Elizabeth says of Mary: "Blessed are you who believed that what was spoken to you by the Lord would be fulfilled."

"Mother of God, pray for us *sinners*" reminds us directly of the human condition. Whatever the circumstances of our life, we know we owe our life to God ultimately and to the mother who bore us more immediately. Moreover, we know that humanity has sinned. The mutual experience of our sinfulness confirms our commonality. We know we sinners stand all together in need of God's salvation in deliverance from our sins. Our universal human predicament, sinful and needing God's mercy, makes for human solidarity. In the Lord's Prayer we pray, "Give *us* our daily bread and forgive *us* our sins for we ourselves forgive everyone in debt to *us*" (Lk 11:4). In the Ave Maria we say simply "pray for *us sinners*." In the French Ave Maria the texts reads "pray for us *poor* sinners (pauvres pécheurs)," and indeed our most radical poverty is our sinfulness. Sin is the absence of being. There can be no greater destitution from which one might pray to be delivered.

Sin is the basic illness. God's grace is the basic cure. Those who ask for cures are always answered, but the cure may not be immediate. God grants us all a delayed cure. We await our death and transfiguration. Every request for our good God grants, but the bestowal is often unrecognized. At the end of our life, however, we will be cured and we will be given everything we ever asked for in being given communion with God. If we have overcome sin at the end of our life, we have overcome all of life's evils, actual and possible. If we achieve union with God in eternity, we have been granted every favor on the face on the earth, for the infinite God lacks no resource to fulfill our life. Unbelief in some form is the root of all sin, and deliverance from unbelief remains the source of all grace. Thus the Ave Maria is specifically a prayer for that salvation in which all other requests and concerns in this life are included implicitly. To believe in the infinite God who made heaven and earth from nothing is ultimately to believe in God who can re-create our body and this world from sin and death. This is salvation. To believe in God is to know that we were given life and that life will be sustained. Indeed in the revelation of Jesus we are given a tangible promise.

If we say we are not sinners, John concludes in his epistle that we are liars (1 Jn 1:10). Matthew was a sinful tax collector, but Jesus called him to repent. Zacchaeus was a guilty tax collector until the Lord came to his house and freed him of his sins. The adulterous woman is told that no one condemns her, but go and sin no more (Jn 8). Paul persecuted Christians, but his former way of life is struck down and he is raised to a new life of faith in Christ Jesus. The Samaritan woman had five husbands, but with none of them did she slake her thirst for love. Jesus said "whoever drinks the water I shall give will never thirst" (Jn 4:14). He came to call sinners (Mt 9:13). The cross and resurrection was the overcoming of sin and death and the promise of eternal life.

"Mother of God, pray for us *sinners*" reads like the prayer of the publican in the back of the temple: "O God, be merciful to me a sinner" (Lk 18:13). Sinners know that they cannot attract love in their wounded condition, unless that love be unconditional. They must be loved in their sinfulness as a mother loves her child in his or her woundedness. Something of that gratuitous quality of love that goes beyond one's deserts and gives life where there is no claim to life captures the tone of this petition in the Ave Maria. The pilgrim's prayer in the classical tradition of Russian devotion is a simple petition: "Lord have mercy on me a sinner."[44] To own simultaneously our sin and the Lord's grace is to stand in the truth that we are a forgiven people and our salvation is yet promised to us. We confess in the creed the "communion of saints and the forgiveness of sins." That condition is the Church of the blessed; it is the kingdom of God. In the communion of saints we pray to and for one another. In our prayer we acknowledge that we are all sinners seeking forgiveness and reconciliation with each other and with God.

If all human beings are sinners, the Good News is embodied in the confession and forgiveness of our sins. The misery of human sinfulness draws forth the mercy of God. The prodigal son is welcomed home by a father whose love is prodigal beyond all expectation. In this "vale of tears" we look for deliverance. The Ave Maria calls upon the mother of God, who gave life to Jesus, to sustain the life of the sinner, wounded and so in need of being loved. Our God is a God of boundless Mercy. Mary is mother of God. Therefore Mary is mother of Mercy. Sinners are hungry for God. As mother of Mercy Mary brings the bread of life to this our mundane life. Karl Rahner writes that pray for us sinners is "a profession of faith in the divine motherhood of the blessed Virgin, and we are confident of our own salvation, because she believed, and in faith, in body and soul and heart, and in her blessed womb, received Jesus Christ our Lord and our eternal salvation. Amen."[45]

Thus the Ave Maria's petition, "Holy Mary, mother of God, pray for us sinners, now and at the hour of our death," can be expanded: Believing Mary, bearer of God who was in Jesus, pray for us who are unbelievers now in this life and in our death that brings us into eternal life. In this regard the Ave Maria as a petitionary prayer does not differ from the Pater Noster, which also asks simply and directly for salvation. Thus, "pray for us sinners" parallels the Lord's Prayer: "give us daily bread and forgive us our sins." We ask Mary for her prayers now; we ask the Father for our daily bread today. We acknowledge to the

mother of Jesus that we need to be prayed for because we are
sinners. We ask the Father of Jesus to give us food for our life
and to feed our soul with the bread of the forgiveness of our
sins. In both prayers we simply and directly pray to live, to be
saved from the death-dealing of our sins, and to be given the life
of the Lord who hears the prayers of the poor, and who came
to call sinners. "Miserable one that I am! Who will deliver me
from this mortal body? Thanks be to God through Jesus Christ
our Lord" (Rom 7:24).

NOW AND AT THE HOUR OF OUR DEATH

The Ave Maria petition concludes without any specific request. It says only to "pray for us." It does specify when to pray for us: "now and at the hour of our death." Why would this temporal concern be included as the only particular in a quite economical prayer of petition? At first blush, it would appear to be saying simply to pray for us *always*. Pray for us now and pray for us then; pray for us in time present and pray for us at time's end. Pray for us now and always, in time and in eternity, in this life and in our coming into the next. In short, pray for us *always*, until the time for prayer has passed. To the shepherds it was announced: "Today in the city of David a savior has been born for you who is Messiah and Lord" (Lk 2:11). And on Calvary Jesus promised the repentant thief: "Today you will be with me in Paradise" (Lk 23:43). As Shakespeare well knew: "All's Well that Ends Well." Whatever the adversity in the divine comedy of human history, if the wedding banquet concludes it all, we have been indeed well served.

Time is a measure of motion. Time is a coordinate of space in which things move. The passage of the earth around the sun gives us our calendar. The rotation of the earth on its axis gives us our clock. We live in a moment that is now, what the medieval theologians called the *nunc fluens*—the passing moment. Nothing else for us is physical life. The past is gone into memory and it recedes as fast as I can write these words: the future is not yet. While there appears to be a long stretch of time ahead of me, I have not even the next second guaranteed by my own resources. Thus, human life is a fragile spark, a moment of light with a great darkness of the past behind it and the mysterious darkness of the future yet ahead of it. This is the human condition. This is finite and contingent existence in the embodied world of space and time. Into this world the Son of God was born of the virgin Mary and became human. The Ave Maria prays to her to pray for us in this our incarnate life, our human life, our moment in time, however brief or however extended. There are only two moments to be concerned about: the now and the then. We are guaranteed only two moments, right now and the moment of our death. At some time, we know not when, those two certain moments will coincide as our last and final one in this life. The now in the Ave Maria petition may prove in practice to be a long succession of moments in time in which we experience our life as a flowing stream, never the same water, but coming from a distant past and flowing out into the ocean of the future as into an eternity. Or this now that is upon me as I write may be the hour of my death; I may not finish this sentence. You may not finish this sentence. All human beings know that they must die. They know that there will be a moment when the now and the hour of death coincide. They know that they do not know when that hour may be. "For you yourselves know very well that the day of the Lord will come like a thief at night" (1 Thes 5:2).[46] And, "Therefore, stay awake, for you know neither the day nor the hour" (Mt 25:13).

Pray for us now and at the end of our time; pray for us always and all ways. Do not let our fear of the future evacuate the radiance of this moment. Let us live in God now, *and* then. The Kingdom of God is within you; the Kingdom of God is now. Nonetheless, the Kingdom of God is not yet. It is both now and to come. The fulfillment of the reign of God awaits the end time. Now is the acceptable time, yet only at the last hour will we see God face to face. We pray to the mother of our Lord for the hour now and the hour then, for our life now and our death then that leads to everlasting life. Escort us along the way to the Lord Jesus, Lord of time and of space, Lord of life and of death, who sits body and soul at the right hand of the Father in the promised fulfillment of this world. You who gave flesh to the Lord of heaven, maiden Mary, give our flesh a prayer to deliver it. Assist us to obtain the eternal moment with Jesus Christ, your son, and God's son, and our only Lord. In his journal Jean Sulivan writes: "*And at the hour of death. Amen.* Death used to light up everything at the end of the Hail Mary. The humble prayer, which seemed only a refrain, was actually a challenge. Mary Immaculate invited us to live in the face of death, not to reject sin but its dictatorship. She stands for active expectation, the plan and the execution of a world of resurrection where it's not a question of dominating or devouring, and there are no longer either men or women, mothers or sons, in the womb of the universal body of love."[47]

"Now and at the hour of our death" suggests a continuity of life, a passage through time, a journey through space. We move from our Christian birth in baptism to the resurrection of the body. Mary in John's Gospel is present in the here and now of the marriage of Cana (Jn 2:1–12), the comedy of the human family. And she is present at the hour of death, at the foot of the cross (Jn 19:25–27), in the tragedy of human death. The annunciation in the life of Mary was but a moment; she would grow in faith and love throughout a lifetime until the hour of death. Her death has been recognized by the Christian community as a special destiny. The Christian tradition of the dormition of Mary widely accepted that she did not die but only fell asleep, or more precisely she died but quickly was raised up and assumed into heaven. With this fulsome background presumed, the Ave Maria seeks her prayerful intercession now and at the hour of death. Similarly, in the Lord's Prayer we pray: "do not subject us to the final test, but deliver us from the evil one," especially and finally at the hour of our death.

Concerning the hour of death one may recall the Gospel story of the daughter of Jairus about whom Jesus says: "Why this commotion and weeping? The child is not dead but asleep" (Mk 5:39). The whole passage about Jairus's daughter and the woman with a hemorrhage (Mk 5:21–43) dovetails with the "now and at the hour of our death." Jesus goes to be with the little girl who is sick unto death at the very hour of her death. In the meantime and in between places, and in the now that is always changing, Jesus is touched by the woman in the crowd and press of people and events that sweep him along. He cures the woman with the hemorrhage even now, and then comes to the assistance of the little girl at the hour of her death. She dies, but she dies unto the life that Jesus raises her up to. She awakens with her hand in his and to the tender concern of him who is the bread of life and who came to her bedside. Jesus asks that she be given something now to eat. We speak even today of falling asleep in the Lord. We imagine Joseph dying with Mary at one side and Jesus holding his hand at the other. John's Gospel places Mary at the side of Jesus dying on the cross. We imagine Mary herself at the end of her days falling asleep and Jesus coming to her side. Our radical illness remains our mortality; our fatal sickness our sinfulness. Pray for us now and at the hour of our death is a prayer to be freed of our sins now by God's coming into our temporal life, and to be given everlasting life at the hour of our death by our coming into God's own eternal life.

II

Since human beings do not know the future, and hence do not know the ending of their time on this earth, they cannot avoid anxiety about the hour of their death. When the Ave Maria petition was being written, harsh conditions of violence, famine, and plague tormented the Christian community of Europe. The preoccupation with temporal death and with deliverance from eternal death in the loss of one's soul was reflected in some of the exaggerations in the liturgy of that period. Elaborate masses for the dead and funeral songs such as the *Dies irae* reveal some of the dreadful consciousness that the moment of death was crucial, its outcome uncertain, and its judgment to be feared. Even to this day we fear death; we hide from it with hospital and funeral home rituals that mask its omnipresence in human life. The success of the hospice program in recent years points to the need people feel to face their death and to accept it with all the support that family, medicine, and religion can bring to bear. The hour of death should be a moment of truth and peace for the person whose last moment it is and a moment of life for their family and friends who need to live with such memories. It is not surprising that a prayer would be addressed to Mary as mother of God at the hour of death. Let us further consider some of the reasons.

Mary might be invoked at the hour of death because death is the last, the most severe, and the incurable illness of the body. Women nursed the sick and dying in so many circumstances; mothers comforted their children and families in time of malady. We use the same word *nurse* for the woman who attends the sick and the woman who feeds the baby at her breast. Women fed everyone in the family; only their bodies provided food. To those just born the milk of their mother brings food to the hungry. To those in the throes of dying, the holy viaticum of the body of Christ fed their souls about to be born into eternal life. Mary had brought the body of Christ into this world, would not Mary be a refuge in the hour of death? She whom the infinite God trusted in God's birthing to this life, should we not trust in our birthing to eternal life? Moreover, sin was the mortal illness of the soul and when severe could bring about that second death that is eternal separation from God. The dying person feared the death of the body and also the spiritual death of his or her soul. Could not prayer to the holy mother of God bring consolation, comfort to the ailing body, and repentance to the sinful soul? Could not Mary be caring nurse to body and soul, just as women and mothers cared for the welfare of their family?

Birth and death support the myth of the "magna mater," the great mother, mother earth, nature as ever life-giving because the inevitable dying demands new birthing always. Nature gives life abundantly, but nature also takes life unceasingly. Women give birth; women prepare the body of their loved ones for burial. We come a naked body into the world and are clothed by our mother. "She wrapped him in swaddling clothes and laid him in a manger" (Lk 2:7). At the end of life, the women around Jesus washed the blood from his naked body and wrapped him in a clean winding sheet for his burial. Women preside at life's beginning and at its ending. Catherina Halkes writes of the moon goddess: "that ancient female image of the rise and fall of the tides, of growth, of fullness and decrease and of light and dark. Very early in human history, the division into four times seven days in the lunar cycles was connected with the female monthly cycle, which was regarded as a primordial image of the constant renewal of life and death, as the primordial unity to birth and death. . . . It is therefore hardly surprising that, throughout the whole history of the veneration of Mary, married women have prayed to her for fertility and that she has been regarded as a powerful advocate 'at the hour of our death'."[48]

Prayer to Mary as woman and mother at the hour of death may trail roots that go deep into the archetypal unconscious of human beings. Women nurse their children at birth with the milk of their body, and they nurse them at death with the care of their hearts. Motherhood is a perduring lifelong relationship in most people's experience. Women await the birthing; and they wait beside the dying and arrange the funeral rituals. The newborn child is immediately placed in the bosom of the happy mother to behold in joy; and the dead body of her child is placed on the lap of the unhappy mother to mourn in sorrow. Mary as joyful mother with child in the madonna has been depicted no more poignantly than Mary as sorrowful mother in the pieta. The womb that welcomes the newly conceived is the womb that welcomes the dead as well, who are born to eternal life. Mother of the living and mother of the dead. Life-accepting in the beginning and life-accepting in the ending. A parallel has been drawn between the virgin womb of Mary which knew no man and the empty tomb of Jesus in which no man had previously been laid to rest. The sovereignty of God is never more manifest than at birth which seems so improbable and resurrection from death which seems so impossible. Womankind has long been connected with the mystery of life and of death coming from the hands of God.

Mary might also be invoked at the hour of death because the hour of judgment was found threatening. Nothing was needed more in that hour than mercy. No love was needed more than a love that was unconditional, a love that was gratuitous, a love that arose from who the person was rather than from what they had accomplished. Such a love was readily seen as a mother's love. It was merciful and not condemning. It was accepting and tender, forgiving of human weakness. A mother's loyalty and commitment to her child regardless of behavior was boundless. To understand this mistaken dichotomy, one has but to contrast two well-known hymns to capture the flavor of a judgment before the bench of a stern and unbending Father-God of righteousness, and the contrasting intercession at the hands of a gracious and accepting mother of God, who embodies tender compassion. The "Battle Hymn of the Republic" captures the Father-God of fearful judgment day: "He is trampling out the vintage where the grapes of wrath are stored. He has loosed the lightning of his terrible swift sword. His truth is marching on." Contrast that song with the "Salve Regina," so beloved in the Middle Ages in its exceeding devotion to the mother of God: "mother of mercy, our life, our sweetness, and our hope. . . . Turn, then, most gracious advocate, thine eyes of mercy upon us, and after this, our exile, show unto us the blessed fruit of thy womb, Jesus. O clement! O loving! O sweet virgin Mary!"

In the Christian life, the outstanding model of a happy death has always been St. Joseph. Because he no longer appears in any of the Gospels after the early years of Jesus, the presumption has been that Joseph died before Jesus. One can easily imagine that at his deathbed he would have known the consolation of Mary his wife and Jesus his son. In Sacred Heart Basilica at the University of Notre Dame there are three different scenes depicting Joseph's death with Mary and Jesus on either side of his bed. No other event in any other saint's life is so frequently portrayed. The Christian hoped for the same kind of deathbed scene.

Christians have also speculated about the death of Mary. Did she die surrounded by the gathered elders of the Christian community? Was there an empty tomb after her burial? Did she die at all? Did she know death but so briefly as to be thought merely the interval of a short sleep? Did she but fall asleep to be awakened in the Kingdom of God? We read in Paul: "Awake, O sleeper, and arise from the dead, and Christ will give you light" (Eph 5:14). In Sacred Heart Basilica mentioned above, the stained glass window in the eastern transept shows Mary in the midst of the apostles at the descent of the Holy Spirit at Pentecost. It is a new day and the early sun illumines that window with morning glory. In the western transept the scene in the window is the death of Mary, which is also depicted amid the gathered community of the apostles. Clearly Mary's presence among the believing community at Pentecost at the birthing of the Church suggests that the church community would indeed be present in her support at her dying. The apocryphal scriptures contain accounts of the death of Mary, and even of the death of Joseph. However, there is nothing clearly known and the canonical scriptures are silent about the death of the Blessed Virgin Mary.[49]

Christians also held up as a sign of hope the last-minute conversion of the repentant thief on Calvary: "today you will be with me in Paradise" (Lk 23:43). In John's account Mary stands at the foot of the cross of Jesus near the good thief who was crucified along with him. For all these many reasons it was easy to see Mary as patron of a happy death and as the saint, and even more than a saint, to whom one might pray with hope at the hour of one's death. Hence the Ave Maria calls upon "Holy Mary, mother of God, pray for us sinners, now and *at the hour of our death.*"

The hour of death for Christians is truly the moment of birth into eternal life. The saints are commemorated on the day of their death. Their feastday is not their birthday, but their deathday, because on that day they were born into everlasting life. The risen Jesus was born unto eternal life and Easter Sunday was the day of his new birth. Mary at the foot of the cross in John's account is given a role to play at the hour of Jesus' death, which is his birth unto life eternal. How easy then to pray to Mary at the hour of any human being's death. She is the *Theotokos*, the birth-giver of God. Could she not assist in the unknown passage from this life to the next? People who have been resuscitated after what to all appearance was their physical death relate almost unanimously that they saw a great light. Some speculate about whether they have seen the heavenly life in some way and returned to their body in this life. Others speculate that such persons have not completely died, and that what they see at that moment may be what they saw when they first were born. They came from the darkness of the womb into the bright light of the sun. Similarly when we die we are born into eternal life. We come from the darkness of the tomb into the dazzling light of the Son of God. It is not difficult to understand why intercessory prayer would most appropriately be directed to the mother of Jesus Christ, Lord of the living and the dead. One might paraphrase the concluding words of the Ave Maria: Holy Mary, birth-giver of the Lord, pray for us sinners now and in our birth to eternal life.

III

In the Ave Maria, the hour of death must surely remind the person praying of the hour of death when Jesus hung on the cross. In John's Gospel the mother of Jesus is given a central place at the foot of the cross in that hour of death. Moreover, the "hour" which had not yet come in the Cana wedding story where Mary previously appeared in John's account has now come in all its importance and glory. From chapter thirteen of John to the end of his Gospel the *hour of Jesus* is entered into deliberately. The "Book of Glory" begins: "Jesus knew that his hour had come to pass from this world to the Father" (13:1). John presents the exaltation of Jesus on the cross, which in John is the glorification and ascension of the one lifted up. From his spear-pierced side the Church is born with water and blood in a pentecostal outpouring of the Holy Spirit. The evangelist places Mary at this crucial place and unique time. To the disciples Jesus has said: "The hour has come for the Son of Man to be glorified" (12:23). And after the giving of his mother to the care of the beloved disciple, John writes: "and from that hour the disciple took her into his home" (19:27). Mary is prominently present at the hour of Jesus' death. In the Ave Maria prayer one can readily recall that presence in seeking her prayer *at the hour of our death.*

The crucifixion scene in John presents a more complex picture than what is found in the synoptic Gospels. Jesus dies with a kind of sovereign composure and that in his death "it is finished." From his side, opened with a lance, blood and water issue. The commentators on this passage usually read the blood and water as symbol of the eucharist and baptism, the foundational sacraments of the Church. The Church is born as human beings are born in blood and water. From the crucified body of Jesus, the Church, the new mother of the living, is drawn from his side, just as Eve was drawn from the side of Adam when he was cast into a deep sleep. And just as Eve is of the same flesh as

Adam, so the Church shared the same risen body of Jesus. Both Adam and Jesus can claim a virgin birth. Mary gave birth to Jesus by the Spirit alone, and creation in the beginning was brought out of virgin nothingness by the Spirit alone. The saints from the baptismal font are all a virginal birth and a new creation by the water and the Holy Spirit. At the Cana wedding Jesus changed water to wine; at the foot of the cross the new-born Church will change wine into the blood of its savior. Then and now "the mother of Jesus was there."

From the symbolic openness of the situation at the foot of the cross in John's account many symbolic readings of Mary have taken rise. Jesus is easily seen on the cross as the new Adam and Mary at the foot of the cross as the new Eve. From the tree Eve picked the forbidden fruit. From the tree of the cross, the tree of eternal life, Jesus presents the fruit of his body: "Unless you eat the flesh of the Son of Man and drink his blood, you do not have life within you" (Jn 6:53). Bultmann and other Protestant theologians have seen Mary at the foot of the cross rather as a symbol of the Jewish synagogue and of the desired bond between the Old and New Testaments. Commentators on John have put forward a variety of symbolic interpretations of Mary at the foot of the cross. Mary is prototype of the Church; Mary is mother of the living. She is widow being cared for by a dying pious son; she is ever-virgin now in the care of John. She is the Jewish mother of all those innocent children violently slain throughout the centuries of human oppression from "Rachel weeping for her children" when Herod would slay the newly born Jesus (Mt 2:18) to the uncounted victims of the Holocaust in the present century. But surely she is the woman who knows about *the hour of death.*

It is unlikely that John in his account of Calvary records literal history, but even if the event as given in the Gospel was chronicle, something more is being given to the reader. John presents Mary in a quite symbolic way. Although it is not imme-diately certain how such a symbolic reading should be construed, nonetheless John opens the way for Mary as symbol of a reality larger than the historical woman and mother of Jesus might have known. She becomes a person of importance and centrality to the Johannine community. No matter how one reads the crucifixion scene in John, Mary surely was associated by the evangelist with the most solemn and magnanimous moments of Jesus' life and death. It was the hour of his glorification, of the passover from this world to the Father. This was the paschal mystery for John, the death and resurrection of Jesus distilled to that moment on Calvary hill. And: "standing by the cross [was] his mother." Surely Christians turn to Mary at the hour of death with some warrant and with a most persuasive precedent. If John put the mother of Jesus at the foot of her son's cross at the hour of his death, can the Christian disciple of Jesus hope for anything more or ask for anything less?

AMEN

The Ave Maria concludes with the customary *Amen* as a closing word. The Book of Revelation ends with these lines: " 'Yes I am coming soon.' Amen! Come, Lord Jesus! The grace of the Lord Jesus be with all" (22:20–21). *Amen* is a Semitic word that means "thus" or "it is true." *Amen* is rooted in the verb *'mn*, which is related to various Hebrew words indicating truth, faith, and trust. In saying *amen* one is saying "yes" to all of life in the providence of God, who is sovereign Lord of all that comes about. Paul writes: "For the Son of God, Jesus Christ, who was proclaimed to you by us, Silvanus and Timothy and me, was not 'yes' and 'no', but 'yes' has been in him. For however many are the promises of God, their Yes is in him; therefore, the Amen from us also goes through him to God in glory" (2 Cor 1:19). At the end of a prayer led by another, the *amen* signifies that the respondent accepts the prayer as his or her own, approves its sentiments, and concurs in its petition. "So be it" in English (*Ainsi soit-il* in French or *Così sia* in Italian) captures something of the content of *amen.* Justin Martyr writes in the second century: "At the end of these prayers [eucharistic prayers] and thanksgiving, all present express their approval by saying 'Amen'. This Hebrew word, 'Amen', means 'So be it!' "[50] In Deuteronomy after each of the imprecations in a list of immoral practices to be shunned by the people of Israel we read: "And all the people shall answer, 'Amen!' " (27:14–26). The word *amen* is so ancient and venerable in Jewish and Christian prayer that it defies adequate translation. The *amen* involves the active participation of the people of God. They must ratify the prayer of their community leader, who collects in a public prayer the many prayers of each individual's heart and soul. That *amen* validates the words of the liturgical prayer. Without it, the congregation is only audience. With a

wholehearted and sincere amen, the person who has soulfully
listened has truly spoken in the silence of their heart the very
same words and with the identical purpose to reach God.

PART THREE

COMMENTARIES

In this part of the book I have gathered a selection of commentaries on the Ave Maria. From patristic times there are innumerable commentaries on the Gospel of Luke and, thus, on the first half of the Ave Maria. My intent is not to survey those biblical studies. In addition, there is an enormous bibliography of Marian writings which have much to do with the themes of the Ave Maria—Mary the mother of Jesus and the premiere patron saint of Christians. This literature is not culled for my purposes here. My focus is on the Ave Maria prayer as such.

The first inclusion is a sermon given by Cyril of Alexandria at the Council of Ephesus (430). At stake was the establishment of the phrase "mother of God" which would become central in the second part of the Ave Maria some thousand years later. Cyril was consecrated Archbishop and Patriarch of Alexandria in 412. The Alexandrian school of theology spoke of the one person of Christ in terms that were easily identified with only one nature in Christ, the divine nature. Hence the *Theotokos* was readily defensible for Alexandrian theology. The Antiochene school of theology spoke of the two natures in Christ, human and divine, in terms that were easily confused with two persons. Hence the reluctance over the word *Theotokos*.

Cyril was an able theologian and astute politician. He was opposed to the overall theological approach of the school of Antioch and suspicious of the rising power of the See of Constantinople (Byzantium or New Rome), which was established by

Constantine I and which would come to dominate eventually the ancient See of Alexandria. Cyril was the dominant voice at the Council of Ephesus, and it is his efforts that led to the acceptance of the term *Theotokos* in the universal Church. Nestorius, whose doctrine was condemned as heretical but who probably was not a Nestorian in the terms that were decried, was subsequently deposed from the See of Constantinople by the Emperor Theodosius II. Cyril was also upheld in this theological dispute by the bishop of Rome, Pope Celestine I.

Cyril died in 444. It was only in 451 at the Council of Chalcedon, however, that the doctrine of the two natures of Christ in the one person was formulated with precision and universal Church assent. Cyril of Alexandria was declared a Doctor of the Church in 1882.

I next include the response of the loyal opposition in a letter of John of Antioch. John was bishop of Antioch in Syria. He was a friend and companion of Nestorius, who was named in 428 the Antiochene bishop of Constantinople, and who was pitted against Cyril of Alexandria at the Council of Ephesus. John of Antioch, who had sent notice of his delay, arrived with his delegation of bishops after the council had already been opened by Cyril. During the period before John's arrival, Nestorius had been excommunicated and his theological doctrine condemned. John then convened a rival council and in turn condemned Cyril of Alexandria. Subsequently the Council of Ephesus excommunicated John. The Council of Ephesus did not so much define doctrine as remove from office proponents of a different doctrine. The resultant schism was healed some two years later when Antioch and Alexandria were reconciled. The "formulary of union" in 433 was contained in a letter from John of Antioch to Cyril of Alexandria. However, divisions and frictions continued between the two schools despite the reconciliation of John and Cyril. John of Antioch died in 441.

The Ave Maria employed as a prayer begins with the Middle Ages, and I include commentaries on the Ave Maria itself by Thomas Aquinas and Mechtild of Helfta. Only the first part of the Ave was said at this time; the second part was yet to be established.

Thomas Aquinas was born circa 1224 in Naples and died in Fossanuova in 1274 while en route to the Council of Lyons. His

Summa Theologica is a monumental work of medieval theological synthesis. His theological writings are voluminous and masterful. His integration of ancient Aristotelian philosophy with classical Christian theology represents an enduring contribution to Catholic theology to this day.

The "Collationes super Ave Maria" are collected in the *Opuscula Theologica* of Thomas. These two or three sermon-conferences on the Ave were given either in Paris or Rome in the last years before his death. They may have been delivered in the vernacular in the parish church of the Dominican priory in Naples during the Lent of 1273, some few months before his death. They are collected in that grouping of Naples Lenten sermon-conferences which includes the Creed, "Collationes super Symbolum," and the Lord's Prayer, "Collationes super Pater Noster." Wherever they were delivered and whatever their origin, they are nonetheless universally considered authentic works of Aquinas. They survive in Latin and are very likely a translation with careful editing by his secretary Reginald of Piperno.

Mechtild (or Mechthild) of Hackeborn or Hackenborn was born circa 1241. She was a nun of the monastery of Helfta in Saxony in southern Germany. Her sister Gertrude (1251–1292) moved the Cistercian monastery near Eisleben to Helfta in 1258, and she became abbess of Helfta, which followed unofficially the Cistercian rule of the Benedictine Order. This sister of Mechtild should not be confused with Gertrude the Great, who was educated at an early age at Helfta by Mechtild herself. This was the golden age of German mysticism, and Mechtild (Matilda in English) received mystical and spiritual revelations which she was persuaded to commit to writing. Mechtild died at the monastery of Helfta in 1299.

With Savonarola in the late fifteenth century we see the whole Ave Maria as it is recited today. His commentary on the Hail Mary is complete and represents one of the few treatises directly devoted to this prayer. Savonarola, or more exactly Girolamo (Jerome) Savonrola, was born in 1452. He entered the Dominican priory in San Marco in Florence, where Fra Angelico had flourished a decade before in painting his simple and soulful frescoes on the walls of the cells of the Dominican friars. Savonarola was a man of ample spiritual resources and serious purpose. In

1482 he became a lector in theology at San Marco and in 1491 was appointed prior. In his role as a prophet to a sinful Christianity and a corrupt Italian Church he preached with great effectiveness to crowds of people gathered in the cathedral of Florence to hear his Sunday sermons. Judged both reformer and extremist, he was excommunicated by Pope Alexander VI in 1497. Savonarola was subsequently tried and condemned, then hung to death and burned in the main square of Florence in 1498.

Savonarola may be considered the earliest witness that we know to the Ave Maria as it is said today. The second part of the Ave Maria given in his commentary and also found written in his own hand inside the cover of one of his prayer books is identical to the contemporary Hail Mary except for the omission of the word "our" in the phrase "hour of *our* death."

From 1850 to 1950 has been called the Marian century because of the definition of the dogmas of the Immaculate Conception and the Assumption. Fulsome Marian literature abounds from this period. I have chosen two pieces by women writing at the end of this period and before the Vatican Council. Both pieces carry a rare mystical quality that is indicative of the depth of insight of Caryll Houselander and Adrienne Von Speyr. Their connection to the Ave Maria is indirect but their relevance will be seen.

Caryll Frances Houselander was born in 1901 and baptized in the Church of England. She became a Catholic at the age of six years, and her autobiography was appropriately entitled *A Rocking-Horse Catholic*. She was educated in convent and in state schools, and she studied art. Her activities included the illustrating of books and the writing of some ten books of her own. Her interest in spirituality was keen and insightful. Her book *The Reed of God* remains to this day one of the few truly perduring works about the blessed virgin Mary written in the twentieth century prior to the Vatican Council. It is as richly readable today as it was the day it was written.

Adrienne Von Speyr was born in 1902. From childhood she was gifted with spiritual and mystical experiences. Her upbringing was in the Protestant faith, but she converted to Catholicism in 1940 during World War II. She studied medicine and practiced as a physician for a number of years. After her conversion and during the years 1941–1955 she wrote or dictated to her confessor some sixty volumes of theological and spiritual thought. Although she had only an ordinary theological background, her work has been found to be exceptional. She was ever a woman of prayer, of charity, and of personal suffering accepted through the mystery of the cross of Christ. Her commentary on John, on Paul, her reflections on prayer and on Mary are outstanding theological endeavors. Her writings on Mary from which we quote represent her earliest book work. Adrienne Von Speyr died in 1967.

From the post–Vatican II Church I have taken two selections. From Pope Paul VI's encyclical letter "Marialis Cultus" I have taken some lengthy excerpts. This is a thoughtful, devout, and irenic treatment of the place of Mary in Christian prayer and liturgy. Its implication for the Ave Maria will be readily understood. Pope Paul VI reigned during the closing years of the Second Vatican Council and its aftermath when the implementation of the council was undertaken amid the many difficulties that change presented to the Church. The decline in Marian devotion was attributed by some people to the work of the Vatican Council, where the treatise on Mary was given a place within the larger treatise on the Church itself (*Lumen Gentium*). To counter the eclipse of Marian devotion, some of which may have been beneficial, Paul VI wrote "Marialis Cultus" as an appeal to a renaissance of the Marian cult using the best insights of modern scripture study and wise liturgical renewal.

I conclude with some recent reflection of Agnes Cunningham, a current theologian. She is a member of the Congregation of the Servants of the Holy Heart of Mary. A professor of theology with special competence in early Church history, she currently teaches patristic theology at the University of St. Mary of the Lake, Mundelein, Illinois. One might expect to see Marian studies continue to develop from the new biblical reading of Mary in the Gospel and some re-symbolization of Mary in the Church that deepens our understanding of her. The Ave Maria will be prayed in the future with just such background.

CYRIL OF ALEXANDRIA

HOMILY XI
ENCOMIUM ON HOLY MARY THEOTOKOS*

Our word shines forth and is filled with grace because of
this illustrious gathering of holy Fathers. Indeed troubled with
vehement sorrow on account of the impious blasphemy of Nestorius, I have raised my voice in this resonant, beautiful, angelic,
and celestial auditorium. These are the teachers of piety, pillars
and summits of faith, unbroken fortifications of it, joyful harbors,
faithful and prudent stewards, wise architects, living celestial nav-
igation and angelic life on earth, comrades of the prophets, col-
leagues of the apostles, presiders over holy Churches, punishers
of wicked blasphemy, wise defenders of our poverty and especially
of our name. These [are the ones] who occupy the beautiful and
deiform throne of the high priesthood, who distill mellifluous
liquids, who are spiritual heralds of divine intelligence, who travel
the four-cornered world with tireless journeys, whom neither
heat, nor tempests of the sea, nor the indomitable fury of the
raging waves, nor violent seasurges keep back, but bounding with
fruitful steps they rejoice in this, having rejected all idleness due
to desire, or rather due to fear before the Lord, and taking up
the cross, gather here as wise vindicators of Mary Theotokos.
On account of which, confirmed in their holy prayers, we give
some small thanks to this city. Therefore I will turn my oration
to the praise of the Theotokos. Hail, city of the Ephesians, in
view of the sea, and especially [hail] because in place of earthly
harbor, angelic and celestial harbors have come to you. Hail,

---

* Patrologiae cursus completus..., Series Graeca, ed. J.-P. Migne, 77:1029–39. The translation
is mine.

beauty of the Asian prefecture, built up on all sides with temples of the saints, [which are] precious pearls. Now worn smooth also by the footsteps of many holy Fathers and patriarchs, you are thus consecrated.

Indeed your very gates, and streets, and harbors are blessed by the revered arrival of the holy Fathers. For where many pastors are gathered, a great congregation of holiness comes about through them: especially these religious, faithful, equals of the angels, [who] drive out all satanic force, and the gentile idolmania of the Porphyrians, the Sabellians, the Phrygians, the Apollinarists, and the Photians, et alteri, and simply all nefarious heresy is confounded and the glory of the orthodox faith is celebrated. Hail also, thrice blessed John the apostle and evangelist, beauty of virginity, teacher of modesty, exterminator of diabolical fraud, overthrower of the temple of Diana, harbor and bulwark of the city of Ephesus, nourisher of the poor, refuge of the afflicted, rest and refreshment of neighbors and travellers. Hail, most pure vessel full of temperance. For to you, Our Lord Jesus Christ, when he was borne up on the cross, handed over the Theotokos, always a virgin, to you a virgin.

Hail also to you Mary Theotokos, Virgin mother, Light-bearer, incorrupt vessel. Hail, Virgin Mary, mother and servant: Virgin indeed, on account of him who is born from you a Virgin; truly mother, on account of him whom you carried in your arms and nourished with your milk; servant, on account of him who first took the form of a servant. For the King has come into your city, or rather into your womb, and again has gone out as he himself wished to do, and your doorway was sealed. You conceived without seed, and you bore in godly fashion. Hail, Mary, dwelling-temple, temple especially holy, such as the prophet David cried out about, saying: "Holy is your temple, wonderful in fairness" [Ps 64:6]. Hail, Mary, most precious thing in all the world; hail, Mary, stainless dove; hail, Mary, inextinguishable lamp; from you is born the Sun of justice. hail, Mary, the place of him who is captured by no place, [you] who had room for the only begotten Word of God, who made sprout the unfading ear of corn without plough and seed. Hail, Mary Theotokos, on account of whom the prophets cry out, and because of whom pastors sing praises to God [in] that tremendous hymn with the angels, saying: "Glory in the highest to God, and peace on earth, to men good will" [Lk 2:14]. Hail, Mary Theotokos, on account of whom the angels dance, archangels exult giving forth tremendous songs. Hail, Mary Theotokos, on account of whom the Magi, led forth by an illustrious star, adore. Hail, Mary Theotokos, on account of whom the election of the twelve apostles is more adorned. Hail, Mary Theotokos, on account of whom, John, though still in the womb of his mother, jumped up, and adored the lamp with perennial light [Lk 2:41]. Hail, Mary Theotokos, through whom ineffable grace issued, about which the Apostle said: "The saving grace of God appeared to all humankind" [Ti 2:11]. Hail, Mary Theotokos, through whom the true light emerged, our Lord Jesus Christ, who says in the Gospels: "I am the light of the world" [Jn 8:12]. Hail, Mary Theotokos, through whom a light shone for those sitting in darkness and in the shadow of death. "For a people who sat in darkness have seen a great light" [Is 9:2]. But what light, unless our Lord Jesus Christ, that true light which illumines everyone coming into this world?" [Jn 1:29] Hail, Mary Theotokos, on account of whom in the Gospels it is proclaimed: "Blessed is the one who comes in the name of the Lord" [Mt 21:9]: on whose account in cities, in villages and islands, Churches of the Orthodox are founded. Hail, Mary Theotokos, through whom emerged the victor of death and exterminator of hell. Hail, Mary Theotokos, through whom issued the fashioner of living matter and the straightener of its prevarication, the leader of the heavenly kingdom. Hail, Mary Theotokos, through whom the beauty of resurrection blossomed and shone forth. Hail, Mary Theotokos, through whom shone forth the tremendous Jordanian baptism of sanctity. Hail, Mary Theotokos, through whom John and the Jordan were sanctified and the devil rejected. Hail, Mary Theotokos, through whom every faithful spirit is saved. Hail, Mary Theotokos, through you the waves of the sea are placated and calmed and carry us fellow servants and fellow ministers with elation and smoothness. Land formerly occupied by thieves is turned to peace with the coming of the holy Fathers. For it is written: "How beautiful are the feet of those evangelizing peace!" [Is 52:7]. What peace? Our

Lord Jesus Christ, herald of peace, who in the holy Gospels said: "My peace I give to you" [Jn 14:27]. What peace? That peace which blasphemous Nestorius would not accept saying, our Lord Jesus Christ is not born Son and Word from Virgin Mary, nor acknowledging the inviolable birth in virginity, nor believing in the voice of the archangel saying: "Hail, Mary, full of grace. The Lord is with you" [Lk 1:28]. Having taken to himself a thoroughly dry leadership, this man, trying to rob the only begotten Son of God of divinity, fashioned the ruin of many and the blasphemy of souls.

JOHN OF ANTIOCH

THE CONFESSION OF JOHN OF
ANTIOCH AND THE EASTERNERS*

Concerning the Virgin Mother of God, how we both hold and speak, and concerning the mode of the Incarnation of the Only-Begotten Son of God, we will perforce declare in few words —not as though we were supplying some deficiency, but as a matter about which there can be no doubt, as we have held from the first, having received it both from the divine Scriptures and from the tradition of the holy fathers—we will declare, I say, in few words, making no addition whatever to the faith put forth by the holy Fathers at Nicaea. For that Faith, as we have already said, suffices both for all knowledge of godliness and for the denunciation of all heretical heterodoxy. And we will make the declaration, not rashly venturing to intrude upon what is beyond our reach, but, while acknowledging our own weakness, barring the way against those who would fain dictate to us, where we are dealing with matters too high for man.

We confess, therefore, our Lord Jesus Christ, the Only-Begotten Son of God, perfect God and a perfect Man, consisting of a rational soul and a body, begotten of the Father before the ages as concerning His Godhead, the same, in the last days, for us and for our salvation, born of the Virgin Mary, as concerning His Manhood: the same of one essence with the Father as concerning

---

* John's letter to Cyril in English translation from Georges Florovsky, *Byzantine Fathers of the Fifth Century*, trans. Raymond Miller and Anne-Marie Dollinger-Labrielle and Helmut Wilhelm Schmiedel (Vaduz, Europa: Büchervertriebsanstalt, 1987) in the *Collected Works of Georges Florovsky*, ed. Richard Haugh, vol. 8, 258–260. Copyright (c) BVA / Büchervertriebsanstalt, Postfach 461, FL – 9490, Vaduz. Reprinted by permission of the copyright owner.

His Godhead and of one essence with us as concerning His Manhood. For of two natures there has been made a union, for which cause we confess one Christ, one Son, one Lord.

In accordance with this sense of the unconfused union, we confess the holy Virgin to be *"Theotokos"* because God the Logos became incarnate and was made man, and from the very conception united to Himself the temple that was received from her. And as to the expressions concerning the Lord in the Gospels and Epistles, we are aware that theologians understand some as common, as relating to one Person, and others they distinguish, as relating to two natures, explaining those that befit the divine nature according to the Godhead of Christ, and those of a humble sort according to His Manhood.

Having been made acquainted then with these sacred words of yours, and finding that we ourselves are of the same mind, for there is "One Lord, One Faith, One Baptism," we gave thanks to God, the Savior of the world, rejoicing with one another that our Churches, both ours and yours, hold a faith in accordance with the divinely inspired Scriptures and with the tradition of our holy Fathers.

But when I learned that some of those who take delight in finding fault were buzzing about like spiteful wasps and were spitting forth odious speeches against me, as though I said that the holy Body of Christ "was brought down from heaven and was not of the holy Virgin," I thought it necessary to say a few words to them about this:—O fools, who know only how to slander, how have you been mispersuaded to take up this perverse notion, how have you fallen sick of so great folly? For you ought by all means to be aware that almost the whole of our contention for the faith has grown out of our confident assertion that the holy Virgin is *"Theotokos."* But if we affirm that the holy Body of Christ, the Savior of us all, was from heaven, and was not born of her, how can she be conceived of as the *"Theotokos"*? For whom in the world did she bear, if it be not true that she bore Emmanuel, according to the flesh? Let them be treated with scorn then, who prate thus about me. For it is no falsehood which the blessed Prophet Isaiah speaks when he says: "Behold the Virgin shall conceive and bring forth a Son and they shall call His name Emmanuel, which being interpreted, is God with us." And it is altogether true which the holy Gabriel said to the blessed Virgin: "Fear not, Mary, for thou hast found favor with God. And behold thou shall conceive in thy womb, and shall bring forth a Son, and shall call His name 'Jesus,' for He Himself shall save His people from their sins."

But when we say that our Lord Jesus Christ is "from heaven and from above," we say it—not as though his holy flesh was brought down from above and from heaven, but we follow rather the divinely-taught Paul, who cries distinctly: "The first man is of the earth, earthly: the second man is from heaven." And we remember moreover the Savior's words: "No one hath ascended up to heaven but he who came down from heaven, the Son of Man," notwithstanding that he was born as to the flesh, as I said just now, of the holy Virgin. But forasmuch as he that came down from above and from heaven, God the Logos, emptied himself, taking the form of a servant, and was called the Son of Man, remaining still what he was, that is, God—(for he is unchangeable and unalterable as to his nature)—therefore he is said to have "come down from heaven," being even now conceived of as one with his own flesh, and he is named also 'Man from heaven,' the same perfect in Manhood, and conceived of as in one Person: for the Lord Jesus Christ is one, although we do not forget the difference of the natures, from which we affirm the ineffable union to have been formed.

But let thy Holiness vouchsafe to stop the mouths of those who say that there was a mixture of confusion or blending of God the Logos with the flesh, for it is likely that some are spreading the report that I hold or say this also. But so far am I from holding anything of the sort that I look upon those as mad who at all imagine that "shadow of turning" can befall the divine nature of the Logos, and that he is capable of change: for he remains what he is always, and hath undergone no alteration. Nor could he ever undergo alteration. Moreover we all acknowledge that the Logos of God is naturally impassible, even though, in his all-wise administration of the mystery, he is seen to attribute to himself the sufferings which befell his own flesh. Thus also the all-wise Peter says, "Christ then having suffered for us in the flesh," and not in the nature of the ineffable Godhead. For in order that he may be believed the Savior of the world, he appropriates to himself, as I said, in view of his Incarnation, the sufferings of his own flesh—as did the Prophet before, who said, speaking in his person, "I gave my back to the scourges, and my cheeks to blows, and my face I turned not away from the shame of spitting."

But that we follow everywhere the sentiments of the holy Fathers, and especially those of our blessed and all-renowned Father Athanasius, refusing to vary from them in the least possible degree, let thy Holiness be assured, and let no one else entertain a doubt. I would have set down many passages of theirs, confirming my own words from them, if I had not been afraid of making my letter too long and therefore tedious. And we in no wise suffer any to unsettle the faith—the Symbol of the Faith I mean—defined by our holy Fathers assembled at Nicaea. Nor assuredly do we suffer ourselves or others either to alter a phrase of what is contained therein, or to go beyond a single syllable, remembering who said, "Remove not the eternal landmarks which thy Fathers set." For it was not they who spoke, but the very Spirit of God the Father, *who proceeds indeed from him* but is not alien from the Son in respect of essence. And in this the words of the holy teachers confirm us. For in the *Acts of the Apostles* it is written: "When they had gone throughout Mysia they attempted to go into Bithynia and the Spirit of Jesus suffered them not." The blessed Paul, too, writes in his Epistle: "They that are in the flesh cannot please God. And you are not in the flesh but in the spirit, if the Spirit of God dwell in you. But if any man have not the Spirit of Christ, he is none of his."

But when any of those who are inclined to pervert the right meaning of my words to what they please, let not thy Holiness marvel, as thou knowest that heretics also of every sort collect arguments in support of their error from the divine Scripture, corrupting by their own evil-mindedness what has been rightly spoken by the Holy Spirit and drawing down in full measure upon their own heads the unquenchable flame.

But since we have learned that some have published a garbled edition of our all-renowned Father Athanasius' orthodox Epistle to the blessed Epictetus, so that many are being injured by it, therefore with a view to what may be useful and necessary to the brethren, we send your Holiness a transcript taken from ancient and correct copies which we have here.

The Lord preserve thee in good health, and interceding for us, most honored brother.

THOMAS AQUINAS

SERMON-CONFERENCES ON THE AVE MARIA*

THE ANGELIC SALUTATION

This salutation has three parts.[1] The Angel gave one part, namely: "Hail, full of grace, the Lord is with thee, blessed art thou among women."[2] The other part was given by Elizabeth, the mother of John the Baptist, namely: "Blessed is the fruit of thy womb."[3] The Church adds the third part, that is, "Mary," because the Angel did not say, "Hail, Mary," but "Hail, full of grace." But, as we shall see, this name, "Mary," according to its meaning agrees with the words of the Angel.[4]

"HAIL MARY"

We must now consider concerning the first part of this prayer that in ancient times it was no small event when Angels appeared to men; and that man should show them reverence was especially praiseworthy. Thus, it is written to the praise of Abraham that he received the Angels with all courtesy and showed them reverence. But that an Angel should show reverence to a man was never heard of until the Angel reverently greeted the Blessed Virgin saying: "Hail."

* From *The Catechetical Instructions of St. Thomas Aquinas*, trans. Joseph B. Collins (New York: Joseph F. Wagner, 1939), 173–180. Copyright was not renewed. The Collins translation into English was based on the Mandonnet Latin edition (1927), which was a revision of the Parma edition (1852–73), and with consultation also of the Vivès edition (1871–80).

THE ANGEL'S DIGNITY

In olden time an Angel would not show reverence to a man, but a man would deeply revere an Angel. This is because Angels are greater than men, and indeed in three ways. First, they are greater than men in dignity. This is because the Angel is of a spiritual nature: "Who makest Thy angels spirits."[5] But, on the other hand, man is of a corruptible nature, for Abraham said: "I will speak to my Lord, whereas I am dust and ashes."[6] It was not fitting, therefore, that a spiritual and incorruptible creature should show reverence to one that is corruptible as is a man. Secondly, an Angel is closer to God. The Angel, indeed, is of the family of God, and as it were stands ever by Him: "Thousands of thousands ministered to Him, and ten thousand times a hundred thousand stood before Him."[7] Man, on the other hand, is rather a stranger and afar off from God because of sin: "I have gone afar off."[8] Therefore, it is fitting that man should reverence an Angel who is an intimate and one of the household of the King.

Then, thirdly, the Angels far exceed men in the fullness of the splendor of divine grace. For Angels participate in the highest degree in the divine light: "Is there any numbering of His soldiers? And upon whom shall not His light arise?"[9] Hence, the Angels always appear among men clothed in light, but men on the contrary, although they partake somewhat of the light of grace, nevertheless do so in a much slighter degree and with a certain obscurity. It was, therefore, not fitting that an Angel should show reverence to a man until it should come to pass that one would be found in human nature who exceeded the Angels in these three points in which we have seen that they excel over men—and this was the Blessed Virgin. To show that she excelled the Angels in these, the Angel desired to show her reverence, and so he said: "*Ave* (Hail)."

"FULL OF GRACE"

The Blessed Virgin was superior to any of the Angels in the fullness of grace, and as an indication of this the Angel showed reverence to her by saying: "Full of grace." This is as if he said: "I show thee reverence because thou dost excel me in the fullness of grace."

The Blessed Virgin is said to be full of grace in three ways. First, as regards her soul she was full of grace. The grace of God is given for two chief purposes, namely, to do good and to avoid evil. The Blessed Virgin, then, received grace in the most perfect degree, because she had avoided every sin more than any other Saint after Christ. Thus it is said: "Thou art fair, My beloved, and there is not a spot in thee."[10] St. Augustine says: "If we could bring together all the Saints and ask them if they were entirely without sin, all of them, with the exception of the Blessed Virgin, would say with one voice: 'If we say that we have no sin, we deceive ourselves and the truth is not in us.'[11] I except, however, this holy Virgin of whom, because of the honor of God, I wish to omit all mention of sin."[12] For we know that to her was granted grace to overcome every kind of sin by Him whom she merited to conceive and bring forth, and He certainly was wholly without sin.

VIRTUES OF THE BLESSED VIRGIN

Christ excelled the Blessed Virgin in this, that He was conceived and born without original sin, while the Blessed Virgin was conceived in original sin, but was not born in it.[13] She exercised the works of all the virtues, whereas the Saints are conspicuous for the exercise of certain special virtues. Thus, one excelled in humility, another in chastity, another in mercy, to the extent that they are the special exemplars of these virtues—as, for example, St. Nicholas is an exemplar of the virtue of mercy. The Blessed Virgin is the exemplar of all the virtues.

In her is the fullness of the virtue of humility: "Behold the handmaid of the Lord."[14] And again: "He hath regarded the humility of his handmaid."[15] So she is also exemplar of the virtue of chastity: "Because I know not man."[16] And thus it is with all the virtues, as is evident. Mary was full of grace not only in the performance of all good, but also in the avoidance of all evil. Again, the Blessed Virgin was full of grace in the overflowing effect of this grace upon her flesh or body. For while it is a great thing in the Saints that the abundance of grace sanctified their souls, yet, moreover, the soul of the holy Virgin was so filled with grace that from her soul grace poured into her flesh from which was conceived the Son of God. Hugh of St. Victor says of this: "Because the love of the Holy Spirit so inflamed her soul, He worked a wonder in her flesh, in that from it was born God made Man." "And therefore also the Holy which shall be born of thee shall be called the Son of God."[17]

MARY, HELP OF CHRISTIANS

The plenitude of grace in Mary was such that its effects overflow upon all human beings. It is a great thing in a Saint when he has grace to bring about the salvation of many, but it is exceedingly wonderful when grace is of such abundance as to be sufficient for the salvation of all human beings in the world, and this is true of Christ and of the Blessed Virgin. Thus, "a thousand bucklers," that is, remedies against dangers, "hang therefrom."[18] Likewise, in every work of virtue one can have her as one's helper. Of her it was spoken: "In me is all grace of the way and of the truth, in me is all hope of life and of virtue."[19] Therefore, Mary is full of grace, exceeding the Angels in this fullness and very fittingly is she called "Mary" which means "in herself enlightened": "The Lord will fill thy soul with brightness."[20] And she will illumine others throughout the world, for which reason she is compared to the sun and to the moon.[21]

"THE LORD IS WITH THEE"

The Blessed Virgin excels the Angels in her closeness to God. The Angel Gabriel indicated this when he said: "The Lord is with thee"—as if to say: "I reverence thee because thou art nearer to God than I, because *the Lord is with thee.*" By the *Lord,* he means the Father with the Son and the Holy Spirit, who in like manner are not with any Angel or any other spirit: "The Holy which shall be born of thee shall be called the Son of God."[22] God the Son was in her womb: "Rejoice and praise, O thou habitation of Sion; for great is He that is in the midst of thee, the Holy One of Israel."[23]

The Lord is not with the Angel in the same manner as with the Blessed Virgin; for with her He is as a Son, and with the Angel He is the Lord. The Lord, the Holy Ghost, is in her as in a temple, so that it is said: "The temple of the Lord, the sanctuary of the Holy Spirit,"[24] because she conceived by the Holy Ghost. "The Holy Ghost shall come upon thee."[25] The Blessed Virgin is closer to God than is an Angel, because with her are the Lord the Father, the Lord the Son, and the Lord the Holy Ghost—in a word, the Holy Trinity. Indeed of her we sing: "Noble resting place of the Triune God."[26] "The Lord is with thee" are the most praise-laden words that the Angel could have uttered; and, hence, he so profoundly reverenced the Blessed Virgin because she is the Mother of the Lord and Our Lady. Accordingly she is very well named "Mary," which in the Syrian tongue means "Lady."

"BLESSED ART THOU AMONG WOMEN"

The Blessed Virgin exceeds the Angels in purity. She is not only pure, but she obtains purity for others. She is purity itself, wholly lacking in every guilt of sin, for she never incurred either mortal or venial sin. So, too, she was free from the penalties of sin. Sinful humans, on the contrary, incur a threefold curse on account of sin. The first fell upon woman who conceives in corruption, bears her child with difficulty, and brings it forth in pain. The Blessed Virgin was wholly free from this, since she conceived without corruption, bore her Child in comfort, and brought Him forth in joy: "It shall bud forth and blossom, and shall rejoice with joy and praise."[27]

The second penalty was inflicted upon man in that he shall earn his bread by the sweat of his brow. The Blessed Virgin was also immune from this because, as the Apostle says, virgins are free from the cares of this world and are occupied wholly with the things of the Lord.[28]

The third curse is common both to man and woman in that both shall one day return to dust. The Blessed Virgin was spared this penalty, for her body was raised up into heaven, and so we believe that after her death she was revived and transported into heaven: "Arise, O Lord, into Thy resting place, Thou and the ark which Thou hast sanctified."[29] Because the Blessed Virgin was immune from these punishments, she is "blessed among women." Moreover, she alone escaped the curse of sin, brought forth the Source of blessing, and opened the gate of heaven. It is surely fitting that her name is "Mary," which is akin to the Star of the Sea (*Maria—maris stella*), for just as sailors are directed to port by the star of the sea, so also Christians are by Mary guided to glory.

"BLESSED IS THE FRUIT OF THY WOMB"

The sinner often seeks for something which he does not find; but to the just man it is given to find what he seeks: "The substance of the sinner is kept for the just."[30] Thus, Eve sought the fruit of the tree (of good and evil), but she did not find in it that which she sought. Everything Eve desired, however, was given to the Blessed Virgin.[31] Eve sought that which the devil falsely promised her, namely, that she and Adam would be as gods, knowing good and evil. "You shall be," says this liar, "as gods."[32] But he lied, because "he is a liar and the father of lies."[33] Eve was not made like God after having eaten of the fruit, but rather she was unlike God in that by her sin she withdrew from God and was driven out of paradise. The Blessed Virgin, however, and all Christians found in the Fruit of her womb Him whereby we are all united to God and are made like to Him: "When He shall appear, we shall be like to Him, because we shall see Him as He is."[34]

Eve looked for pleasure in the fruit of the tree because it was good to eat. But she did not find this pleasure in it, and, on the contrary, she at once discovered she was naked and she was stricken with sorrow. In the Fruit of the Blessed Virgin we find sweetness and salvation: "He that eateth My flesh . . . hath eternal life."[35]

The fruit which Eve desired was beautiful to look upon, but that Fruit of the Blessed Virgin is far more beautiful, for the Angels desire to look upon Him: "Thou art beautiful above the sons of men."[36] He is the splendor of the glory of the Father. Eve, therefore, looked in vain for that which she sought in the fruit of the tree, just as the sinner is disappointed in his sins. We must seek in the Fruit of the womb of the Virgin Mary whatsoever we desire. This is He who is the Fruit blessed by God, who has filled Him with every grace, which in turn is poured out upon us who adore Him: "Blessed be God and the`Father of our Lord Jesus Christ, who hath blessed us with spiritual blessings in Christ."[37] He, too, is revered by the Angels: "Benediction and glory and wisdom and thanksgiving, honor and power and strength, to our God."[38] And He is glorified by men: "Every tongue should confess that the Lord Jesus Christ is in the glory of God the Father."[39] The Blessed Virgin is indeed blessed, but far more blessed is the Fruit of her womb: "Blessed is He who cometh in the name of the Lord."[40]

NOTES

1. In the translation I have substituted "human beings" for "men" when the intent is generic. In the endnotes I have standardized the biblical references. The NAB is used for abbreviations.

2. Lk 1:28.

3. Lk 1:42.

4. "Most fittingly has the Holy Church of God added to this thanksgiving [i.e., the Hail Mary] a petition also and an invocation to the most holy Mother of God. This is to impress upon us the need to have recourse to her in order that by her intercession she may reconcile God with us sinners, and obtain for us the blessings necessary for this life and for life eternal" ("Roman Catechism," *On Prayer*, Chapter V, 8).

5. Ps 103:4.

6. Gn 18:27.

7. Dn 7:10.

8. Ps 54:8.

9. Jb 25:3.

10. Song 4:7.

11. 1 Jn 1:8.

12. *De natura et gratia*, c. xxxvi. Elsewhere St. Thomas says: "In the Angelic Salutation is shown forth the worthiness of the Blessed Virgin for this Conception when it says, 'Full of grace'; it expresses the

Conception itself in the words, 'The Lord is with thee'; and it foretells the honor which will follow with the words, 'Blessed art thou among women' " (*Summa Theol.*, III, Q. xxx, art. 4).

13. St. Thomas wrote before the solemn definition of the Immaculate Conception by the Church and at a time when the subject was still a matter of controversy among theologians. In an earlier work, however, he pronounced in favor of the doctrine (*I Sent.*, c. 44, Q. i, ad. 3), although he seemingly concluded against it in the *Summa Theologica*. "Yet much discussion has arisen as to whether St. Thomas did or did not deny that the Blessed Virgin was immaculate at the instant of her animation" ("Catholic Encyclopedia," art. "Immaculate Conception"). On December 8, 1854, Pope Pius IX settled the question in the following definition: "Mary, ever blessed Virgin in the first instant of her conception, by a singular privilege and grace granted by God, in view of the merits of Jesus Christ, the Saviour of the human race, was preserved exempt from all stain of original sin."

14. Lk 1:38.

15. Lk 1:48.

16. Lk 1:34.

17. Lk 1:35.

18. Song 4:4.

19. Eccl 24:25.

20. Is 58:11.

21. "The Blessed Virgin Mary obtained such a plenitude of grace that she was closest of all creatures to the Author of Grace; and thus she received in her womb Him who is full of grace, and by giving Him birth she is in a certain manner the source of grace for all human beings" (*Summa Theol.*, III, Q. xxvii, art. 5). St. Bernard says: "It is God's will that we should receive all graces through Mary" (*Serm. de aquæductu*, n. vii). Mary is called the "Mediatrix of all Graces," and her mediation is immediate and universal, subordinate however to that of Jesus.

22. Lk 1:35.

23. Is 12:6.

24. Antiphon from the Little Office of Blessed Virgin.

25. Lk 1:35.

26. "*Totius Trinitatis nobile Triclinium.*"

27. Is 35:2.

28. 1 Cor 7:34.

29. Ps 131:8.

30. Prv 13:22.

31. Here St. Thomas contrasts the fruit of the forbidden tree for Eve with the Fruit of Mary's womb for all Christians.

32. Gn 3:5.

33. Jn 8:44.

34. 1 Jn 3:2.

35. Jn 6:55.

36. Ps 44:3.

37. Eph 1:3.

38. Rv 7:12.

39. Phil 2:11.

40. Ps 117:26.

MECHTILD OF HELFTA

THE BOOK OF SPECIAL GRACE*

On a certain Saturday when *Salve Sancta Parens* would be
sung, she [this maiden] said to the Blessed Virgin Mary: "O
Queen of heaven, if only I were able to greet you with the most
tender greeting that the human heart ever devised, I would do
so most willingly." Immediately the glorious Virgin appeared to
her with the Angelic salutation written in letters of gold upon
her breast, and she said:

> Never has anyone devised anything beyond this salutation, nor
> would anyone be able to salute me more tenderly than the one
> who greets me with reverence as God the Father greeted me with
> this word *Ave*, thereby confirming me in his omnipotence, so
> that I might be preserved from every woe of guilt. The divine
> Son of God also in his divine wisdom so brightened me that I
> might become the most shining star, by which heaven and earth
> are illumined. This name of *Mary*, which means star of the sea,
> should be so noted. The Holy Spirit as well, penetrating me with
> all her divine sweetness, made me so gracious by her grace in order
> that everyone who seeks grace through me would find it. This is
> indicated by the words, *full of grace*. Also in these words, *The Lord
> is with you* I am mindful of the ineffable union and work which
> the whole Trinity accomplished in me, when the substance of my
> flesh was joined to the one person of divine nature, so that God

* From the *Liber Specialis Gratiae* [Book of Special Grace] in *Revelationes Gertrudianae et
Mechtildianae,* ed. the Benedictines of Solesmes, vol. II (Paris: H. Oudin Bros., 1877), in
the Prima Pars, ch. 42, pp. 126–27. The translation of the Latin is mine. See also *The Books
of Gostyle Grace of Mechtild of Hackeborn*, the critical edition of a Middle English translation
with ample introduction and commentary by Theresa A. Halligan (Toronto: Pontifical
Institute of Mediaeval Studies, 1979).

150

became human and a human being became God. What I would feel in that hour of joy and sweetness no human being would be able to experience to the full. Through [these words] *Blessed are you among women* every creature acknowledges with wonder and gives witness to me as blessed and exalted above every creature both in heaven and on earth. Through [these words] *Blessed is the fruit of your womb* the most excellent and most efficacious fruit of my womb is extolled, he who gave life to every creature, sanctified and blessed them in all eternity.

SAVONAROLA

EXPOSITION BY THE MOST REVEREND BROTHER IN CHRIST, JEROME OF FERRARA, OF THE ORDER OF PREACHERS CONCERNING THE PRAYER TO THE GLORIOUS VIRGIN. COMPOSED BY HIM IN THE VERNACULAR AT THE REQUEST OF CERTAIN DEVOUT NUNS OF FERRARA.*

Ave, Maria, Gratia Plena; Dominus Tecum: Benedicta tu in Mulieribus, et Benedictus Fructus Ventris tui Iesus. Sancta Maria, Mater Dei, ora pro Nobis Peccatoribus Nunc et in Hora Mortis. Amen.

This most devout and angelic salutation which is offered up daily by our most holy Church through the mouths of her devoted sons and daughters to the most glorious mother of her beloved spouse, Jesus Christ, was composed by the Holy Spirit, partly through the lips of the angel Gabriel, partly through the lips of St. Elizabeth, mother of St. John the Baptist, and partly through the lips of Holy Church. When the angel Gabriel was sent from heaven to earth to be the ambassador of the incarnation of the Son of God, he greeted the Virgin of Virgins in this fashion: AVE GRATIA PLENA; DOMINUS TECUM: BENEDICTA TU IN MULIERIBUS.

Later, when the Virgin went to visit St. Elizabeth, after she had greeted her, feeling the Holy Spirit within herself, St. Elizabeth, among the other words she spoke in praise of so great a

---

* From Savonarola's 1496 commentary on the Ave Maria, "Esposizione sopre l'orazione della Vergine," and published in *Marian Library Studies*, New Series, 10 (Dec., 1978): 118-129. The critical Italian translation was done by Mario Ferrara and the English translation by James Ferrigno. *Marian Library Studies* is published by The Marian Library at the University of Dayton in Ohio. Fr. Theodore Koehler wrote the introductory and editorial remarks for this presentation of the commentary on the Ave Maria by Savonarola. Reprinted by permission of The Marian Library, University of Dayton, Dayton, OH 45469–1390.

virgin and mother, said in a loud voice, BENEDICTUS FRUCTUS VENTRIS TUI.

Still later, it pleased Holy Church to add the other parts. And so this sweetest of prayers was perfected; and, in order that devout young virgins may the more devoutly say it, I intend to explain it in the vernacular, maintaining a simple and lowly style that I consider them capable of comprehending; and I beg them all to offer it up for me now and then, to the mother of my Lord and Savior, Jesus Christ, who is one God with the Father and the blessed Holy Spirit forever and ever. Amen.

AVE. This is a word of greeting and it can be translated into the vernacular: "May God save you," or "May you be saved." As if I were to say "I wish you to be saved." And in this manner we greet those we love and whose salvation we desire almost as though we want to express our desire by saying "I pray to God that He may bring you every good and that He bring you to salvation, just as I desire." And therefore the angel who loved Mary, as if he were happy at her well-being, and wishing her to have even more of God's grace than she already had, at the moment he entered, said, AVE, which means, "May you be saved." As much as to say, "I am happy that you are in the grace of God, and I wish Him to raise your state to even greater glory." And in the same way, when we begin to pray to her, first we say AVE, that is, "May you be saved." This does not mean that we wish God to give her a salvation she does not already possess; but through this our wish, we show her our love for her, and not only are we happy at her glory, but also desirous that she have much triumph, and that it may endure forever and ever. Amen. And so we say AVE almost as if we were saying "Mary, we are happy at your eternal glory, and we wish you to continue in it eternally. Just as we know that it will endure without any doubt, we desire for you every good and every crown."

MARIA. The archangel did not say "Mary," calling her by her own name, rather he said AVE, GRATIA PLENA, changing her name and instead of calling her *Maria* he called her "full of grace," since at that moment the virgin was being raised from a lowly state to a very high one. And so the Angel called her "full of grace" almost changing her name to indicate the change in her state. This our Redeemer did with St. Peter (whose name had been Simon) since he had changed state. He wished him to be called Peter[1] as the foundation rock and head of the Church. And Holy Church does the same with those who have been made pope, as do the religious orders with those who enter the religious life. But the Church has given Mary her own name, that is, Mary, humbling itself before her and confessing it has need of her help. For Mary means *My Lady*, or *Illuminated*, and *Illuminatrix*, or *Star of the Sea* as St. Jerome says. Hence the Church humbly confesses it has need of her holy hand when it says to her "Hail, Mary" as if it were saying "May you always be saved, *My Lady* and my *Illuminatrix* and *Star and Harbor of my tribulations*." And therefore this name is glorious, holy and sweet. Glorious because it means "My Lady." And the Virgin is lady and queen not of a province only, but of all creatures, angelic, terrestrial and infernal, because she is the spouse of Him who is King of the Universe, that is, of God the Father Almighty, since Jesus Christ is the true child of them both. She is the Mother of Jesus Christ, the King of heaven and earth, who is one substance with the Father. She is the tabernacle of the Holy Spirit, who is one God with the Father and the Son; for the Father, and the Son and the Holy Spirit are one God eternally blessed. And since the Father wishes His spouse to be honored by all creatures, the Son has the same wish for His mother, and so does the Holy Spirit for His tabernacle.

In her, this name Mary is also holy in the highest degree, that is to say, pure. It signifies that unstained Virgin of whose most pure blood the Son of God made His own holy little body. Hence Mary means "Illuminated" and "Illuminatrix," because having been purified, she, with celestial light, has illuminated the entire universe; for remaining in the glory of her virginity, she gave birth on earth to the eternal light, Jesus our Lord. O happy and blessed Virgin, shining like a radiant morning star, you have merited to bear and to bring forth to the world the splendor of paradise. And so you are holy, that is, confirmed in grace and purified by that light which illuminates all men and women who are born into this world. And your name too is holy.

Moreover, it is sweet because it means star of the sea; and in truth the holy Virgin is the star of this sea, of this world full of storm and tribulation; [a star] to which we must lift our eyes when we feel [the blows of] fortune, for she is powerful to help and most merciful and totally desirous of our salvation. And therefore sweet is this name which means that which gives us a thousand sweet consolations, that is, the star of the sea which always comforts us.

GRATIA PLENA. "Full of grace"; grace is a very great treasure, a most precious jewel, a light, a splendor, a most pure garment for the soul. It most intimately joins the rational creature to her most sweet spouse, Jesus Christ, by means of a clear and immaculate knowledge and a sincere and unfeigned love, [such that] anyone who does not possess it, thinks he has nothing in this world; and he who does have it, guards it from thieves lest it be stolen from him, since he would lose more treasure than the whole world is worth. This is the manna which lets us walk serenely through the desert of this world. This is the pearl for which we should sell and scorn everything else. This is the treasure which enriches every man who has merited to have it, for when grace enters the soul, it brings with it every virtue: faith, hope, charity, justice, temperance, fortitude, prudence, humility, patience, obedience, meekness, peace, eternal joy and true wisdom, and all other virtues. It makes the soul pleasing in the sight of God, and worthy of reverence in the sight of angels; for through grace, God dwells in our souls. Now some are wealthy in this grace, and others are somewhat lacking. For God does as temporal lords do, who distribute their wealth to different officials, more to some, less to others, according to their station and the authority of the offices they hold. Thus the Lord of Lords distributes His grace according to the responsibilities [of each], and so He gives more to him to whom He has committed more, and less to him to whom He has committed less. He gives as much to each as he needs in order to perform the duties assigned to him by God. Hence it is recorded that St. Stephen was full of grace because he had as much as he needed for the duty assigned to him. But our Redeemer was full of grace because He possessed all graces, and in as perfect a way as it is possible to have them. And after Him, His most sweet mother was full of grace, and so there has never been a creature, nor will there ever be one (except the soul of Christ), which had or will have as much grace as the glorious Virgin had. Through this grace, the true and living God is her true and only begotten child, [a privilege] which was granted to no other creature but her. And so *gratia plena* says it well: *full of grace*. And this was the pledge and the ring by which the Eternal Father called for her in marriage through the angel. And so Gabriel quickly offered it to her, after the greeting; and even now we say "gratia plena," for she is in heaven filled with every perfection of grace and glory, and in the highest triumph.

DOMINUS TECUM. The archangel said, most appropriately, "The Lord is with you"; the Lord, because He is lord of all things. In Ferrara, of course, the Duke is called "lord." Likewise in Milan is the Duke called "lord," since in Ferrara there is no other "lord" than the Duke Hercules, and in Milan it is no other than the Duke of Milan; but anyone from Venice would not say "lord" in reference to the Duke of Milan because he is not lord of Venice; rather he would say "the Duke of Milan." And so in Ferrara the King of France is not called "lord," and if you said "the lord has made war with the Duke of Burgundy," one in Ferrara would believe that you were talking about Duke Hercules and not about the King of France. But if we wish to speak of that king, we could not call him "lord" in Ferrara, but King of France, since he is not lord of Ferrara. And so each lord (ruler) in his own country is called "lord," but in another country he is more restrictedly called "lord of Ferrara," or "of Milan," or of some other country. And since God is lord of all creatures and extends His lordship to all places, He must in all places be called Lord. When the angel wished to say that God was with the virgin, he quite properly said "the Lord," as if to say "he Who alone is Lord is with you, Mary," because the others who are called "lord" are ministers or officers of God rather than lords. And He is lord of the universe.

Blessed are you, therefore, O holy Virgin, who have found grace with the true Lord. He is with you in privileged manner, one that has never been nor ever will be accorded to any other creature; for in all other creatures, He dwells through grace spiritually, but in you God dwells spiritually and physically. The Father is with her as a spouse with his beloved spouse and also like a father with his most dear child; the Son is with her like a son with his longed-for mother. And He was with her and in her like a guest in His beloved shelter; He dwelt first in her mind, then in her blessed womb. O happy palace to have been worthy to receive such a guest and Lord! The Holy Spirit is with her like balm in a precious ivory vessel, for He filled it with every fragrance and virtue and celestial sweetness. O blessed Virgin who were made the city and palace of the entire Trinity, daughter and spouse of the Father, mother of the Son, and temple of the Holy Spirit. Truly the Lord is with you more than with any other creature and so we very fittingly say, "The Lord is with you."

BENEDICTA TU IN MULIERIBUS. "Blessed are you among women." This benediction appropriately follows after he has said to her "the Lord is with you," for since the Lord is with her, His blessing follows; but it is to be noted that to bless is nothing more than to speak well [of someone]. We bless those of whom we speak well. It is true that the Lord blesses His creatures in one way; and His creatures bless God in another way, because the blessing of God is nothing other than doing good, as St. Thomas says. Hence when He does good to His creature, it is called blessing the creature, because God's saying and doing are one and the same thing. As David the prophet says, "He spoke and it was done," which means that He spoke and commanded, and it was done immediately. And so His speaking well [blessing] is doing good for His creatures. But our blessing of God is nothing other than praising and thanking Him. And so the three youths who were placed in the fiery furnace, which by divine power brought them good rather than harm, thanking God for this and calling the other creatures to equal thanks, began their canticle in this manner: *Benedicite Omnia Opera Domini Domino, etc.*, which means nothing other than "Thank the Lord you creatures and works of the Lord."

So that when we bless the Lord, it is the same as if we thanked him. Likewise, when we bless creatures, we are only praising God and thanking Him for the favors He has done for those creatures or else really desiring that God do them some good favor. Hence when a mother says to her son, "I bless you and pray that God may bless you," it is as much as to say, "I wish God to give you His grace, and I pray to Him to do this." Or if he has this grace, it is the same as saying, "I give thanks to God for granting you His grace, and I pray that he preserve and increase it." Then too it is possible that our blessing of creatures means doing good, just as we read that Isaac blessed his son Jacob because he made him his heir and set him as lord over his brothers. So to sum up, for God, to bless is to do good. For us, to bless God is to give Him thanks for benefits received, and to bless creatures is to thank God for the graces they have, or to praise Him for those graces, or to pray that they may have such graces, or to do them some good, as Isaac did to Jacob. We therefore say to the glorious Virgin, "Blessed are you among women"; and first blessed by God, who has adorned her with greater gifts and graces than any other woman or any other creature can be compared, because He is joined in one person with the divine and glorious Word. As St. John says, to Christ Jesus was given the Holy Spirit without measure and from Him as from the head, this spirit has been communicated to the whole Church; but after Him, we rightly believe that His most beloved mother was endowed with greater grace than any other creature, angelic or human. And so she has truly been blessed by God. And she is moreover blessed by all creatures in heaven and on earth in as much as the angels and men and women thank God for having deigned in her to make one of our sisters His very mother. And moreover they praise her every day for having been so worthy that she could harbor the Son of God Eternal in her shelter (*ospizio*) for which reason the world is freed from the infernal chains. And note that he says to her "among women" and not "among men" because she is blessed above all creatures for no less a reason than that her blessedness consists uniquely in conceiving and giving birth to the Son of God without detriment to the glory of her virginity, something that was never before heard of nor ever granted to any woman. And since childbirth is proper to women and not to men, the archangel therefore says, *"Blessed are you among women* because you will have this unique privilege among them, that you will be a virgin and a mother; other women, if they are virgins, are not mothers, and if they are mothers, are not virgins. But you will have one and the other privilege, that you will be a mother and will not lose your virginity." And consequently the glorious virgin is truly blessed among all women.

ET BENEDICTUS FRUCTUS VENTRIS TUI. "And blessed is the fruit of your womb." If we consider the holy child of the glorious virgin in His human nature, God has blessed Him above every other creature, in view of the fact that He has filled him with all the graces to be had from Him. And His soul is more splendid and more radiant than are all the seraphim. And His body, already glorified, is more splendid than the sun and more beautiful than the firmament and the empyrean heaven, while those most noble, blessed spirits desire to see themselves reflected in His sweet face, as St. Peter the apostle says. And He is blessed by God, inasmuch as He has filled him with every grace and has made Him lord over all creatures, and has given Him a name which is above all other names, since Jesus Christ, who is a true man, son of one of our women, is true God, living Son of God the Father all-powerful. And in heaven He has a Father without a mother; and on earth a mother without a father, since the eternal Father generated Him eternally from His substance when he was not yet a creature. And His mother temporally generated Him, remaining a virgin before, during and after parturition, without the intervention of any man. This, then, is that fruit in which are concealed all the treasures of God's wisdom, and all the graces which sustain heaven and earth. This is that blessed fruit which all creatures should thank and bless. This, finally, is the holy fruit with which no creature in heaven or on earth can be compared in sanctity, and who is the universal redeemer of the entire human race. And so He is truly blessed by God and must be blessed by all creatures, and every day, heaven with its church triumphant and earth with its church militant bless Him and praise Him forever and ever. Amen. O therefore blessed fruit, and blessed the vessel which produced it, and [blessed] those sacred breasts that nourished Him and the most chaste hands that swathed Him. O blessed Mary, tell me, I pray you, and do not turn away from me, a sinner, [tell me] who is this fruit of your womb? It is He who has created the sky and the stars, who commands and is quickly obeyed, who makes hell tremble, who is revered in heaven, who makes the blessed spirits triumph, the bread of angels, food of travelers, comfort of the afflicted, hope of the good, love of our hearts, teacher of the apostles, prince of martyrs, light of confessors, spouse of virgins, highest sweetness of all blessed souls. He is our hope; there is none other than he. One who does not hope in you, O blessed fruit, lives in vain; indeed, he is dead. For you are our life. He who does not hope in you, sweet Jesus, vainly lives his time and years, and in the end will find himself deceived. You are therefore, my Lord, the blessed fruit of the holy womb of our Lady, the Virgin Mary, most pure and blessed, blessed as to divinity and blessed as to humanity—blessed by God and by all creatures, blessed flower, blessed lily, blessed fruit of the Blessed Virgin. I bless You and Your holy mother and glorify You forever and ever. Amen.

JESUS. This name, "Jesus," is most powerful, venerable and gentle. Most powerful because it signifies that most powerful Lord who has routed the prince of darkness from this world. Hence the infernal Demon trembles at the power of this name. This is the name by which the apostles would revive the dead; in the name of Jesus, they freed the sick; in the name of Jesus, they cast out demons; in the name of Jesus, they restored sight to the blind; in the name of Jesus, they baptized the infidels. This is the name, which, when we call upon it, lets us overcome the enemy of human nature, and every diabolical temptation. This is the name which softens adamantine hearts, that breaks boulders, that causes injuries to be forgiven, that makes chaste the dissolute, that humbles the proud, that makes the avaricious generous, the wrathful gentle, and fills the envious with charity. This is the name that surpasses the greatest minds, that brings kingdoms low, that makes empires bend, that humbles princes and finally, that subjects the whole world to its dominion. And therefore it is most powerful, of infinite virtue. It is to be venerated, moreover, because it must be honored by every creature. Indeed, I have noted at times the name of some temporal lord given reverence which should be given at the mention of the celestial king. Whoever does not give reverence to this name of Jesus must be considered as an infidel Turk; indeed, worse than a Turk, because the Turks have great reverence for Him, perhaps more than many Christians. Certainly, when Jesus is mentioned, we should bow to the ground. And that is why St. Paul the Apostle says, since Jesus Christ "was humiliated even unto death—I say, to death on the cross for us—God has exalted Him and has given Him a name above all other names, so that at the name of Jesus, every knee should bend. And every creature, celestial, terrestrial and infernal, must pay Him reverence," and acknowledge that the one signified by this name Jesus, is in the glory of God the Father, made lord of the universe. Moreover, this name of Jesus is gentle because Jesus means the same as "savior," and certainly salvation is sweet to him who feels death close upon him. We were all dead; for at least we had to descend into the prison of Limbo. But the Savior Jesus has freed us all, provided we do not fall short in our own efforts. And so what can be sweeter to our ears than to hear this gentle name; what can be sweeter to our tongue and softer to our hearts, most sweet Jesus? This name is sweet to sinners because it promises them indulgence for their sins. It is sweet to the just because this name gives them hope of a reward for their labors. And so St. Paul the Apostle, had it written in his heart; he sowed it in all his epistles so that in almost every sentence, this name is found. Likewise one reads of St. Ignatius, who, when the cruel tyrant had him beaten and subjected to diverse tortures, did not cease to call upon this name, Jesus Christ. And so when those butchers and executioners asked him why he called so much upon that name, he answered "because I have it written upon my heart"; and after he died, they opened his heart and found (in the center of that holy heart) written in letters of gold, [the name] Jesus Christ. Moreover, I have heard from a reliable person that a young virgin bride of Christ was so in love with Him that whenever she heard this name of Jesus spoken, it seemed that an arrow pierced the roots of her heart. And she would faint from spiritual sweetness, and would lie as if dead. And so this name is most gentle and penetrates human hearts.

SANCTA MARIA MATER DEI. "Holy Mary, Mother of God": we have spoken above of the Virgin's name. Holy, as we were saying earlier, means pure or even firmly established. And so Holy Mary, that is, pure and immaculate, and confirmed in the vision of God. Holy Mother Church sings of this through Mary's person: *Et sic in Syon Firmata Sum*, which means "and thus am I established firmly in Zion." Zion means "Behold" and signifies the city of God where one beholds and contemplates the Holy Trinity. And so we say "Holy Mary," which almost means "O Mary most pure, and confirmed in the highest contemplation of the supreme Trinity." And then follows Mother of God. O incomparable praise! What more can be spoken in praise of Mary? This word is so great and so high that I believe that anyone who thinks about it will agree that nothing more glorious can be said to the glorious Queen of the heavens. This praise surpasses all praise. This one includes all her praises: Mother of God! Indeed, mother and virgin; mother without husband; mother intact, mother entire, mother innocent; mother immaculate. Mother of whom? mother of God; mother of her Creator; mother of her Father; mother of her Redeemer; mother of her Spouse; mother of the Creator of the universe; mother of the Father of angels. And so she is mother even of the angels; mother of the Father of human nature, hence mother of human nature; mother of the Father of all creatures, therefore, mother of all creatures. O blessed Mary, O most clement mother, turn your merciful eyes toward your children and make them worthy of seeing your beloved and only begotten Son, blessed Christ Jesus forever and ever. Amen.

ORA PRO NOBIS PECCATORIBUS. "Pray for us sinners" because we are ashamed to go before the throne of God's majesty on account of the great number and frequency of our sins; so we turn to you, as to the one who is most merciful, having given birth to the sources of pity, and we say, "Pray for us sinners," because we are not equal to the task. And note that one must not ask so great a virgin anything contrary to our salvation, for in this we should be doing her an injury and we should not be heard; nor should anyone obstinate in sin ask, for he would not deserve to be heard, but rather would tempt her and her son. Therefore if you are weighed down with sins, do not be obstinate, but rather repentant, run to her feet with confidence and say, "Ora pro nobis peccatoribus," that is, "you, Mother of God, to whom the son can deny nothing, you, spouse to whom the husband can deny nothing, you, great queen, mother of pity and our mother, for which reason you must have compassion on us, pray not only for me alone, but for all us sinners here on earth." And do not doubt that you will be heard.

NUNC. "In the present time," that is, during the years and days of our life, and truly, Mother of God, you must pray for us out of compassion as long as our life endures in this present time, for we are in this world as though in a great and heavy sea full of shoals; and our tiny boat, that is, our nature, is very fragile, and every hour we encounter a thousand contrary winds with rain and storms. On one side, the adversary of human nature, on another, the perverse world, and on still another, the flesh; who could defend himself against so many snares? And therefore, Holy Mother, pray for us that God may forgive us in the present time for our sins, and give us strength in temptations and tribulations. Pray, Mary, in the present time, when we need but one thing, which is the love of your beloved Son. Pray, therefore, for us, most sweet Mother, to your Son that He may forgive us our sins, and that He may deeply penetrate our heart with your sweet love; and that He grant us perseverance in this until death.

ET IN ORA MORTIS. "And in the hour of our death." If ever we have need of the Mother of God, we shall need her most of all at the moment of our death, when he who gains the victory will nevermore lose the crown. And whoever loses the war can never hope to have triumph. And on the other hand, at that moment, man is in the greatest of bodily anguish, for death is a most terrible thing; and also spiritual [anguish] because of remorse of conscience. And because of the Demon

who in that most important hour importunely molests the soul
as much as he can. O how bitter is death for sinners! And that
is why Scripture says, "*O mors, quam amara est memoria tua homini
pacem habenti in substantiis suis,*" which means, "O death, how
bitter is your memory to the wealthy man who possesses in peace
his temporal substance." O blessed are they who find themselves
in that moment having observed God's commandments during
their lifetime. And therefore it is necessary that in the hour of
death, the Virgin pray for us to her most sweet Son, and that she
hold out to us her benign hand and remove us from so much
anguish. We read that this is the way she at that hour has deigned
to give her mercy to many of her devotees, coming in person to
meet them and lead them into holy paradise.

AMEN. This word, according to St. Jerome, means, "It is
true." Hence according to this interpretation, it is properly
placed at the end of the salutation to the Queen of the heavens,
as though it confirmed what has been said. It is as if we said, "It
is true, Mary, that you are full of grace and that the Lord is with
you; and that you are blessed among women. And blessed is the
fruit of your womb. And that you are holy and mother of God."
Amen also means "in truth," as though we said: "Those praises
that I have spoken of you are true," or as if one said "God, who
is truth, is witness to them." It also means "Let it be done." And
so at the end of the prayer we say *Amen,* that is, "Let it be done";
as if we plainly said, "I beg you, my Lady, that what I ask of you
be done; please do not deny me."

This, then, is the salutation which is so pleasing to the
Queen of the heavens that I have read that she once deigned
to appear before a young virgin who every day offered it to her
many times. And she said to her, "My child, I am very pleased that
you offer me this prayer each day. And most of all when I hear
you say the words *The Lord is with you,* because it almost makes
me feel as though I were still carrying in my womb my most
sweet Son. Hence I admonish you to persevere in this prayer and
to say it with greater attention than you do." When the maiden
was thus aroused, she diminished the number of *Hail Marys* and
said fewer of them but with greater attention because one *Hail*

Mary spoken with the attention of the mind and the devotion of love is more welcome than a hundred spoken hastily and with wandering mind; for God and his mother want our heart. It is true that St. John in the Apocalypse said he saw a woman clothed with the Sun and crowned with twelve stars, with the moon beneath her foot. And some see in this the Virgin Mary, who was clad with the sun of justice, Jesus Christ, and full of the Holy Spirit, and crowned with the twelve apostles amongst whom she remained after Christ's Ascension; she had beneath her foot, the moon, that is, the fleeting things of this world.

And if anyone wishes to make a short crown [or rosary], to say it more devoutly, let him for the sun, say four *Paternosters*, for the twelve stars, let him say twelve *Hail Marys*, and for the moon, let him say the *Magnificat*, which teaches us to crush the arrogance of this world. I have also read that a man once passing through a desert, saw some assassins and in fear began to say the *Hail Mary*, and quickly the virgin appeared and for every *Hail Mary* that he spoke, drew from his mouth a beautiful flower and made a garland of them and after it was finished, she disappeared. And having seen this, the thieves were converted to the faith.

And so I pray that each young virgin and every other person who may be pleased by this little book which I have put together for those who are unlettered, and most of all, for all the little virgins of Christ, handmaidens of the Queen of the angels, that they may sometimes wish to offer this prayer to the Mother of our Savior in remission of my sins. So that we may all find ourselves one day in that celestial fatherland to enjoy with the glorious Virgin the possession of her most sweet Son who is one God with the Father and the blessed Holy Spirit forever and ever. Amen.

NOTE

1. *Peter.* in Italian, Savonarola has: *Pietro* which is similar to *pietra* (stone) and thus suggests the Hebrew play of words: Jesus called Simon: *Kepha* (rock). Our English *Peter* comes from the Latin *petra* (stone).

CARYLL FRANCES HOUSELANDER

INTRODUCTION*

When I was a small child, someone for whom I had a great respect told me never to do anything that Our Lady would not do; for, she said, if I did, the angels in heaven would blush.

For a short time this advice "took" in me like an inoculation, causing a positive paralysis of piety.

It was clear to me that all those things which spelt joy to me were from henceforward taboo—blacking my face with burnt cork, turning somersaults between props against the garden wall, putting two bulls eyes into my mouth at the same time—all that was over! But even if I faced a blank future shackled with respectability, it was still impossible to imagine Our Lady doing anything that I would do, for the very simple reason that I simply could not imagine her doing *anything at all.*

The inoculation of piety wore off quickly, and so completely that when the sunset warmed the sky over our tangled garden with a pink glow, I thought that it must be the faint reflection of the rosy blush that suffused all heaven!

This would not be worth recording but for one thing, namely, that the wrong conception of Our Lady which I had is one that a great many other people have, too; a very great many people still think of Our Lady as someone who would never do anything that we do.

To many she is the Madonna of the Christmas card, immobile, seated forever in the immaculately clean stable of golden straw and shining snow. She is not real; nothing about her is real, not even the stable in which Love was born.

---

* From *The Reed of God* (New York: Sheed and Ward, 1944), pp. ix–xiii. Copyright Sheed and Ward. Reprinted by permission of Sheed and Ward, Kansas City, Missouri.

There are two things today which make it difficult for many people to love Our Lady.

First that she is pure and virgin. There is nothing so little appreciated by the world today as purity, nothing so misunderstood as virginity.

In many minds virginity is associated only with negative qualities, with impotence—impotence of body and mind, emotional and spiritual impotence.

Unfortunately, there are not only wise virgins in this world but unwise ones, foolish virgins; and the foolish virgins make more noise in the world than the wise, giving a false impression of virginity by their loveless and joyless attitude to life. They cause us to turn with a sign of relief to the page in the Missal which announces the splendid feast of a holy woman who was neither a virgin nor a martyr.

These foolish virgins, like their prototypes, have no oil in their lamps. And no one can give them this oil, for it is the potency of life, the will and the capacity to love.

We no longer think of virginity as the first fruits laid upon the fire of sacrifice, but rather as a windfall of green apples, which are hard and sour because the sun has never penetrated them and warmed them at the core.

Virginity is really the whole offering of soul and body to be consumed in the fire of love and changed into the flame of its glory.

The virginity of Our Lady is the wholeness of Love through which our own humanity has become the bride of the Spirit of Life.

It is this very fact which refutes the other mistaken idea about Our Lady, namely, that she is not human.

When we are attracted to a particular saint, it is usually the little human details which attract us. These touches bridge the immense gap between heroic virtue and our weakness. We love most those saints who before they were great saints were great sinners.

But even those who were saints from the cradle are brought closer to us by recorded trifles of their humanness. How dear to us St. Catherine of Sienna is, because she loved her garden, because she made up little verses and gilded tiny oranges to humor a difficult Pope. How close she comes to us in her friendships: in the motley company of poets, politicians, soldiers, priests, and brigands; men who idolized her; and not only men, for St. Catherine was not only the most dynamic woman in history but also the best friend to other women that ever lived. Such things almost make us forget that she was fiercely ascetic, that for years she was fed only on the Blessed Sacrament, and that she was an ecstatic: her agony for the world's sin is hidden under the beautiful cloak of her love for sinners.

Of Our Lady such things are not recorded. We complain that so little is recorded of her personality, so few of her words, so few deeds, that we can form no picture of her, and there is nothing that we can lay hold of to imitate.

But it is Our Lady—and no other saint—whom we *can* really imitate.

All the canonized saints had special vocations, and special gifts for their fulfillment: presumption for me to think of imitating St. Catherine or St. Paul or St. Joan if I have not their unique character and intellect—which indeed I have not.

Each saint has his special work: one person's work. But our Lady had to include in her vocation, in her life's work, the essential thing that was to be hidden in every other vocation, in every life.

She is not only human; she is humanity.

The one thing that she did and does is the one thing that we all have to do, namely, to bear Christ into the world.

Christ must be born from every soul, formed in every life. If we had a picture of Our Lady's personality, we might be dazzled into thinking that only one sort of person could form Christ in himself, and we should miss the meaning of our own being.

Nothing but things essential *for us* are revealed to us about the Mother of God: the fact that she was wed to the Holy Spirit and bore Christ into the world.

Our crowning joy is that she did this as a lay person and through the ordinary daily life that we all live; through natural love made supernatural, as the water at Cana was, at her request, turned into wine.

In the world as it is, torn with agonies and dissensions, we need some direction for our souls which is never away from us; which, without enslaving us or narrowing our vision, enters into every detail of our life. Everyone longs for some such inward rule, a universal rule as big as the immeasurable law of love, yet as little as the narrowness of our daily routine. It must be so truly part of us all that it makes us all one, and yet to each one the secret of his own life with God.

To this need, the imitation of Our Lady is the answer; in contemplating her we find intimacy with God, the law which is the lovely yoke of the one irresistible love.

ADRIENNE VON SPEYR

MARY AND THE ANGEL*

Mary's meeting with the angel is like the summation of her entire preceding life of contemplation. It is the first thing we learn about her. We do not know who she is, we do not know her past. But when we learn that she saw the angel, the whole composition of her soul becomes visible. The angel which appears is the fulfillment of her prayer, not in the sense that she had prayed for the appearance or prepared herself for it, but rather in the sense that she has held herself in readiness for a mission still unknown to her. She has lived in an attitude of prayer, and in virtue of this life she is capable in the crucial moment of seeing and obeying the angel who comes to her. Both vision and obedience flow from the same source in her; from the openness toward the mission which God may give her, when and in whatever way he likes. Her obedience is the prototype of every future instance of Christian obedience, which draws its whole meaning from the life of prayer and the perception of God's will. For Mary, however, God's will in its certainty has not yet become apparent. She is still waiting for the declaration of this will. She is ready in prayer to accept it even when she does not know what she will be accepting. She knows perfect indifference; and whoever among the generations of future Christians knows about the meaning and the extent of indifference will owe this knowledge most of all to the Mother.

---

*From *Handmaid of the Lord*, trans. E. A. Nelson (San Francisco: Ignatius Press, 1985), pp. 27–29 and 41–43. Copyright 1985 Ignatius Press, San Francisco. All rights reserved. Reprinted by permission of Ignatius Press. The *Handmaid of the Lord* was first published in 1948 under the title *Magd des Herrn*.

The angel comes to her. She sees him with her own eyes, in the form proper to him both in his essence and as an apparition. But her gaze does not stop at the angel; she sees, in him and behind him, the whole of heaven, straight up to God. For her the angel is no indistinct supernatural phenomenon but an exact, precise figure which is at the same time the clear and definite revelation of God himself. In being ready to obey the word of the angel, she knows with certainty that she is obeying God's voice. There is no hesitation in her, no interruption; she does not need to reassure herself, to ask anyone, to await any human judgment. The angel's appearance is unconditional for her; it is the clear answer to her faith. All her prayer until now has been aimed at this, although a moment before she had no idea what would befall her. The appearance of the angel is the determinate answer to her entire, still indeterminate readiness, and it commits her at once to this same determination which has become manifest to her as the will of God.

Therefore the angel, without introducing himself, can begin at once with his salutation: "Hail, full of grace." In his first greeting he immediately gives her the title which is her due, because he has no doubt that she will accept everything. Without having spoken it, she has already said Yes through her entire attitude, through her constant waiting for the way God had reserved for her. And so the angel goes further and says, "The Lord is with thee." She has not yet conceived the Lord and yet he is already with her, for he has chosen her as his mother with the same certainty that the angel now demonstrates. The Lord also knew that she would accept everything even this, to have him as her Son. The whole salutation is not so much the preparation of a new, yet-to-be-created situation as the expression of one which has already long existed and which, through the words, is simply more clearly defined. The angel shows Mary her situation; he does not create it. Through the greeting she achieves possession of self-knowledge; but she herself seems in this to be standing already in the service of heaven. The salutation sounds like a retrospect of her entire attitude until now, and we are not told when her mission had begun. The greeting promises a coming event; she is going to conceive the Son, she does not yet have him physically in her. But her mission she possesses already; it is much older than the conception. And so the promise of the Lord who is to come is the verification of the Lord who is already there in the mission which she received at the beginning. That the Lord is with her is so much a part of her being that it simply cannot be thought of otherwise; since her coming into being in God's eternal thought, she has not been thought of otherwise than in the Lord's company, in communion with the Lord. She herself did not know that the Lord was so much in her; but *he* knew that he was her eternal companion. Between her life and the Lord's eternal life there exists no gap; she could not live this life without being, even during temporal existence, wholly within eternal life.

THE VISITATION

"In those days Mary arose and went with haste into the mountains to a city of Judah, and she entered the house of Zechariah and greeted Elizabeth." The Mother must take this course, for she must adhere to the community to which the angel indicated the way, the basis of which lies not only in the two women and in the manner of their conception but equally in the mission of their children. Mary arises in haste because she stands, with respect to God, in a relationship of vowed obedience. The angel in his words had left much merely implied, offered only parenthetically; it is for her sense of obedience, given to her by God when she made her vow, to bring these implications to realization and to let the slightest hint be her command.

At the greeting from the Lord's Mother, the child stirs in Elizabeth's body, and this movement is the occasion which draws Elizabeth's attention to the New Thing which has occurred. Through the stirring of her child she is filled with the Holy

Spirit, and the prophetic spirit enters her; she begins to know the supernatural and other-worldly event which has happened in Mary. And thus she greets her with a wholly new and strange form of address. No time passes between the movement of the child, the filling with the Holy Spirit, and the greeting. Elizabeth finds the right form of address, but the words she speaks receive their truth for her in the very movement in which they are spoken: she has the same experience as prophets and Christians who speak in the Spirit and suddenly say things which they themselves had never guessed and which affect the listeners just as abruptly and unexpectedly, and all the more deeply for it. In the speaker as well as the receiver, it is the sudden intervention of the Holy Spirit.

This effect of the Spirit which fills Elizabeth is like an aftereffect of the angel's visit to Mary. At his appearance he had explained to her with words what was going to occur; at the Mother's appearance, Elizabeth, through the Spirit, grasps the whole matter at once without words. For Mary brings the fragrance of the angel with her, and her entire undiminished surrender as well. She appears like someone who has been disturbed at prayer, someone who, by looking up, clearly shows that another is suddenly taking up in his world the space which only a second before was filled by the angels praying with him.

So Elizabeth cries out in a loud voice, the voice of the Spirit in her: "Blessed art thou among women, and blessed is the fruit of thy womb." Both Mother and Child are blessed and given benediction; Elizabeth does not distinguish at all between the Mother's blessing and the Son's. She grasps that the two form a unity and that this unity is the result of a very special grace which in this moment envelops both of them and is spread over them both without distinction. It is divine grace; for she understands that Mary's Son is God; she knows it through the Holy Spirit who begot the Child in the Mother. But since the occasion of this knowledge in Elizabeth was the stirring of her own son, she grasps at the same time that between herself and her child and between her mission and the mission of her child, a unity likewise exists; she further grasps that these two unities are themselves related. All these relationships together form one great unity; all four missions participate in something unique which stems from the one Spirit of God.

One mother was barren, the other was virginal. In the first God worked a miracle by changing something in her body before she conceived in a natural way. He changed nothing in the virginity of Mary but gave her the seed from above. But this he does not do until after the first miracle was already worked. The fruit of the barren one, who is to give birth first, is John, the forerunner of the Lord. He also comes into being by the election of God, who chose a barren woman as mother for him and in doing so has already entered the path at the end of which he will make the Virgin a mother. Thus John becomes the forerunner of the Lord; his very coming into existence calls attention to him. The fruitfulness of the barren one is an outward sign which will attract the gaze of men more strongly than the fruitfulness of the Virgin; just as John in the desert will be a sign, visible at a distance, pointing to the Lord who passes as an inconspicuous youth. . . .

PAUL VI

THE BLESSED VIRGIN AS THE MODEL
OF THE CHURCH IN DIVINE WORSHIP*

In accordance with some of the guidelines of the Council's teaching on Mary and the Church, we now wish to examine more closely a particular aspect of the relationship between Mary and the liturgy, namely, Mary as a model of the spiritual attitude with which the Church celebrates and lives the divine mysteries. That the Blessed Virgin is an exemplar in this field derives from the fact that she is recognized as a most excellent exemplar of the Church in the order of faith, charity and perfect union with Christ,[1] that is, of that interior disposition with which the Church, the beloved spouse, closely associated with her Lord, invokes Christ and through him worships the eternal Father.[2]

Mary is *the attentive Virgin*, who receives the word of God with faith, that faith which in her case was the gateway and path to divine Motherhood, for, as Saint Augustine realized, "Blessed Mary by believing conceived him (Jesus) whom believing she brought forth."[3] In fact, when she received from the angel the answer to her doubt (cf. Lk 1:34–37), "full of faith, and conceiving Christ in her mind before conceiving him in her womb, she said, 'I am the handmaid of the Lord, let what you have said be done to me' (Lk 1:38)."[4] It was faith that was for her the cause of blessedness and certainty in the fulfillment of the promise: "Blessed is she who believed that the promise made her by the Lord would be fulfilled" (Lk 1:45). Similarly, it was faith with which she, who

---

* From the encyclical letter "Marialis Cultus" (1974), paragraphs 16–23 and 28. The English translation is from the Vatican, and the edition used was published by the United States Catholic Conference (Washington, D.C.: 1974), pp. 12–16 and 20. Text not copyrighted.

played a part in the Incarnation and was a unique witness to it, thinking back on the events of the infancy of Christ, meditated upon these events in her heart (cf. Lk 2:19, 51). The Church also acts in this way, especially in the liturgy, when with faith she listens, accepts, proclaims and venerates the word of God, distributes it to the faithful as the bread of life[5] and in the light of that word examines the signs of the times and interprets and lives the events of history.

Mary is also the Virgin in prayer. She appears as such in the visit to the Mother of the Precursor, when she pours out her soul in expressions glorifying God, and expressions of humility, faith and hope. This prayer is the Magnificat (cf. Lk 1:46–55), Mary's prayer par excellence, the song of the messianic times in which there mingles the joy of the ancient and the new Israel. As Saint Irenaeus seems to suggest, it is in Mary's canticle that there was heard once more the rejoicing of Abraham who foresaw the Messiah (cf. Jn 8:56)[6] and there rang out in prophetic anticipation the voice of the Church: "In her exultation Mary prophetically declared in the name of the Church: 'My soul proclaims the glory of the Lord. . . .'"[7] And in fact Mary's hymn has spread far and wide and has become the prayer of the whole Church in all ages.

At Cana, Mary appears once more as the Virgin in prayer: when she tactfully told her Son of a temporal need, she also obtained an effect of grace, namely, that Jesus, in working the first of his "signs," confirmed his disciples' faith in him (cf. Jn 2:1–12).

Likewise, the last description of Mary's life presents her as praying. The Apostles "joined in continuous prayer, together with several women, including Mary the Mother of Jesus, and with his brothers" (Acts 1:14). We have here the prayerful presence of Mary in the early Church and in the Church throughout all ages, for, having been assumed into heaven, she has not abandoned her mission of intercession and salvation.[8] The title Virgin in prayer also fits the Church, which day by day presents to the Father the needs of her children, "praises the Lord unceasingly and intercedes for the salvation of the world."[9]

Mary is also *the Virgin-Mother*—she who "believing and obeying . . . brought forth on earth the Father's Son. This she did, not knowing man but overshadowed by the Holy Spirit."[10] This was a miraculous Motherhood, set up by God as the type and exemplar of the fruitfulness of the Virgin-Church, which "becomes herself a mother . . . for by her preaching and by baptism she brings forth to a new and immortal life children who are conceived by the power of the Holy Spirit and born of God."[11] The ancient Fathers rightly taught that the Church prolongs in the sacrament of Baptism the virginal Motherhood of Mary. Among such references we like to recall that of our illustrious predecessor, Saint Leo the Great, who in a Christmas homily says: "The origin which (Christ) took in the womb of the Virgin he has given to the baptismal font: he has given to water what he had given to his Mother; the power of the Most High and the overshadowing of the Holy Spirit (cf. Luke 1:35), which was responsible for Mary's bringing forth the Saviour, has the same effect, so that water may regenerate the believer."[12] If we wished to go to liturgical sources, we could quote the beautiful *illatio* of the Mozarabic liturgy: "The former (Mary) carried Life in her womb; the latter (the Church) bears Life in the waters of baptism. In Mary's members Christ was formed; in the waters of the Church Christ is put on."[13]

Mary is, finally, the Virgin presenting offerings. In the episode of the Presentation of Jesus in the Temple (cf. Lk 2:22–35), the Church, guided by the Spirit, has detected, over and above the fulfillment of the laws regarding the offering of the firstborn (cf. Ex 13:11–16) and the purification of the Mother (cf. Lv 12: 6–8), a mystery of salvation related to the history of salvation. That is, she has noted the continuity of the fundamental offering that the Incarnate Word made to the Father when he entered the world (cf. Heb 15:5–7). The Church has seen the universal nature of salvation proclaimed, for Simeon, greeting in the Child the light to enlighten the peoples and the glory of the people Israel (cf. Lk 2:32), recognized in him the Messiah, the Saviour of all. The Church has understood the prophetic reference to the Passion of Christ: the fact that Simeon's words, which linked in one prophecy the Son as "the sign of contradiction" (Lk 2:34) and the Mother, whose soul would be pierced by a sword (cf. Lk 2:35), came true on Calvary. A mystery of salvation, therefore, that in its various aspects orients the episode of the Presentation in the Temple to the salvific event of the Cross. But the Church herself, in particular from the Middle Ages onwards, has detected in the heart of the Virgin taking her Son to Jerusalem to present him to the Lord (cf. Lk 2:22) a desire to make an offering, a desire that exceeds the ordinary meaning of the rite. A witness to this intuition is found in the loving prayer of Saint Bernard: "Offer your Son, holy Virgin, and present to the Lord the blessed fruit of your womb. Offer for the reconciliation of us all the holy Victim which is pleasing to God."[14]

This union of the Mother and the Son in the work of redemption[15] reaches its climax on Calvary, where Christ "offered himself as the perfect sacrifice to God" (Heb 9:14) and where Mary stood by the Cross (cf. Jn 19:25), "suffering grievously with her only-begotten Son. There she united herself with a maternal heart to his sacrifice, and lovingly consented to the immolation of this victim which she herself had brought forth"[16] and also was offering to the Eternal Father.[17] To perpetuate down the centuries the Sacrifice of the Cross, the divine Saviour instituted the Eucharistic Sacrifice, the memorial of his death and Resurrection, and entrusted it to his Spouse the Church,[18] which, especially on Sundays, calls the faithful together to celebrate the Passover of the Lord until he comes again.[19] This the Church does in union with the saints in heaven and in particular with the Blessed Virgin,[20] whose burning charity and unshakeable faith she imitates.

Mary is not only an example for the whole Church in the exercise of divine worship but is also, clearly, a teacher of the spiritual life for individual Christians. The faithful at a very early date began to look to Mary and to imitate her in making their lives an act of worship of God and making their worship a commitment of their lives. As early as the fourth century, Saint Ambrose, speaking to the people, expressed the hope that each of them would have the spirit of Mary in order to glorify God: "May the heart of Mary be in each Christian to proclaim the greatness of the Lord; may her spirit be in everyone to exult in God."[21] But Mary is above all the example of that worship that consists in making one's life an offering to God. This is an ancient and ever new doctrine that each individual can hear again by heeding the Church's teaching, but also by heeding

the very voice of the Virgin as she, anticipating in herself the
wonderful petition of the Lord's Prayer—"Your will be done"
(Mt 6:10)—replied to God's messenger: "I am the handmaid of
the Lord. Let what you have said be done to me" (Lk 1:38).
And Mary's "yes" is for all Christians a lesson and example of
obedience to the will of the Father, which is the way and means
of one's own sanctification.

It is also important to note how the Church expresses in
various effective attitudes of devotion the many relationships that
bind her to Mary: in profound veneration, when she reflects on
the singular dignity of the Virgin who, through the action of
the Holy Spirit, has become Mother of the Incarnate Word; in
burning love, when she considers the spiritual Motherhood of
Mary towards all members of the Mystical Body; in trusting invocation, when she experiences the intercession of her Advocate
and Helper;[22] in loving service, when she sees in the humble
Handmaid of the Lord the Queen of mercy and the Mother of
grace; in zealous imitation, when she contemplates the holiness
and virtues of her who is "full of grace" (Lk 1:28); in profound
wonder, when she sees in her, "as in a faultless model, that
which she herself wholly desires and hopes to be";[23] in attentive
study, when she recognizes in the Associate of the Redeemer,
who already shares fully in the fruits of the Paschal Mystery, the
prophetic fulfillment of her own future, until the day on which,
when she has been purified of every spot and wrinkle (cf. Eph
5:27), she will become like a bride arrayed for the bridegroom,
Jesus Christ (cf. Rv 21:2).

Therefore, venerable Brothers, as we consider the piety that
the liturgical tradition of the universal Church and the renewed
Roman Rite expresses towards the holy Mother of God, and as
we remember that the liturgy through its preeminent value as
worship constitutes the golden norm for Christian piety, and
finally as we observe how the Church when she celebrates the
sacred mysteries assumes an attitude of faith and love similar to
that of the Virgin, we realize the rightness of the exhortation that
the Second Vatican Council addresses to all the children of the
Church, namely "that the cult, especially the liturgical cult, of the
Blessed Virgin be generously fostered."[24] This is an exhortation

that we would like to see accepted everywhere without reservation and put into zealous practice. . . .

It is also necessary that exercises of piety with which the faithful honor the Mother of the Lord should clearly show the place she occupies in the Church: "the highest place and the closest to us after Christ."[25] The liturgical buildings of Byzantine rite, both in the architectural structure itself and in the use of images, show clearly Mary's place in the Church. On the central door of the iconostasis there is a representation of the Annunciation and in the apse an image of the glorious Theotokos. In this way one perceives how through the assent of the humble Handmaid of the Lord mankind begins its return to God and sees in the glory of the all-holy Virgin the goal towards which it is journeying. The symbolism by which a church building demonstrates Mary's place in the mystery of the Church is full of significance and gives grounds for hoping that the different forms of devotion to the Blessed Virgin may everywhere be open to ecclesial perspectives.

The faithful will be able to appreciate more easily Mary's mission in the mystery of the Church and her preeminent place in the Communion of Saints if attention is drawn to the Second Vatican Council's references to the fundamental concepts of the nature of the Church as the Family of God, the People of God, the Kingdom of God and the Mystical Body of Christ.[26] This will also bring the faithful to a deeper realization of the brotherhood which united all of them as sons and daughters of the Virgin Mary, "who with a mother's love has cooperated in their rebirth and spiritual formation,"[27] and as sons and daughters of the Church, since "we are born from the Church's womb, we are nurtured by the Church's milk, we are given life by the Church's Spirit."[28] They will also realize that both the Church and Mary collaborate to give birth to the Mystical Body of Christ since "both of them are the Mother of Christ, but neither brings forth the whole (body) independently of the other."[29] Similarly the faithful will appreciate more clearly that the action of the Church in the world can be likened to an extension of Mary's concern. The active love she showed at Nazareth, in the house of Elizabeth, at Cana and on Golgotha—all salvific episodes having vast ecclesial importance—finds its extension in the Church's maternal concern that all men should come to knowledge of the truth (cf. 1 Tm 2:4), in the Church's concern for people in lowly circumstances and for the poor and weak, and in her constant commitment to peace and social harmony, as well as in her untiring efforts to ensure that all men will share in the salvation which was merited for them by Christ's death. Thus love for the Church will become love for Mary, and vice versa, since the one cannot exist without the other, as Saint Chromatius of Aquileia observed with keen discernment: "The Church was united . . . in the Upper Room with Mary the Mother of Jesus and with his brethren. The Church therefore cannot be referred to as such unless it includes Mary the Mother of our Lord, together with his brethren."[30] In conclusion, therefore, we repeat that devotion to the Blessed Virgin must explicitly show its intrinsic and ecclesiological content; thus it will be enabled to revise its forms and texts in a fitting way.

NOTES

1. Cf. II Vatican Council, Dogmatic Constitution on the Church, "Lumen Gentium," 63: AAS 57 (1965), p. 64.

2. Cf. II Vatican Council, Constitution on the Sacred Liturgy, "Sacrosanctum Concilium," 7: AAS 56 (1964), pp. 100–01.

3. Sermo 215, 4: PL 38, 1074.

4. Ibid.

5. Cf. II Vatican Council, Dogmatic Constitution on Divine Revelation, "Dei Verbum," 21: AAS 58 (1966), pp. 827–28.

6. Cf. *Adversus Haereses* IV, 7, 1, 990–91; S. Ch. 100, t. II, pp. 454–58.

7. Cf. *Adversus Haereses* III, 10, 2: PG 7, 1, 873; S. Ch. 34, p. 164.

8. Cf. II Vatican Council, Dogmatic Constitution on the Church, "Lumen Gentium," 62: AAS 57 (1965), p. 63.

9. Cf. II Vatican Council, Constitution on the Sacred Liturgy, "Sacrosanctum Concilium," 83: AAS 56 (1964), p. 121.

10. II Vatican Council, Dogmatic Constitution on the Church, "Lumen Gentium," 63: AAS 57 (1965), p. 64.

11. Ibid., 64: AAS 57 (1965), p. 64.

12. Tractatus XXV (In Nativitate Domini), 5: CCL 138, p. 123; S. Ch. 22 bis, p. 132; cf. also Tractatus XXIX (In Nativitate Domini), 1:

CCL ibid., p. 147; S. Ch. ibid., p. 178; Tractatus LXIII (De Passione Domini), 6: CCL ibid., p. 386; S. Ch. 74, p. 82.

13. M. Ferotin, Le "Liber Mozarabicus Sacramentorum," col. 56.

14. "In Purificatione B. Mariae," Sermo III, 2: PL 183, 370; *Sancti Bernardi Opera*, ed. J. Leclercq & H. Rochais, vol. IV (Rome: 1966), p. 342.

15. Cf. II Vatican Council, Dogmatic Constitution on the Church, "Lumen Gentium," 57: AAS 57 (1965), p. 61.

16. Ibid., 58: AAS 57 (1965), p. 61.

17. Cf. Pius XII, Encyclical Letter "Mystici Corporis": AAS 35 (1943), p. 247.

18. Cf. II Vatican Council, Constitution on the Sacred Liturgy, "Sacrosanctum Concilium," 47:AAS 56 (1964), p. 113.

19. Ibid., 102, 106: AAS 56 (1964), pp. 125–26.

20. ". . . deign to remember all who have been pleasing to you throughout the ages, the holy Fathers, the Patriarchs, Prophets, Apostles. . . and the holy and glorious Mother of God and all the saints. . . . may they remember our misery and poverty, and together with us may they offer you this great and unbloody sacrifice": *Anaphora Iacobi fratris domini syriaca: Prex Eucharistica*, ed. A. Hanggi & I. Pahl (Fribourg: Editions Universitaires, 1968), p. 274.

21. *Expositio Evangelii secundum Lucam*, II 26: CSEL 32, IV, p. 55; S. Ch. 45, pp. 83–84.

22. Cf. II Vatican Council, Dogmatic Constitution on the Church, "Lumen Gentium," 62: AAS 57 (1965), p. 63.

23. II Vatican Council, Constitution on the Sacred Liturgy, "Sacrosanctum Concilium," 103: AAS 56 (1964), p. 125.

24. II Vatican Council, Dogmatic Constitution on the Church, "Lumen Gentium," 67: AAS 57 (1965), pp. 65–66.

25. II Vatican Council, Dogmatic Constitution on the Church, "Lumen Gentium," 54: AAS 57 (1965), p. 59. Cf. Paulus VI, "Allocutio ad Patres Conciliares habita, altera exacta Concilii Oecumenici Vaticani Secundi Sessione," 4 December 1963: AAS 56 (1964), p. 37.

26. Cf. II Vatican Council, Dogmatic Constitution on the Church, "Lumen Gentium," 6, 7–8, 9–11: AAS 57 (1965), pp. 8–9, 9–12, 12–21.

27. Ibid., 63: AAS 57 (1965), p. 64.

28. St. Cyprian, "De Catholicae Ecclesiae unitate," 5: CSEL 3, p. 214.

29. Isaac de Stella, Sermo LI, "In Assumptione B. Mariae": PL 194, 1863.

30. Sermo XXX, I: S. Ch. 164, p. 134.

AGNES CUNNINGHAM

THE MESSAGE*

In order to understand the meaning of the Church's teaching in calling Our Lady "*Theotokos*," it is necessary to have some idea of the art style in which this image of Mary is presented. We have to try to understand what the icon is meant to be, if we want to hear the Word Mary brings to us; if we would see the Image Mary shows us.

The word, icon, comes from a Greek word (EIKON) which means *image*. The Jews of the Old Testament were forbidden, by law, to produce images, in order to preserve the purity of their worship of an invisible god, Yahweh. This prohibition was also a preparation for their acceptance of God's revelation in Christ, the Icon (Image) of God par excellence. Indeed, as the Fathers of the Church tell us, when God created man (*HOMO*) in the beginning, it was "in the image" of God, that is, *in* the Word of God and *according to* the Image of God.

In A.D. 843, the Council of Constantinople definitively reaffirmed the veneration of icons, following the iconoclast crisis and the destruction of sacred images by those who rejected all representations of God, Christ, Mary and the saints. What the iconoclasts failed to grasp was the theological and spiritual reality which constituted the heart and the essence of the icon.

The elements of an icon are simple. They include the *sacred* (sacred time, sacred space) and the *beautiful*. Both of these elements exact from the iconographer the discipline of mind and

* From *The Significance of Mary* (Chicago: Thomas More Press, 1988), pp. 35–39. Copyright The Thomas More Association. Reprinted by permission of The Thomas More Association, Chicago, Illinois.

spirit which leads to contemplation and the discipline of hand
and eye which leads to the mastery of a difficult technique.

From the earliest ages of Christianity, the followers of Jesus
knew how to engage in *visual* as well as in *verbal* theology. We
in the West are more familiar with a theology that came to
us in words. Words were spoken in catechetical instruction, in
sacramental preparation or in liturgical celebration. Words were
proclaimed in discourse, polemic or apologetic. Words were pastoral: in homilies and sermons; they were enlightening: through
exegesis and reflection. The documents that come to us in the
Scriptures and from the centuries of the patristic age (c. A. D. 95–
608 [West]/A.D. 759 [East]) bear witness to the rich development
and significant contribution of a theology that was written to be
read and spoken to be heard.

The visual transmission of the Good News of Jesus Christ
also emerged early in the Christian experience. The walls of
the rock-cave churches of Cappodocia, for example, are adorned
with every story of the Old and New Testaments necessary for
Christian instruction and adornments in catacombs, on sarcoph-
agi, wherever Christians assembled. Christians were instructed,
whether they were literate or illiterate. The tradition of Christian art was established. Iconography developed through three
periods or ages, each one of which was marked by specific characteristics in the evolution of a "visual theology." The golden age
of iconography occurred in the fourteenth century.

The person who aspires to be an iconographer must be
willing to submit to the intense spiritual discipline that initiates
one to the art of contemplation. The icon is a symbol of a mystery
that is present, represented in and entered into through the
icon. The icon is meant to touch the mind, the heart and the
imagination with its message. It communicates an Epiphany—a
manifestation—of a presence that is transcendent. The iconographer must be able to contemplate the reality of the mystery he or
she plans to represent. The iconographer must let the mystery
inspire whatever representation will best transmit the meaning
and message of the transcendent.

The second discipline to which the iconographer must submit is the discipline of the art. Icons are painted on wood,

frequently, the wood of the cypress tree. A slightly depressed area is prepared, so that a natural frame is formed around the main area. A coat of adherent is spread so that canvas, covered by a layer of alabaster powder, can be fixed in place. As much as possible, the colors used by the artist must be taken from natural powders mixed with the yolk of an egg. When the painting is finished, a protective coat of the best linseed oil, mixed with various resins, is added. This furnishes a resistant, impenetrable finish which protects and preserves the original splendor of the colors.

Iconographic rules regarding the use of material, colors, lines or adornment are strictly indicated. The art of iconography is jealously guarded, passed on from a master to his disciples. Surprising as it may seem, no two icons—even those of the same subject, even in the same "school"—are ever identical. The discipline of the art is transformed by the discipline of contemplation. The result is a masterpiece that is solemnly blessed to become the focus-point for entrance into prayer and for personal contact with a heavenly presence and mystery.

Why this lengthy description of what seems to be a technical procedure: the painting of an icon? Quite simply, the painting of an icon is, actually, a spiritual experience both for the iconographer and for one who gazes on the finished products as well as a process which reflects an ever-deepening knowledge and veneration of the presence and the mystery into which we enter through prayerful reflection on the icon. In the case of the *Theotokos*, this is strikingly true.

St. John Damascene has said that the entire mystery of the economy of salvation is contained in the one word, *Theotokos*. We need time, as an iconographer does, to grasp the many dimensions of beauty revealed in the image of the God-bearing Mother. She is the new Eve, the figure of the new creation, yet she is one of us. In the words of the poet, Gerard Manley Hopkins, the icon of the *Theotokos*, like the Mother of God herself, has only one thing to do: "To let God's glory through." The luminous quality of the true icon is one of its most symbolic characteristics.

The icon of the *Theotokos* affirms the Church's ancient, never-changing belief that Mary is truly Mother of God. She is Mother of Jesus Christ, true God and true Man. She is Mother of the Child to whom she gave birth and Mother of the Body of Christ, the Church. The three stars on her forehead and shoulders proclaim her virginity before, during and after the birth of her child. The colors she wears declare that she is human with us, but exalted and royal, a true queen. The child is clothed in garments and colors that proclaim divinity and humanity. So too does the gesture of his right hand, with two fingers raised to signify the two natures that are his and the other three joined to affirm the Trinity of persons in God. The book he carries is the book of the Scriptures. In later representations of the *Theotokos*, the artist has shown us what the child sees: the instruments of the Passion, held by ministering angels with veiled hands. . . .

FINAL WORDS

THE PRAYER OF THE GOSPEL:
THE MADONNA

It is a truism that to love someone one must first know them. We say to know someone is to love them. To understand everything is to forgive everything. Love comes out of knowledge. Christian living comes out of knowing the stories of Christianity. Martha's service and practical devotion needs to emerge from her sister Mary's knowledge and love of the word of God embodied in Jesus. In particular the Christian needs to know the story of the passion and resurrection of Jesus Christ. The stories of those men and women connected with his life are also helpful. Each Christian must come to cry the Gospel with their life story in imitation of Jesus. Mary is the oldest memory of the first church.[1] Her story is also our story. In essence her life is told in the first part of the Ave Maria.

Through the centuries religious people have been story-tellers. During the Passover meal the Jews to this day relate the story of the Exodus and the passing over from the slavery of Egypt to the freedom of God's people. The refrain in that sacred meal relates their perennial hope: "Next year in Jerusalem!" It reminds the believer that it is as important to know where one is going as from where one has come. Stories have endings as well as beginnings. Christians re-present the last supper of Jesus Christ before his passover from death to life in his passion and resurrection. They keep alive the paschal mystery by telling the story and then by living out its implications. They await in hope the messianic banquet in the kingdom of God at the endtime.

187

Next year in the heavenly Jerusalem! In the eucharist the faithful declare: "When we eat his body and drink his blood we proclaim his death until he comes."

In the Apostles' Creed we proclaim our faith in Jesus Christ who "descended into hell." He went down to the household of the dead. He remembered them. In solidarity with them all, he came to the abode of darkness. To the good thief crucified with him he said: "Today you will be with me in Paradise" (Lk 23:43). In the communion of saints we cherish the being and eternal value of every human being. None is to be forgotten before the face of God. Their story will live on in God's mind. It may be retold by the Church in its stories of the saints. The lives of the saints give flesh and blood memory to the communion of saints. The martyrology is a sacred record of the heroic lives and deaths of the Christian faithful.

One can understand why the survivors of the Jewish Holocaust must labor while there is yet time to compile a record. No name must be omitted; no moment of anguish must be allowed to be obliterated. We must remember the dead and so give them new life. In *The Gulag Archipelago* Alexander Solzhenitsyn retrieved every scrap of memory of those awful years like precious crumbs of a sacred loaf of bread. No fragment must be lost. These stories of human anguish are too holy to be left unsung. The dead must live in our memory, and we in God's. The criminal must be brought to justice; the victim must be brought to honor, with his or her story retold.

When we die we hope that God will remember our story. We will lose in death all that depends upon this mortal flesh. When we enter into resurrection, we hope that God will re-member our life in whatever deserves to perdure. We count on remaining in the mind of God who sustains us even now. If we break bread in the eucharist "in memory of" the Lord Jesus, we also hope our particular story and our very bones will be remembered by God and placed in the book of life to be ever told just as the sweet anointing of the feet of Jesus by the unknown woman in the Gospel (Lk 7:37–50) is ever told "in memory of her." Retelling the history of Mary joins her life story to the sweep of narrative theology that makes up the four Gospels.

All saints from the first to last pray in an incarnational solidarity with the mother of Jesus. If Mary is not a believer and among the saved, she who carried the Word made flesh in her body, she who lived in Nazareth for thirty years with her unique son whose father-God was Abba, then who can hope to approach the incarnate Lord? Of course Mary's union must finally be a spiritual one, that of the disciple and friend, and not just the mother and caregiver. Beginning as infant and mother, Jesus and Mary ended as companions in faith. We might imagine them somewhat as Augustine and Monica, who after twenty years of growth in faith in God, spoke to each other lovingly of highest heaven in their last days together in Ostia Antiqua. Of Mary as portrayed in the Gospels, one commentator concludes: "The overall impression left by the material in the Gospels about Mary is that no Evangelist made a concerted effort to give Mary more significance than she actually had in the ministry of Jesus; that no Evangelist attempted to paint a purely idealized portrait of her; and that no Evangelist attempted to portray a strictly Christian (i.e., non-Jewish) picture of Jesus' mother."[2] Mary is the Church ever coming to know the Lord.

At the same time, Mary is held to be the paradigm of the Christian. She is the woman of faith. She is the first Christian catechumen who heard the word of God announced in her heart. She is the first disciple who brings Christ to her family in the visitation. At Cana she is the first Christian to intercede in prayer. On Calvary hill she is the first witness of a Christian death. She is the first churchwoman to receive the Holy Spirit at its descent on Pentecost day. Mary is the only person to know Jesus from the moment of the birth of his body in Bethlehem to the birth of his body the Church in the mystery of the Holy Spirit at Pentecost. The mother of Jesus thus becomes the premiere Christian, the woman of a faith that grows from her Jewish origin to her Christian centrality. She becomes the quintessential Christian, the mother of faith in Jesus just as Abraham was considered the father of faith in Yahweh.

Jesus on the cross dies as the representative of oppressed humanity, victim of countless injustices. In the Gospels one can see a convergence of the story of Jesus and the story of Mary. The

Ecce Homo yields the *Pieta.* The resurrection of Jesus leads to the assumption of Mary. In life they were associated, would they not be together in death? One imagines an intimacy between Jesus and Mary that is profound, and one that began while Jesus was still unborn. The bonding between child and its mother stems from her loving welcome of the new life within her. One imagines that Jesus had facial features that reminded others of his mother; perhaps he had her eyes. One imagines that had the Son of God become human as a woman, the living God would have looked like Mary. Fra Angelico's simple overall-white painting of the coronation of Mary captures something of the mystical communion between Jesus and Mary. The virgin mother is portrayed so humbly, with head bowed, and with no adornment. No one else is present at the coronation. There is no triumph and no trumpet. They are alone and silent, in the hidden presence of the Spirit, before the unseen throne of God. Low Mariology and high Mariology seem reconciled in this fresco of Mary in pure and simple glory. She is the Many taken up into the One. She is the human condition transfigured into union with the divine. She is glorified with her son Jesus and crowned by his own hand.

To Mary we pray thus. The Lord is with you in the beginning, be with us in the ending. Pray for us who are in the same communion of saints, the same mystical body, who share the same cosmos of grace. Walk with us as we walk with you. Be with us, Mary, as we are with you. Be mindful of us as we remain of you. From the first hour of the Lord Jesus to the last hour of the last disciple, be with all the saints. As the Lord was with you first and in the beginning, may Our Lord be with us all in the ending at the hour of our death. The madonna enfolds the pieta; the incarnation of Jesus implicates the final coming in glory of the Son of Man who is Son of God.

THE PRAYER OF THE CHURCH:
THE PIETA

In the human condition the flesh is born and the body dies. On Calvary hill Jesus dying must leave his mother from whom he received his body in order to go to the Father from whom he holds his life. He is stripped of his earthly clothes; he lays down his body on the cross. We are our body; we are human; we are mortal. We are dust and from dust we came. God is the potter and we are the clay. No advice is more poignant: *memento mori*. Remember, you are to die. The second part of the Ave Maria reminds us of our need of prayer particularly when we are alone "at the hour of our death." We do not save ourselves nor give ourselves eternal life. This is the human condition. Our hearts are restless, and they will not rest until they rest in God.[3]

Who cares about each one of us? This is the human predicament. Who will cherish my flesh? If a human being remains vulnerable, who will answer the body's fierce claim to live? Who will care about me? To whom do this tender flesh and fragile bones matter? Human bodies are readily abused, ravaged by disease, and inevitably grow old. The flesh can be undone by famine, tortured by design, crushed by accident, burned by fire, and enfeebled by the implacable passage of time. Children are abused in body and in soul. The eyes grow blind, the ears deaf, the memory and mind may be lost. Cancer of the body and drug addiction of the soul consume in agony. Many human beings are heartbroken, alone, and desolate in their despair. Unbelief erodes all hopes. Earthquake from below and nuclear holocaust from above enkindle anxiety. The sinner is inwardly devastated and the victim is outwardly ravished. The human body and soul are naked before the "thousand slings that mortal flesh is heir to." Simone Weil's essay, "A Poem of Force," speaks insightfully

191

of the awful inevitability of necessity, which is dramatized in the Trojan War of Homer's *Iliad*.[4] From the dawn of our history human violence could be recognized as a vicious circle of wounds and bitterness that no one could halt because the equanimity to sue for peace was always being destroyed by the violence being inflicted that enraged the heart and maddened the mind. The folly of war is self-perpetuating like a forest fire that feeds on the on-going combustion caused by its own heat. Human misery is a chain reaction that no one can stop. The flesh always suffers. The human being is familiar with grief everywhere. Who then will cherish my flesh? Who will be my life-giver, my healing and loving touch? Who will raise me up again when I am cold and dead? Who will gather up this bare bones flesh?

We come naked into the world, and we leave naked. Our life is a challenge to strip away the masks we wear, to see through the veils we impose, to undo our concealment and camouflage. After their sin Adam and Eve hid themselves in the woods from the face of God. Who shall cherish our naked flesh? C. S. Lewis wrote about a woman's flight from God in his novel *Till We Have Faces*.[5] All her life she had been hiding her face from herself and everyone else behind a black veil. Only in death does she recognize herself in her narrow fears. She finally sees how she was forgiven and loved during her life more than she ever knew. In our general anxiety and mortality we pray: "Holy Mary, mother of God, pray for us sinners now and at the hour of our death."

Mary wraps the naked baby boy in swaddling clothes and lays him in a manger. Naked he dies on the cross, and the women wrap his body in a shroud for burial. Madonna and pieta. Birth and death. The Christmas story is told of a woman and her newborn son, and the Easter story of a dead man and the women at the tomb. Women preside at the entrance of human beings and at their exit. They wrap the living body for warmth and they wrap the dead body against the chill of the grave. Women enfold human flesh. We are mothered into life and we are mothered out of life. We are birthed into this life and birthed into eternal life. Our flesh is the blessed fruit of the womb, and our flesh yet needs succor at the hour of our death. Both Eve in the beginning of the old dispensation and Mary in the beginning of the new dispensation are "mother of the living." In a novel of Herman Hesse, Goldmund on his deathbed says to Narcissus: "Without a mother one cannot love. Without a mother one cannot die."[6] No human being creates or loves himself or herself. We must be cherished by another because we are not self-generating nor self-sufficient.

Mary is called "mother of God." Perduring motherhood remains a human imperative because there is perennial dying. An acceptance of motherhood is an acceptance of mortality. The reproduction of the body is the acknowledgment of our finitude. There is birth because there is death. There is Christmas because there is Easter. There is the fruit of the womb because there is the hour of death. There is Mary as madonna because there is Mary as pieta. The wedding wine of Cana prefigures the paschal wine of the last supper. Annunciation is linked to resurrection. The evangelical prayer of part one of the Ave Maria leads to the ecclesial prayer of part two. What God has begun in Mary with the body of Jesus God will finish with the body of all humanity, the body of Christ. So we pray to the mother of Jesus Christ: pray for us now and at the hour of our death. Amen.

THE HAIL MARY AS THE
PRAYER OF THE HOLY SPIRIT

The first part of the Ave Maria is the Christmas story of the madonna and child. The second part is the Easter story of a love stronger than death. Little wonder that Mary who is mother of the body of Jesus was easily symbolized as mother of the Church, the historically extended spiritual body of Jesus. Little wonder that the Ave Maria speaks of the mystery of birth in part one and of the mystery of death in part two. Mary is the woman who knew Jesus in the Nazareth descent of the Spirit at the annunciation of the conception of Jesus, and she knew the Jerusalem descent of the Spirit at the Pentecost annunciation of the conception of the Church. Part one of the Ave parallels the joyful wedding of Cana; part two the passion of Calvary where Mary stood at the foot of the cross. Upon Mary in part one and upon the Church in part two the Holy Spirit descends with the fullness of the life of Jesus who is Lord. The Ave Maria contains the Spirit-filled words of Gabriel, of Elizabeth, and of holy mother Church. One Spirit, the Spirit of God, speaks in the Ave Maria in three voices.[7] The Holy Spirit thus overshadows the whole Ave Maria, which may well be seen as a prayer of the Spirit alive in the life of Mary and alive in the life of the Church.

Given an emphasis on the Holy Spirit in an in-depth understanding of the Ave Maria, let us compare the first two chapters of Luke's Gospel, which tell of the infancy of Jesus, and the first two chapters of Luke's Acts of the Apostles, which tell of the infancy of the Church.[8] In the opening chapters of the third Gospel, we are told of the descent of the Holy Spirit and the conception of Jesus by the Virgin Mary: "The Holy Spirit will come upon you" (1:35). In the opening chapters of the Acts we are told of the descent of the Holy Spirit and the birth of the Church

194

among the disciples gathered in prayer in the upper room (1:8 and 2:1–13). The account of the birth of Jesus makes a parallel with the account of the birth of the mystical body of Jesus that is the Church. After the reception of the word of God and the overshadowing of the Holy Spirit, Mary hastens on a mission into the hill country to assist her kinswoman. Elizabeth herself is filled with the Holy Spirit when Mary carrying Christ embraces her. After the rushing wind and the tongues of fire descend upon the assembly of the disciples of Jesus in Pentecost, Peter hastens on a mission to address the crowds come on pilgrimage to Jerusalem. The Spirit touches their hearts. They understand the apostle's words about the life and death of Jesus. Despite the barriers that the Babel of their many different tongues created to keep them apart, they become through the Spirit a unified community enabled to hear the word of God.

The descent of the Holy Spirit suffuses both parts of the Ave Maria. Mary's experience is the Church's as well. The annunciation to Mary is a Pentecost, and Pentecost announces the indwelling of the Holy Spirit in the hearts of the faithful. The Holy Spirit hovered over the waters in the beginning, and the created world in all its grandeur emerged from the dark primordial chaos: "'Let there be light.' . . . And God saw that the light was good" (Gn 1:3–4). The world was the first womb of God's creation. And the manifestation of the Spirit continues. The glory of God, the Shekinah, hovered over the ark that housed the covenant tables, in a cloud by day and in a pillar of fire by night (Ex 24:16–18 and 40:34–38). The Holy Spirit descends upon Jesus at his baptism in the Jordan, and a voice proclaims: "This is my beloved Son, with whom I am well pleased" (Mt 3:17). In baptism within the Church of Jesus Christ, the Holy Spirit sanctifies the waters and new life in the Spirit is born from the font of holy mother Church. When Jesus is transfigured on Mt. Tabor he is overshadowed by the cloud of the glory of God, and a voice declares: "This is my chosen Son; listen to him" (Lk 9:35). Luke uses the same Greek word, *episkiazein*, in the transfiguration account for this overshadowing as he does when writing of the Spirit's conception of Jesus in the womb of Mary. On the cross Jesus breathes forth his *spirit* just before the soldier breaks his heart with a lance, "and immediately blood and water flowed out" (Jn 19:34). In John's Gospel this is the Pentecostal birth of the Church from the wounded side of Jesus. The Church is taken from the body of Jesus as Eve from the rib of Adam or even as Jesus from the womb of Mary. Adam proclaims Eve "flesh of my flesh" (Gn 2:23). Paul speaks of "the Church, which is his [Jesus'] body" (Eph 1:22). Jesus at the last supper gives his life saying "This is my body" (Lk 22:19).

In the eucharistic commemoration of the last supper we pray: "Let your Holy Spirit come upon these gifts so that they may become for us the body and blood of Jesus Christ, our Lord." The wine is changed into his blood as water was changed into wine at the wedding at Cana. "And the mother of Jesus was there." The Church lives by the Holy Spirit. Mary was filled with the Holy Spirit. "Mary is prototypical of the Church which is constituted by the gift of the Spirit."[9] Both Elizabeth at the visitation and the apostles (the Church) at Pentecost receive the Holy Spirit in the company of Mary the mother of the Lord. One might imagine why Leonardo Boff would go so far as to say the Holy Spirit was "spiritualized" in Mary in an analogous way as the Son of God was embodied in Jesus.[10] Gerard Manley Hopkins's sonnet, "God's Grandeur," offers hope of renewal to a tired and abused world by appealing to the perennial vivification by the Holy Spirit: "Because the Holy Ghost over the bent / World broods with warm breast and with ah! bright wings."[11] The Ave Maria should be seen as a prayer whose understanding depends on an understanding of the Holy Spirit.

THE HAIL MARY AS PARADIGM PRAYER

The Ave Maria is freedom prayer. Mary's Magnificat has been prayed not only as her prayer of praise to God but also as the song of Christian solidarity with the poor and oppressed who are especially loved and saved by God.[12] Mary is a woman of the poor. She suffers as a minority person. Her sex was oppressed throughout the civilized world. Deprived of education and political power, women raised the children and did a great deal of the work that sustained domestic life. Mary lived in an oppressed land, occupied by a foreign armed force. Her son died as a convicted criminal hung in torments as a spectacle in a shameful and humiliating public crucifixion. Mary represents all the women of the world that yearn for justice for their sex, for justice for all their family, and for life without violence. She represents the starving and oppressed masses of men and women who have never been given a life of dignity. The "option for the poor" that has been championed by contemporary liberation theology finds in Mary and her Magnificat prayer to the God who feeds the poor and "sends the rich away empty" a patron saint. Thy Kingdom come. The Ave Maria addresses the mother of the poor.

The Ave Maria is people prayer. To appreciate the Ave Maria will require of the Christian a sympathy with popular piety. Such devotion is often marked with excess and sometimes with an enthusiasm that is carried away to inappropriate expression. Religion would have more decorum and order were it to exclude the enthusiasts, the half educated, and the mistakenly motivated from its midst. In an effort to include anyone and everyone, religion is vulnerable to what its followers may distort, however well intentioned their practice. With friends like these, one might remark, who needs enemies? Yet, Christians are asked to carry one another's burdens, and to entrust prayer to people who in

197

turn may diminish it. The wheat and the weeds must be allowed to grow together because their roots are inextricably entwined. Only at the end of time will the harvest be altogether pure. The Church is married to the faithful for better or for worse, and while one may urge improvement one is prepared to bear shortcomings. Devotion to Mary and the prayer in her name have sometimes suffered at the hands of all those who welcome her memory. There have also been great discoveries in popular prayer. All enthusiasm, however wholesome, may seem ridiculous taken out of context. In this regard Newman points out how foolish love letters might appear when reproduced in a police report. Yet love letters are not without their profound value. The incarnation as portrayed succinctly and poignantly in the madonna with child in arms is such an astonishing truth and dazzling beauty that no fulsome reaction of any kind can come as a complete surprise. How can one limit the kinds of delight that human beings might find in this woman and her child who is the infinite God? "When once we have mastered the idea, that Mary bore, suckled, and handled the Eternal in the form of a child, what limit is conceivable to the rush and flood of thoughts which such a doctrine involves?"[13] The Ave Maria is a folk prayer, a pilgrim's prayer, a publican's prayer, a people prayer.

The Ave Maria is body prayer. The Hail Mary is often said in a repetitious way. It is a prayer associated in the minds and hearts of many devotees with the beads of the rosary. The beads fingered with fervor and love pursue a silent and tactile prayer. Many religions employ hand beads to occupy the body in prayer, especially when the head is distracted and the flesh is weary. Many persons recognize the worth of the rosary as prayer in those numbing and mindless moments such as grief, heavy weariness, and serious illness. It is a favorite Catholic prayer at wake services for just that reason. One can actually pray the rosary always, and especially when lethargy or listless feelings or dullness of mind eliminate more attention-demanding kinds of prayer.[14] Then one's fingers, long familiar with the consolation of the beads, do the praying without effort and even without words. Some people use the recitation of the Ave Maria as a kind of mantra that accompanies their own meditation upon the mysteries of the life and death of Jesus Christ. Others have found that they simply cling to God when they pray the Hail Mary, and that it is a way of dwelling with the incarnate Lord in all of the ineffable ramifications of the mystery of salvation. Lacordaire is reported to have said: "Love has but few words to utter; and, while it is ever repeating these words, it never repeats itself."[15] The Ave Maria at its best is not a way of saying many prayers, nor a way to "babble like the pagans, who think that they will be heard because of their many words" (Mt 6:7). It is a way of praying always by dwelling within the mystery of God incarnate. Paul writes: "Rejoice always. Pray without ceasing. In all circumstances give thanks, for this is the will of God for you in Christ Jesus" (1 Thes 5:17–18). While I do not suggest Paul prayed the Ave Maria, I do think many Christians have come to "pray always" with this prayer that their lips have learned by old habit and their minds and hearts absorbed. It is a centering prayer of ancient beauty ever old and ever new. The Ave Maria is embodied prayer.

The Ave Maria is simple prayer. Prayer is the expression of faith. The decision to believe involves a recognition that God needs no explanation; it is my existence that begs justification. Religion often seems a complicated business—many doctrines and various histories. And yet only one thing is necessary: to believe in God with all of one's heart and strength, body and soul. All else would be included, just as to cling to the roots of a tree brings along the stem and even the fruit. Prayer may also seem complicated. There are so many methods and so many books. Yet to pray is simple. We need only turn to God who has already turned to us. Sin is a failure to pray because one does not believe. Prayer is a mystery of faith. We thereby acknowledge God's great love for us, a "love stronger than death" (Cant 8:6). The blind beggar at the side of the road in Luke (18:35–43) asks Jesus for nothing but to see. He would view things as they are in reality; he would know the truth. In prayer we ask to see in this dark night of faith our soul's passage to the God who loves us. Implicit in prayer is recognition of God's sovereignty and resourceful care for our life. Nothing more is required, though a good deal more might be added. The Ave Maria is such a simple prayer. "Mary pondered all these things in her heart."

The Ave Maria is perduring prayer. The godless do not recognize God in their life and hence they do not pray. To those who have seen a vision of an angel announcing tidings of great joy, or a Beatrice who points to a love that moves the sun and stars, or any moment of joy that can never be forgotten, the desire to dwell in prayer that recalls the spirit's revelation is fierce. The problem for the believer is what to do when the angel departs, when Beatrice dies, when the children gathered around the oak tree at the ending of *The Brothers Karamazov* must separate in this life. It's then in darkness that generations have found it blessed to repeat those words, those words prayed around well-worn beads, those words of Gabriel, Elizabeth, and mother Church. The few and familiar words of the Hail Mary, murmured by innumerable brothers and sisters in the Lord, recall how the incarnate mystery of God took its origin and how our life will be fulfilled despite the terrors of the night.

THE HAIL MARY IN
CHRISTIAN PRAYER LIFE

What is the future of the Hail Mary in Christian prayer? Is that an impossible question to ask, or an arrogant one to propose?

The first part of the Ave Maria has perdured in the Church from early post-apostolic origins. The prayerful yoking of Gabriel's annunciation with Elizabeth's spirit-filled exclamation dates from fifteen hundred years ago or earlier. In the Lucan account Mary certainly knew something profound about Jesus in the beginning of his life, but she also came to believe in him fully over a lifetime and probably most of all in the resurrection revelation. She was providentially chosen to be the mother of Jesus, but we do not need to conclude that an exaltation of a later Mary is the explicit message of Gabriel's invocation of her as "full of grace." It is enough to say that Luke tells us she was especially graced by God to be the mother of Jesus. Thus in the Ave Maria all Christians can readily claim Mary as a "sister in faith" and a believer first of all.[16]

The biblical clarification of another Mary in the Gospels, Mary of Magdala, may shed light on what process is involved in restoring a more authentic Gospel biography. Mary of Magdala has been considered the prototype of the repentant sinner, the prostitute with a heart of gold, the image of unfaithful and adulterous Israel that turns from idolatrous earthly loves to the one true love of God. The image of Mary Magdalene is culled from the Gospels and conflated with the story of the unnamed sinful woman who washes the feet of Jesus with her tears and dries them with her hair (Lk 7), and with the story of Mary of Bethany who anoints the feet of Jesus (Jn 12). In point of fact Mary of Magdala is neither the sinner of the town nor the sainted Mary of Bethany

201

who sat at the feet of Jesus. She is a woman whom Jesus cured of "seven devils" (Jn 8), very likely a serious mental illness. She was one of the women who followed Jesus and took care of his material needs. Her Gospel vocation is not that of the repentant prostitute who spends the remainder of her life in penance and contemplation. The proper re-symbolization of Mary Magdalene displays the woman first entrusted with the resurrection Good News, and empowered to bring the Gospel of the risen Christ to the apostles (Jn 20). Mary of Magdala is a woman of mission within the Church, and indeed the apostle to the apostles. Mary of Magdala stands before the mystery of the resurrection as the original witness, just as Mary of Nazareth stands as the original witness of the mystery of the incarnation. To see Mary Magdalene in this light is to re-symbolize a woman of the Gospel in a way that is more faithful to the biblical text. Such a reading frees her from a distorted biography, however edifying, and restores to her a vocation even more marvelous before God.

The relationship of contemporary women to Mary of Nazareth remains a complex one. The re-symbolization of Mary of Magdala sketched above may prove a helpful example for those women who find Mary of Nazareth problematic as typically presented in the dominant Mariology of a given age in the Church. A biography of Mary that would stay close to the Gospel texts and reclaims the human Mary, prototypical woman of faith, original believer in Christ, and emerging disciple will give Mary back to her sisters in a fresh way. That re-symbolization of Mary will assist the enormous efforts of the world in the twentieth century to effect the liberation of women and the establishment for the first time in history of a sexual equality in all areas of human qualification and endeavor. Sebastian Moore has called this contemporary moment of truth about women an axial revolution in the world on a scale parallel to the time of ancient Greek tragedy when men were separating themselves from tribal consciousness in order to seek their individual personal destiny. The struggle of women's liberation will find support in the life of Mary, a timeless woman whose freedom transcends her historical boundaries.

The second part of the Ave Maria presents two problems for the future. The first problem is the invocation of *Holy Mary*

Mother of God. That one long phrase includes an implicit definition of motherhood and of the divinity that anyone taking
these words on their lips must supply. That understanding of the
mystery of woman/mother and Jesus/God can be more or less
ample. *Holy Mary* echoes the evangelical words "full of grace,"
and *mother of God* echoes "blessed among women."[17] At the same
time the symbolization of Mary goes beyond what Luke says. The
symbolization of Mary began in earnest with the Gospel of John,
where she is conspicuously and deliberately placed at the pivot
points of Jesus' life—the beginning of his public ministry at Cana
and the ending of his public life with his death on Calvary. The
Theotokos of Cyril of Alexandria at the Council of Ephesus is yet
a further symbolization of Mary that has been chosen especially
by the Church. Whatever future symbolization of Mary, *Theotoko*s
will perdure in its substantial truth. The Greek word of history
can hardly be replaced. What can be more fully understood is
the depth of the mystery that T*heotokos* imperfectly reveals to
the heart of the faithful Christian. The further comprehension
of Mary in the Gospels and *Theotokos* in Marian theology will
depend on how deeply we come to understand womankind and
motherhood, along with the mystery of the incarnation of the
Father's only son in Jesus of Nazareth. If the symbolization of
the past has been unbiblical in any way, or failed to comprehend
the richness of women and men in their interrelationship with
each other and with God, then we will have to rediscover the
perennial truth of *Theotokos* in symbols that do not lose the past
and yet claim the future.

The second problem in the church words of the Ave Maria
stems from the never fully understood mystery of Christian
prayer, and of the intercessory prayer to the saints in particular. This is where Protestant objection lies and where any rap-
prochment with Catholics and Protestants needs to begin.
Differing ecclesiologies finally divide us. The role of Mary in
the New Testament need not prove the grounds for division. All
Christians understand that Mary is not God. She is one of the
saints, and indeed preeminent among them, both by the several
and crucial Gospel passages that position her at the heart of the
mystery of Christ Jesus and by the long tradition of the Church.

We will have to appropriate not only Mary-*Theotokos*. We will have to comprehend further the richness of the communion of saints, the integral Church *with whom* we always pray and not only *to whom* we pray.

There may in the end be no fully persuasive argument for prayer to the mother of Jesus. Marian prayer comes out of a tradition that many, but not all, Christians embrace and which satisfies a deep orientation that stems from the earliest years of their life. By that I mean that the prayers people prefer are often ones that come trailing memories of family and church, of first experience and long familiarity. I still recall with delight a prayer taught to me by the pastor of our parish who came to our elementary school classroom for a brief visit. He urged us to say a short one-line prayer, "Divine infant of Bethlehem, come and take birth in our hearts," fourthousand times during Advent. That was the then-popular estimate of the years of waiting before the coming of Christ. We children tried to keep count of our prayers. To this day, I say the prayer frequently. It is grooved in my brain, and my tongue is bent to those particular sounds. On my deathbed and comatose I might mumble just those words. There is no sterling defense for that particular prayer; it does not demonstrate exceptional theology. But whatever its shortcomings, it has lifted my mind and heart to God over a lifetime. And so it may be with the Ave Maria. Its virtues are many, but they will not be compelling to everyone. It is by no means the only resource of Christians at prayer. Nonetheless, the Hail Mary remains an ancient, sacred, and oft-spoken Christian prayer familiar from childhood to most Catholic folk and framed in a few words of fathomless profundity.

APPENDIX I

MARY IN THE NEW TESTAMENT

PAUL Galatians 4:4–5 — (Less surely 1:19 and 4:28–29, and Romans 1:3–4 or Philippians 2:6–7)

MARK 3:31–35 (see also 20–21) — The family of Jesus comes to visit him (see also Matthew 12:46–50 and Luke 8:19–21 and also 11:27–28)

6:1–6a — Jesus visits Nazareth (see also Matthew 13:54–58 and Luke 4:16–30)

MATTHEW 1:1–17 — Genealogy (see also Luke 3:23–38)

1:18–25 — Annunciation to Joseph

2:1–23 — Birth and infancy of Jesus

12:46–50 — The family of Jesus comes to visit him (see also Mark 3:31–35 (20–21), and Luke 8:19–21 (also 11:27–28)

13:54–58 — Jesus visits Nazareth (see also Mark 6:1–6a and Luke 4:16–30)

LUKE 1:26–38 — Annunciation to Mary

1:39–56 — Visitation to Elizabeth

2:1–21 — Birth and infancy of Jesus

2:22–40 — The Presentation in the Temple

2:41–52 — Finding in the Temple

3:23–38 — Genealogy (see Matthew 1:1–17)

4:16–30 — Jesus visits Nazareth (see also Mark 6:1–6a and Matthew 13:54–58)

8:19–21 — The family of Jesus comes to visit him (and 11:27–28). See also Mark 3:31–35 (20–21) and Matthew 12:46–50

Acts 1:13–14 — Prayer at Pentecost time

JOHN 2:1–12 — The wedding at Cana

19:26–27 — Mary and the beloved disciple at the foot of the cross (Less surely 6:42, 7:1–10 and 41–43, 8:41)

Revelation 12 — The woman and the dragon

APPENDIX II

BIBLICAL TITLES*

Lk 1:28	Greeted by the angel Gabriel
Lk 1:28	Full of grace
Lk 1:31	Mother of Jesus
Lk 1:32	Mother of the Son of the Most High
Lk 1:32	Mother of the Son of David
Lk 1:33	Mother of the King of Israel
Lk 1:35	Mother by act of the Holy Spirit (and Mt 1:20)
Lk 1:38	Handmaiden of the Lord
Mt 1:23	Virgin, Mother of Emmanuel (from Is 7:14)
Jn 1:14	You in whom the Word became flesh
Jn 1:14	You in whom the Word dwelled amongst us
Lk 1:41	Blessed amongst all women
Lk 1:43	Mother of the Lord
Lk 1:43	Happy are you who have believed in the words uttered by the Lord
Lk 1:48	Lowly handmaid of the Lord
Lk 1:48	Called blessed by all generations
Lk 1:48	You in whom the Almighty worked wonders
Lk 1:55	Heiress of the promises made to Abraham
Lk 1:37	Mother of the new Isaac
Lk 2:7	You who gave birth to your firstborn at Bethlehem
Lk 2:7	You who wrapped your child in swaddling clothes and laid him in a manger

---

*List taken from John P. Kenny, *The Meaning of Mary for Modern Man* (Melbourne, Spectrum: 1980), pp. 141–142, who took this table from A. M. Roquet, *La Vie Spirituelle*, Vol. 119, No. 553 (Oct., 1968), pp. 213–217. I have made some slight adaptations of the text for my own purposes. Note that this list is a maximal attempt to find references to Mary in the New Testament, and that not all readers, including myself, would be so inclusive. I have put an asterisk by those items that seem to me questionable. Roquet includes some references to Old Testament texts, which are generally considered to be even more problematical, and which I omit.

Gal 4:4	Woman from whom Jesus was born
Lk 2:11	Mother of the Saviour (and Mt 1:21)
Lk 2:11	Mother of the Messiah (and Mt 1:16)
Lk 2:16	You who were found by the shepherds with Joseph and the newborn child
Lk 2:19, 51	You who kept and meditated all things in your heart
Lk 2:22	You who offered Jesus in the Temple
Lk 2:28	You who put Jesus into the arms of Simeon
Lk 2:33	You who marvelled at what was said of Jesus
Lk 2:35	You whose soul a sword should pierce
Mt 2:11	Mother found together with the child by the Wise Men
Mt 2:14	Mother whom Joseph took into refuge in Egypt
Lk 2:42	You who took the child Jesus to Jerusalem for the Passover
Lk 2:46	You who searched for Jesus for three days
Lk 2:46–49	You who found Jesus again in his Father's house
Lk 2:51	Mother whom Jesus obeyed at Nazareth
*Mk 6:3	Model of widows
Jn 2:1–12	Jesus' compassion at the marriage feast at Cana
Jn 2:5	You who told the servants, "Do as he shall tell you"
Jn 2:11	You who gave rise to Jesus' first miracle
Mt 12:50	Mother of Jesus for having done the will of the Father in heaven
*Lk 10:42	Mary who chose the better part
Lk 11:28	Blessed for having heard the word of God and kept it
Jn 19:25	Mother standing at the foot of the cross
Jn 19:26–27	Mother of the disciple whom Jesus loved
Acts 1:14	Queen of the Apostles, persevering in prayer with them
*Apoc 12:1	Woman clothed with the sun
*Apoc 12:1	Woman crowned with twelve stars
*Apoc 12:2	Sorrowful Mother of the Church
*Apoc 12:5	Glorious Mother of the Messiah
*Apoc 21:2	Image of the new Jerusalem
*Apoc 22:1	River of living water, flowing from the throne of God and the Lamb

APPENDIX III

VERSIONS OF THE AVE MARIA

Gabriel's Salutation to Mary in Greek: Luke 1:28

καὶ εἰσελθὼν ὁ ἄγγελος πρὸς αὐτὴν εἶπε,
Kai eiselthōn ho angelos pros autēn eipe,
And came the angel to her said,

Χαῖρε κεχαριτωμένη. ὁ Κύριος μετὰ σοῦ,
Chaire, kecharitōmenē ho Kurios meta sou,
Hail, favored-one the Lord with you,

εὐλογημένη σὺ ἐν γυναιξίν.
eulogēmenē su en gunaixin.
blessed you among women.

kai	coordinating conjunction
eiselthōn	verb, participle, aorist, active, nominative, masculine, singular
ho	definite article, nominative, masculine, singular
angelos	noun, nominative, masculine, singular
pros	preposition, takes accusative
autēn	pronoun, accusative, feminine, third person, singular
eipe	verb, indicative, aorist, active, third person, singular
Chaire	verb, imperative, present, active, second person, singular functions as a sentential particle
kecharitōmenē	verb, participle, perfect, passive, vocative, feminine second person, singular

---

The New Testament in Greek: The Gospel According to St. Luke, edited by the American and British Committees of the International Greek New Testament Project (Oxford: Clarendon Press, 1984), 11. Note that the Angel Gabriel is given a further text, "blessed are you among women," which has been much disputed here.

ho	definite article, nominative, masculine, singular
Kurios	noun, nominative, masculine, singular
meta	preposition, takes genitive
sou	pronoun, genitive, second person singular
eulogēmenē	verb, participle, perfect, passive, nominative, feminine, second person, singular
su	pronoun, genitive, second person singular
en	preposition, takes dative
gunaixin	noun, dative, feminine, plural

Elizabeth's Greeting of Mary in Greek: Luke 1:42

καὶ ἀνεφώνησεν φωνῇ μεγάλῃ καὶ εἶπεν,
Kai anephōnēsen phōnē megalē kai eipen,
And she exclaimed with cry loud and said,

Εὐλογημένη σὺ ἐν γυναιξί,
Eulogēmenē su en gunaixi,
Blessed you among women,

καὶ εὐλογημένος ὁ καρπὸς τῆς κοιλίας σου.
kai eulogēmenos ho karpos tēs koilias sou.
and blessed the fruit of womb your.

kai	coordinating conjunction
anephōnēsen	verb, indicative, aorist, active, third person, singular
phōnē	noun, instrumental dative, feminine, singular
megalē	adjective, instrumental dative, feminine, singular
kai	coordinating conjunction
eipen	verb, indicative, aorist, active, third person, singular
eulogēmenē	verb, participle, perfect, passive, nominative, feminine, second person, singular
su	pronoun, nominative, second person, singular

The New Testament in Greek: The Gospel According to St. Luke, edited by the American and British Committees of the International Greek New Testament Project (Oxford: Clarendon Press, 1984), 20.

en	preposition, takes dative
gunaixi	noun, dative, feminine, plural
kai	coordinating conjunction
eulogēmenos	verb, participle, perfect, passive, nominative, masculine, third person, singular
ho	definite article, nominative, masculine, singular
karpos	noun, nominative, masculine, singular
tēs	definite article, genitive, feminine, singular
koilias	noun, genitive, feminine, singular
sou	pronoun, genitive, second person, singular

The Latin Text

Ave, Maria,
Gratia plena,
Dominus tecum.
Benedicta tu in mulieribus,
Et benedictus fructus ventris tui, Jesus.

Sancta Maria,
Mater Dei,
Ora pro nobis peccatoribus,
Nunc et in hora mortis nostrae.
Amen.

The English Text

Hail Mary,
Full of grace,
The Lord is with thee,
Blessed art thou among women,
And blessed is the fruit of thy womb, Jesus.

Holy Mary,
mother of God,
pray for us sinners,
Now and at the hour of our death.
Amen

Some texts have changed *thee* and *thou* to "you," and *thy* to "your."

NOTES

Introduction

1. Epiphanius, *Haereses*, 78:24, in Henri Daniel-Rops, *The Book of Mary*, trans. Alistair Guinan (New York: Hawthorn, 1960), 136–137. On Epiphanius, see also Hilda Graef, *Mary: A History of Doctrine and Devotion*, vol. 1 (New York: Sheed and Ward, 1963), 70–73.

2. *Haereses*, 79:7, in Paul Palmer, *Mary in the Documents of the Church* (London: Burns and Oates, 1953), 49.

3. John de Satge, *Down to Earth: The New Protestant Vision of the Virgin Mary* (Wilmington, N.C.: Consortium Books, 1976), 139.

4. Frank E. Brightman, ed., *Liturgies Eastern and Western*, comp. Charles Edward Hammond, vol. 1 (Oxford: Clarendon, 1896), 56 and 128.

5. An ancient form of the Ave Maria. See Adalbert Hamman, ed., *Early Christian Prayers*, trans. Walter Mitchell (Chicago: Regnery, 1961), 76. This text, written in Greek on a Coptic ostracon, was discovered in the late nineteenth century in the area of Luxor in Egypt. Its condition was fragmentary, and it was reconstructed by F. E. Brightman and edited and published by Walter E. Crum, *Coptic Ostraca* (London: Kegan and Paul, 1902), Text #518, p. 3. The date of origin is sixth or seventh century. A more literal translation of the last two lines might read: "because you have conceived Christ the Son of God, the redeemer of our soul." See Gabriele Giamberardini, *Il Culto Mariano in Egitto*, vol. 1, publicazioni dello Studium Biblicum Franciscanum, analecta 6 (Jerusalem: Franciscan Printing Press, 1975), 226. The Alexandrian liturgy of Saint Mark changes the ending slightly to read: "Because you have generated the Savior of our souls" (Giamberardini, 232).

6. Brightman, *Liturgies Eastern and Western*, 218.

7. See the Antiphonary (*Liber Antiphonarius*) traditionally ascribed to Gregory the Great. *Patrologiae cursus completus . . . , Series Latina (PL)*, ed. J.-P. Migne, 78:657.

8. Herbert Thurston, "Our Popular Devotions: The Angelus," *The Month* 97 (May 1901): 490.

9. See *The Catholic Encyclopedia*, s.v. "Hail, Mary," 7:110-112.

10. Herbert Thurston, *Familiar Prayers: Their Origin and History* (London: Burns and Oates, 1953), 101.

11. Jean Laurenceau, "Les Débuts de la Recitation Privée de L'Antienne Ave Maria en Occident avant la Fin du 11e Siècle," *Du Cultu Mariano Saeculis VI-XI: Acta Congressus Mariologici Mariani Internationalis in Croatia anno 1971 celebrati* (Rome: Pontificia Academia Mariana Internationalis, 1972), 245.

12. See *The Catholic Encyclopedia* 7:110-112. See also Laurenceau, "Les Débuts de la Recitation," 246.

13. Daniel-Rops, *Book of Mary*, 91.

14. The original text in Greek is a fragmentary piece of papyrus, and some reconstruction was required to present a coherent text for publication. Various liturgies, both East and West, have further adapted the text of this prayer to their particular devotional situation. There is thus no one standard Greek text to which everyone subscribes. For an exhaustive treatment of the "Sub Tuum," see Giamberardini, *Il Culto Mariano*, 69-97 and 273.

15. *Dublin Review* 10 (1868): 320-361.

16. Palmer, *Mary in the Documents of the Church*, 54.

17. Laurenceuau, "Les Débuts de la Recitation," 238.

18. See *The Catholic Encyclopedia* 7:110-112.

19. Giamberardini, *Il Culto Mariano*, 277. The text reads: "Sancta Maria, Mater Dei, ora pro nobis, inquam, Peccatoribus. Amen."

20. Ibid., 278. See also pp. 234-235. The translation of the Italian is mine.

21. "Decretum Generale" of the Sacred Congregation of Rites, *Acta Apostolicae Sedis* 47 (1955): 222.

22. See Marcel Mahe, "Aux Sources de Notre Rosaire," *Supplement de la Vie Spirituelle* 16 (February 1951): 101-120. This article gives a careful overview of the history of the rosary. For further study of the rosary see Herbert Thurston, *The Month* 96 (October 1900): 403-418; (November 1900): 513-527; (December 1900): 620-628; 97 (January 1901): 67-79; 97 (February 1901): 172-188; 97 (March 1901): 286-304; 97 (April 1901): 382-404. See also Hans-Urs von Balthasar, *The Threefold Garland: The World's Salvation in Mary's Prayer*, trans. Erasmo Leiva-Merikakis (San Francisco: Ignatius Press, 1982); Romano Guardini, *The Rosary of Our Lady*, trans. H. Von Schuecking (New York: P. J. Kenedy and Sons, 1955); Rosemary Haughton, *Feminine Spirituality: Reflections on the Mysteries of the Rosary* (New York: Paulist, 1976); Maisie Ward, *The Spendour of the Rosary* (New York: Sheed and Ward, 1945) and Maisie

Ward, "Elements and Office of the Rosary," in *The Mary Book*, ed. Frank Sheed (New York: Sheed and Ward, 1950), 316-335; Eithne Wilkins, *The Rose-Garden Game: A Tradition of Beads and Flowers* (New York: Herder and Herder, 1969); and Francis Michael William, *The Rosary: Its History and Meaning* (New York: Kaiser, 1953).

The history of the Angelus is quite complex. For further study see *The Catholic Encyclopedia*, s.v. "Angelus," by Herbert Thurston, 1:486-488. See also his serially published articles in *The Month*: "Our Popular Devotion: The Angelus," 98 (November 1901): 483-499; "The Curfew Bell," 98 (December 1901): 607-616; "Compline or Curfew Bell—Which?" 99 (January 1902): 61-73; "The Mid-Day Angelus," 99 (May 1902): 518-532; "The Antiquity of the Angelus," 103 (Jan. 1904): 57-67. See also *Dictionnaire de Théologie Catholique*, s.v. "Angelus," by U. Berlière, 1:1278-81; and *Dictionnaire d'Archéologie Chrétienne et de Liturgie*, s.v. "Angelus," by W. Henry, 1:2068-78.

23. The most helpful source remains Raymond Brown, K. P. Donfried, J. A. Fitzmyer, and J. Reuman, *Mary in the New Testament: A Collaborative Assessment by Protestant and Roman Catholic Scholars* (Philadelphia: Fortress Press, 1978). Also quite useful is John McHugh, *The Mother of Jesus in the New Testament* (Garden City, N.Y.: Doubleday, 1975). See also John Galot, *Mary in the Gospel*, trans. Maria Constance (Westminster, Md.: Newman, 1965). Any commentary on the pertinent scripture passages may be useful. Particularly comprehensive is Raymond Brown, *The Birth of the Messiah: A Commentary on the Infancy Narratives in Matthew and Luke* (New York: Doubleday, 1977). Quality commentaries on Luke's Gospel, such as that of A. Plummer, of I. H. Marshall, and of J. Fitzmyer are also quite helpful. See also Mary in the New Testament in the appendix.

24. See the annunciation account attributed to Abraham in Genesis 17, to Gideon in Judges 6, to the parents of Samson in Judges 13, and to Hannah in 1 Samuel 1. The annunciation to Joseph in Matthew 1, to Zachary in Luke 1, and to the shepherds in Luke 2 seems also to borrow from such Old Testament sources. The word "annunciation" in Greek is *euangelismos*, which might be translated as good tidings, or good news, or the evangel, i.e., the Gospel.

25. *Mary in the New Testament* was written by Raymond Brown, but with the collaboration and group authorization as indicated.

26. Ibid., 119.

27. Lawrence Cunningham, *Mother of God* (San Francisco: Harper and Row, 1982), 31.

28. See Jacques Hervieux, ed., *The New Testament Apocrypha*, trans.

Dom Wulstan Hibberd (New Haven: Hawthorn, 1960). Also *The Apocryphal New Testament*, ed. and trans. Montague James (Oxford: Clarendon, 1953), and *The Apocryphal New Testament*, Jones-Wake translation of 1820 (New York: P. Eckler, 1927).

29. See the writings of Carl Jung, for example.

30. See Michael Carroll, *The Cult of the Virgin Mary: Psychological Origins* (Princeton: Princeton University Press, 1983).

31. Leonardo Boff, *The Maternal Face of God: The Feminine and Its Religious Expressions*, trans. Robert R. Barr and John W. Diercksmeier (San Francisco: Harper and Row, 1987), 242.

32. Ibid., 100-101.

33. See E. B. Pusey's *Eirenicon* (London: Gilbert and Rivington, 1865) and John Henry Newman's response, *A Letter to the Rev. E. B. Pusey* (New York: Lawrence Kehoe, 1866).

34. See Thomas O'Meara, *Mary in Protestant and Catholic Theology* (New York: Sheed and Ward, 1966), 111-137. See also Walter Tappolet, ed., *Das Marienlob des Reformatoren* (Tubingen: Katzmann-Verlag, 1962), 125.

35. Statement by the Permanent Commission on Interchurch Relations of the Presbyterian Church, U.S.A., *Christian Century* 72 (June 1955): 756-758.

36. "De Salutatione Angelica," in *Migne, PL* 204:472.

37. *PL* 204:472.

38. "The Mother of Jesus in the New Testament" in *Mary in the Churches*, ed. Hans Kung and Jurgen Moltmann, trans. Marcus Lefebure (New York: Seabury, 1983), 9.

39. Elizabeth Johnson, "The Marian Tradition and the Reality of Woman," *Horizons* 12 (1985): 135.

40. Marcello Azevedo, *Vocation for Mission: The Challenge of Religious Life Today*, trans. John Diercksmeier (New York: Paulist, 1988), 56.

Part One

1. Gabriel here seems to appear as a person, and not just a personification. The proper name suggests something more than the "angel of the Lord" as metaphor for the communication of God. Fitzmyer notes that the name Gabriel means "God is my hero/warrior." See Joseph Fitzmyer, *The Gospel According to Luke, I-IX*, Anchor Bible, vol. 28 (New York: Doubleday, 1981), 328. Also see Gabriel in the Book of Daniel 8:16 and 9:20–25. Gabriel's stature as a leader of the good angels in the poetry of Dante and Milton remains immense.

2. See the footnote to Luke 1:19 in the *New American Bible.*

3. Galot, *Mary in the Gospel,* 1–77.

4. See Stanislas Lyonnet, "Chaire and Kecharitōmenē," *Biblica* 20 (1939): 131–141. A good summary of this entire issue can be found in McHugh, *Mother of Jesus,* 37–52.

5. Max Thurian, *Mary, Mother of the Lord, Figure of the Church,* trans. Neville B. Cryer (London: Faith Press, 1963), 16.

6. Brown, *Mary in the New Testament,* 126–132.

7. Ibid., 131–132. Fitzmyer also defends "hail" as the preferable translation. See *Gospel According to Luke,* 345.

8. McHugh, *Mother of Jesus,* 52.

9. F. Zorell, "Maria, Soror Mosis, et Maria Mater Dei," *Verbum Domini* 6 (1926): 257–263.

10. Bonaventura Rinaldi, *Mary of Nazareth: Myth or History,* trans. Mary F. Ingoldsby (Westminster, Md.: Newman, 1966), 220.

11. Daniel-Rops, *Book of Mary,* 38.

12. See Aquinas, "Collationes super Ave Maria," in *The Three Greatest Prayers,* trans. Lawrence Shapcote (London: Burns, Oates, and Washbourne, 1937), 30–38.

13. Richard Klaver, *The Litany of Loreto* (London: Herder, 1954), 4–5.

14. Fitzmyer, *The Gospel According to Luke,* 344. See also Fitzmyer, *The Genesis Apocryphon of Qumran Cave I* (Rome: Biblical Institute Press, 1971), 162.

15. See E. Vogt, "De Nominis Mariae Etymologia," *Verbum Domini* 26 (1948): 163–168. See also John Baptist Bauer, "De Nominis 'Mariae' vero Etymo," *Marianum* 19 (1957): 231–234.

16. Andrew Key, "The Giving of Proper Names in the Old Testament," *Journal of Biblical Literature* 83 (1964): 55–59.

17. This suggested possible reading came to me through a conversation with scripture scholar Eugene Ulrich.

18. Attributed to Anthony of Padua, but the reference is not known to me.

19. Hannah in Hebrew means "highly favored one." Luke's story of Mary in the infancy narratives shows parallel passages with Hannah's story (1 Sm 1).

20. Brown, *The Birth of the Messiah,* 326–327. Fitzmyer also concludes that "full of grace" refers to Mary's being favored for the particular mission of bearing Jesus. See *Gospel According to Luke,* 345–346.

21. An earlier translation in the New American Bible read: "Rejoice, O highly favored daughter!" The Phillips translation reads:

"Greetings to you, Mary, O favoured one!" The Living Bible reads: "Congratulations, favored Lady!" Both of these translations take some liberty with the biblical texts.

22. Boff, *Maternal Face of God*, 101–102.

23. Stephen Benko, *Protestants, Catholics, and Mary* (Valley Forge, Penn.: Judson Press, 1968), 108.

24. Reginald Fuller, "A Note on Luke 1:28 and 38," in *The New Testament Age: Essays in Honor of Bo Reicke*, vol. 1, ed. William Weinrich (Macon, Ga.: Mercer University Press, 1984), 201–206.

25. This insight is usually attributed to St. Augustine among others. See his Sermon #25, in Migne, *PL* 46:937.

26. The declarative is preferred over the optative by Fitzmyer, *Gospel According to Luke*, 346; by Brown, *Mary in the New Testament*, 126; and by others.

27. For example, Boaz greets the reapers with "The Lord be with you" as his ordinary salutation (Ru 2:4). It was apparently a common form of greeting.

28. Fitzmyer, *Gospel According to Luke*, 346; and Brown, *Mary in the New Testament*, 132.

29. McHugh, *Mother of Jesus*, 72.

30. Nicholas Cardinal Wiseman, *Essays on Various Subjects*, vol. 1 (London: Charles Dolman, 1853), 76–77. The Rheims translation of the New Testament, done in the sixteenth century, reads, "*Our* Lord is with you."

31. See Brown, *Mary in the New Testament*, 126; and Fitzmyer, *Gospel According to Luke*, 346. A footnote to Luke 1:43 in the New American Bible declares that even before the birth of Jesus, Mary was recognized by Elizabeth as "mother of the Lord," understood as Lord God.

32. See McHugh, *Mother of Jesus*, 48–50.

33. Old Testament quotations are taken from the Revised Standard Version.

34. See Boff, *Maternal Face of God*, 100–101.

35. See the following passages: Is 62:5; Song 2:8–14; Rv 19:7 and 21:2–3.

36. See McHugh, *Mother of Jesus*, 71–72. Alfred Plummer argues that verses 42–45 in Luke make up a canticle of Elizabeth of two strophes of four lines each. See *A Critical and Exegetical Commentary on the Gospel according to Saint Luke* (Edinburgh: T. and T. Clark, 1901), 27. See also Brown, *The Birth of the Messiah*, 333.

37. Brown, *Mary in the New Testament*, 77–83.

38. The story of Judith and the story of Esther are usually not regarded as historical events.

39. See also Luke 1:65, 2:33, and 2:50. Brown makes just this point about the memoirs of Mary. See *Mary in the New Testament*, 152. An excellent treatment of Mary's pondering of the mystery of God can be found in Ben Meyer, "But Mary Kept All These Things . . . ," *Catholic Biblical Quarterly* 26 (1964): 31–49.

40. In the Greek, *blessed* in Luke 1:45 is not *eulogēmenē* but rather *makarios*, which means *happy* is she who. The beatitudes make use of this same word.

41. See also Genesis 30:2; Deuteronomy 7:13 and 28:4

42. Francis J. Sheed, ed., *The Mary Book* (New York: Sheed and Ward, 1950), 39.

43. "De Salutatione Angelica," Migne *PL* 204:477.

44. George Maloney, *Mary, the Womb of God* (Denville, N.J.: Dimension Books, 1976), 14.

45. Gerard Manley Hopkins, "The Wreck of the Deutschland," *Poems and Prose of Gerard Manley Hopkins* (Harmondsworth: Penguin, 1953), 14.

46. Boff, *Maternal Face of God*, 151.

47. Thurian, *Mary, Mother of the Lord*, 37.

48. See Thomas Aquinas, *The Three Greatest Prayers*, 30–38.

Part Two

1. Thomas Aquinas, *The Sermon Conferences of St. Thomas Aquinas on the Apostles' Creed*, trans. and ed. Nicholas Ayo, C.S.C. (Notre Dame, Ind.: University of Notre Dame Press, 1988), 53.

2. Thomas Aquinas, *Summa Theologica* I , q. 25, a. 6.

3. Boff, *Maternal Face of God*, 166.

4. Daniel Rops, *Book of Mary*, 91. The text reads: "In a subterranean sanctuary in Alexandria which dates from the third century, a fresco represents the Marriage Feast at Cana, and in it the Mother of Christ is seen speaking to the servants. She is specifically indentified as *Haghia Maria* or Holy Mary."

5. Cunningham, *Mother of God*, 121; emphasis added. In Latin this prayer is known as the *Sub Tuum Presidium*: "We fly to thy patronage, O Holy Mother of God. Despise not our petitions in our necessities; deliver us always from all dangers, O glorious and blessed Virgin." Text and translation taken from Cunningham.

6. Vatican II used all three Latin phrases: *Dei Genitrix, Deipara,* and *Mater Dei. Mater Dei,* however, was not the customary translation of *Theotokos* in Vatican documents through the centuries.

7. Whether or not Mary knew that Jesus was the Son of God as later councils would define the mystery of the incarnation is much more debatable. Raymond Brown writes that one "ought not to assume that Mary had explicit knowledge of Jesus as 'the Son of God' during his lifetime" (*Mary in the New Testament,* 119). Note that one may still conclude that Mary knew something very special about the mystery of Jesus during his lifetime, and that along with the disciples she would have known much more of who Jesus truly was after the resurrection.

8. See Kari Borresen, "Mary in Catholic Theology," in *Mary in the Churches,* 48–59.

9. Maloney, *Mary, the Womb of God,* 65. Margaret Healy translates *Theotokos* as "the one-bearing-God." Donald Attwater translates the same term as "God bearer" or "God's forth-bringer."

10. Henricus Denzinger, *Enchiridion Symbolorum,* 29th ed. (Freiburg: Herder, 1953), paragraph 148.

11. John Henry Newman, *The New Eve* (Westminster, Md.: Newman, 1952), 34.

12. John Damascene, "De Fide Orthodoxa," III, 12, in Migne, *PG* 94:1029.

13. Cyril Vollert, *A Theology of Mary* (New York: Herder and Herder, 1965), 57–58.

14. Caroline Walker Bynum, *Holy Feast and Holy Fast: The Religious Significance of Food to Medieval Woman* (Berkeley, Calif.: University of California Press, 1987), 275.

15. The medieval theology of eucharistic consecration understood the priest as agent to bring the body of the Lord to the altar.

16. The female ovule was discovered by Karl Ernst Von Baer in 1827.

17. Elizabeth Johnson, "Marian Tradition and the Reality of Women," 116–135.

18. Wordsworth's poem, "Sonnet to the Virgin."

19. The title of Marina Warner's controversial book, *Alone of All Her Sex* (New York: Knopf, 1976).

20. See Elizabeth Moltmann-Wendel, "Motherhood or Friendship," in *Mary in the Churches,* 17–25.

21. Johnson, "Marian Tradition and the Reality of Women," 117.

22. Ibid.

23. Boff, *Maternal Face of God,* 121.

24. See Moltmann-Wendel, "Motherhood or Friendship."

25. Augustine quoted in Newman, *New Eve*, 73.

26. Augustine, "De Verbis Evangelli matth., vers 41–50," in Migne, *PL* 46:937. The text reads: "Plus est felicius discipulam fuisse Christi, quam matrem fuisse Christi. Ideo Maria beata erat, quia, et antequam pareret, magistrum in utero portavit."

27. See Patrick Bearsley, "Mary the Perfect Disciple: A Paradigm for Mariology," *Theological Studies* 41 (1980): 461–504. I am especially indebted to this article and to Elizabeth Johnson's text cited above.

28. McHugh, *Mother of Jesus*, 153.

29. Newman, *New Eve*, 44.

30. Quoted in Maloney, *Mary, the Womb of God*, 172.

31. Newman, *New Eve*, 39.

32. Peter Brown, *The Cult of the Saints: Its Rise and Function in Latin Christianity* (Chicago: University of Chicago Press, 1981), 6. Brown explores Latin patronage and devotion to the saints with sympathetic insight and vast erudition.

33. Maloney, *Mary, the Womb of God*, 172–173.

34. Paragraph 62.

35. Newman, *New Eve*, 42.

36. See Anthony J. Tambasco, *What Are They Saying About Mary?* (New York: Paulist, 1984), 69.

37. "Woman Listening" (unpublished) in Sara Maitland, *A Map of the New Country: Women and Christianity* (London: Routledge and Paul, 1983), 185.

38. Jaroslav Pelikan, *Mary: Image of the Mother of Jesus in Jewish and Christian Perspective* (Philadelphia: Fortress Press, 1986), 85.

39. See Bertrand de Margerie, "Ecumenical Problems in Mariology," *Marian Studies* 26 (1975): 180–203. In this article, which I think suffers from some exaggeration, an account of eastern prayer *for* Mary is given. I am indebted to the author.

40. Augustine, *Confessions*, Book 11, Paragraph 13. The Latin reads: "anni tui dies unus, et dies tuus non cotidie, sed hodie. . . . " *Cotidie* is a variant of *quotidie*, which is composed of two words, *quot dies*, meaning so many days or everyday.

41. Augustine, "Letter to Lady Proba," #130, *Fathers of the Church*, vol. 18 (New York: Newman Press, 1953).

42. See Tambasco, *What Are They Saying About Mary?* 69–70.

43. Desiderius Erasmus, "Votive Ode," in Therese Lentfoehr, ed., *I Sing of a Maiden* (New York: Macmillan, 1947), 120.

44. *The Way of a Pilgrim*, trans. R. M. French (New York: Seabury, 1965).

45. Karl Rahner, *Mary, Mother of the Lord*, trans. W. F. O'Hara (New York: Herder and Herder, 1963), 62.

46. See also 2 Pt 3:10; Mt 24:43; and Rev 3:3.

47. Jean Sulivan, *Morning Light: The Spiritual Journal of Jean Sulivan*, trans. Joseph Cunneen and Patrick Gormally (New York: Paulist, 1988), 63.

48. Caterina Halkes, "Mary and Women," in *Mary in the Churches*, 66–74.

49. The *Transitus Mariae* gives an account of a new burial grave, the assumption of Mary with the coming of Jesus, whom she yearned to be with, to escort her to heaven. The History of Joseph the Carpenter tells of the death and assumption of Joseph. Both of these works are found in the early apocrypha. See Jacques Hervieux, ed., *The New Testament Apocrypha*, trans. Dom Wulstan Hibberd (New York: Hawthorn, 1960).

50. Justin Martyr, "First Apology," Paragraph 65, in *Justin Martyr: Fathers of the Church*, trans. Thomas Falls (New York: Christian Heritage, 1948).

Final Words

1. Mary as "memory of the Church," attributed to a sermon by John Paul II as quoted in Hans Urs von Balthasar, *Mary for Today*, trans. Robert Nowell (San Francisco: Ignatius Press, 1987), 35.

2. Ben Witherington, III, *Women in the Ministry of Jesus* (Cambridge: Cambridge University Press, 1984), 99–100.

3. Augustine, *The Confessions*, chapter 1.

4. *The Iliad; or the Poem of Force*, trans. Mary McCarthy (New York: Politics, 1947).

5. *Till We Have Faces A Myth Retold* (London: G. Bles, 1956).

6. Richard Rohr, "The Church Without Mary," in *Mary, the Spirit and the Church*, ed. Vincent P. Branick (Ramsey, N.J.: Paulist, 1980), 7–27. Rohr quotes from *Narcissus and Goldmund*, trans. Ursule Molinaro (New York: Farrar, Strauss and Giroux, 1968), 314–315.

7. Stefano Apicella, *Le Glorie della Vergine-Madre nella Salutazione Angelica* (Cava dei Tirreni: Stab. Tip del Populo, 1885), xix.

8. I am indebted to Rene Laurentin's writings for this idea, though I have seen it mentioned by other authors.

9. Tambasco, *What Are They Saying About Mary?* 75.

10. Boff, *Maternal Face of God*, 101.

11. *Poems and Prose of Gerard Manley Hopkins* (Harmondsworth: Penguin, 1953), 27.

12. See Gebara and Bingemer, *Mary, Mother of God, Mother of the Poor*; Jegen, *Mary According to Women*, and Brennan, *The Sacred Memory of Mary*.

13. Newman, *New Eve*, 49.

14. Edward Schillebeeckx, *Mary, Mother of the Redemption* (London: Sheed and Ward, 1964), 164–171.

15. Quoted in Klaver, *Litany of Loreto*, 220.

16. See Patricia Noone, *Mary for Today* (Chicago: Thomas More Press, 1977).

17. Apicella, *Le Glorie della Vergine-Madre*, 387.

BIBLIOGRAPHY OF THE AVE MARIA

An asterisk signifies a book that I found particularly helpful in this work.

BIBLICAL STUDIES

Mary in the New Testament

*Brown, Raymond, K. P. Donfried, J. A. Fitzmyer, and J. Reumann. *Mary in the New Testament: A Collaborative Assessment by Protestant and Roman Catholic Scholars.* Philadelphia: Fortress Press, 1978.

McHugh, John. *The Mother of Jesus in the New Testament.* Garden City, N.Y.: Doubleday, 1975.

Mary in the First Chapter of Luke

*Brown, Raymond. *The Birth of the Messiah: A Commentary on the Infancy Narratives in Matthew and Luke.* New York: Doubleday, 1977.

Fitzmyer, Joseph. *The Gospel According to Luke I-IX.* Anchor Bible, vol. 28. New York: Doubleday, 1981.

Marshall, I. Howard. *The Gospel of Luke: A Commentary on the Greek Text.* Grand Rapids, Mich.: Eerdmans, 1978.

Plummer, Alfred. *A Critical and Exegetical Commentary on the Gospel According to Saint Luke.* Edinburgh: T. and T. Clark, 1901.

HISTORICAL STUDIES

Giamberardini, Gabriele. *Il Culto Mariano in Egitto.* Vol. 1. Pubblicazioni dello Studium Biblicum Franciscanum, Analecta 6. Jerusalem: Franciscan Printing Press, 1975. See pages 69–97 and 224–238 in particular.

*Graef, Hilda. *Mary: A History of Doctrine and Devotion.* New York: Sheed and Ward, 1963. See pages 229–233 in particular. See also her shorter version, *The Devotion to Our Lady.* New York: Hawthorn, 1963.

Laurenceau, Jean. "Les Débuts de la Recitation Privée de L'Antienne Ave Maria en Occident avant la Fin du 11th Siècle." In *De Cultu Mariano Saeculis VI-XI: Acta Congressus Mariologici Mariani Internationalis in Croatia anno 1971 celebrati.* Rome: Pontificia Academia Mariana Internationalis, 1972. See pages 231–246.

Lazzarini, P. *Il Saluto dell'Angelo: Studio Storico, Critico, Esegetico dell' Ave Maria.* Milan: Editori Daverio, 1972.

*Martins Terra, J. E. "A Ave Maria à Luz do Antigo Testamento." In *A Oração no Antigo Testamento.* São Paulo: Ediçoes Loyola, 1974. See pages 191–221 in particular.

Montagna, Davide. "La Formula dell' Ave Maria a Vicenza in un Documento dell 1423." *Marianum* 26 (1964). See pages 234–236.

Roschini, P. Gabriele M. "L'Ave Maria." *Marianum* 5 (1943): 177–185.

Thurston, Herbert. "Our Popular Devotions: The Angelus." *The Month* 97 (1901): 483–499. This article, which is preliminary to an extented treatment of the Angelus, is concerned with the Hail Mary.

*Thurston, Herbert. "The Origins of the Hail Mary." In *Familiar Prayers: Their Origin and History.* London: Burns & Oates, 1953. See pages 90–114 in particular. This material first appeared serially in "The Origins of the Hail Mary," *The Month* 121 (February 1913): 162–176, and "The Second Part of the Hail Mary," *The Month* 121 (April 1913): 379–384. It was republished with some additions from his unpublished notes in the book cited above after the author's death in 1939.

Wilkins, Eithne. *The Rose-Garden Game: A Tradition of Beads and Flowers.* New York: Herder and Herder, 1969. See pages 64–79 in particular.

LITURGICAL STUDIES

Barre, Henri. "La Liturgie Romaine." In *Prières Anciennes de L'Occident a la Mère du Sauveur.* Paris: P. Lethielleux, 1963. See also "Sancta Maria, Ora pro Nobis."

Brightman, Frank E., editor. *Liturgies Eastern and Western.* Compiled by Charles Edward Hammond. Oxford: Clarendon, 1896. See pages 56, 128, and 218 in particular.

Crum, Walter E., editor. *Coptic Ostraca.* London: Kegan, Paul, 1902. See page 3 and the introduction in particular.

Giamberardini, Gabriele. *Il Culto Mariano in Egitto.* Vol. 1. Pubblicazioni dello Studium Biblicum Franciscanum, Analecta 6. Jerusalem: Franciscan Printing Press, 1975.

Hamman, Adalbert, editor. *Early Christian Prayers.* Trans. Walter
Mitchell. Chicago: Henry Regnery, 1961. See pages 76–77 in particular.

PATRISTIC COMMENTARIES

I know of no Patristic commentaries on the Ave Maria as such. Any
commentary on the Gospel of Luke, however, would comment upon
the salutation of Gabriel and of Elizabeth, which made up the Ave Maria
as it was generally known and recited until the end of the Middle Ages.

MEDIEVAL COMMENTARIES

Aquinas, Thomas. *The Catechetical Instructions of St. Thomas Aquinas.*
Trans. Joseph Collins. New York: J. F. Wagner, 1939.
Aquinas, Thomas. *The Three Greatest Prayers: Commentaries on the Our
Father, the Hail Mary, and the Apostles' Creed.* Trans. Laurence Shap-
cote. London: Burns, Oates, & Washburne, 1937.
Baldwin, Abbot of Canterbury. "De Salutatione Angelica." In Migne, *PL*
204: 467–478. English translation in *Spiritual Tractates*, vol. 1. Trans.
David N. Bell. Cistercian Fathers Series 38. Kalamazoo: Cistercian
Publications, 1986.
Mechtild of Hackenborn. *The Booke of Gostlye Grace.* Ed. Theresa Halli-
gan. Toronto: Pontifical Institute of Medieval Studies, 1979.
Waldeby, John. *John Waldeby, O.S.A.,c. 1315–c. 1372: English Augustinian
Preacher and Writer; with a Critical Edition of His Tract on the "Ave
Maria."* Critical edition by Margaret Josephine Morrin. Rome:
Analecta Augustiniana, 1975. This book is a reprint of articles
appearing in *Analecta Augustiniana* 35 (1972): 7–80; 36 (1973):
5–79; 37 (1974): 162–198.

MODERN COMMENTARIES

*Apicella, Stefano. *Le Glorie della Vergine-Madre nella Salutazione Angelica.*
Cava dei Tirreni: Stab. Tip del Populo, 1885.
*Boff, Leonardo. *A Ave-Maria: O Feminio e o Espirito Santo.* Petropolis:
Vozes, 1980.
de Beaulieu, Ernest-Maria. *Mois de Marie des Amis de St. Francis: L'Ave
Maria Commenté.* Arras: Brunet, 1936.
Diether, Lawrence. *Ave Maria: A Short Commentary on the Hail Mary.*
Chicago: Carmelite Press, 1934.

Fritsch, Ad. *La Vierge Marie dans les Prières Liturgiques.* Paris: Rene Hatron, 1896.

Girardey, Ferreol. *"The Mother of My Lord": Or an Explanation of the Hail Mary.* St. Louis, Mo.: B. Herder, 1921.

Laborde, J. *L'Ave Maria ou Excellence de la Salutation Angélique.* Paris: Retaux-Bray, 1888.

Lawrence of Brindisi. *La Madonna nell'Ave Maria e nella Salve Regina.* Roma: Libreria Mariana Editrice, 1959. Saint Lawrence was a sixteenth-century doctor of the Church.

Lazzarini, P. *Il Saluto dell'Angelo: Studio Storico, Critico, Esegetico dell' Ave Maria.* Milan: Editori Daverio, 1972.

Le Buffe, Francis Peter. *Our Father, Hail Mary.* New York: America Press, 1931.

*Martins Terra, J. E. "A Ave Maria à Luz do Antigo Testamento." In *A Oração no Antigo Testamento.* São Paulo: Ediçoes Loyola, 1974. See pages 191–221 in particular.

Occhiuzzo di Cedraro, Vito. *Il Negozio de' Secoli: Compendiate nell'Angelico Saluton o Sia Lezioni Teologiche, Scritturali, e Morali sulla Spiega dell'Ave Maria.* Naples: Barnaba Cons., 1816.

Pedro Barona de Valdivieso. *Tractado sobre el Ave Maria.* Salamanca: Renaut, 1596.

Raimond, Joseph. *Ave Maria.* Langres: Ami du Clerge, 1961.

Roschini, Gabriele. *Ma Mère!* Sherbrooke: Apostolat de la Press, 1957.

*Savonarola, Jerome. *The Lord's Prayer and the Angelical Salutation.* London: Catholic Truth Society, 1899. See also *Marian Library Studies* 10 (1978): 81–129.

Val D'Eremao. *The Hail Mary: Or, Popular Instructions and Considerations on the Angelical Salutation.* London: Burns and Oates, 1891.

Vandeur, Eugene. *Hail Mary.* Trans. John H. Collins. Westminster, Md.: Newman Press, 1954.

Van Zeller, Hubert. *Our Lady in Other Words: A Presentation for Beginners.* Springfield, Ill.: Templegate, 1963.

Westerveld, Ivo. *A "Ave Maria" Meditata e Explicada.* Petropolis: Vozes, 1955.

ENCYCLOPEDIA ARTICLES

(All of these articles contain further bibliography)

*The Catholic Encyclopedia, 7:110–112, s.v. "Hail Mary" by Herbert Thurston.

The New Catholic Encyclopedia, 1:1123. s.v. "Ave Maria" by R. Steiner and 6:898, s.v. "Hail Mary," by A. A. DeMarco.

Dictionnaire d'Archéologie Chrétienne et de Liturgie, 10:2043–2062, s.v. "Marie" (Je vous salue) by H. Leclercq.

Dictionnaire de Spiritualité, 1:1162–1166, s.v., "Ave Maria" by Herbert Thurston.

Dictionnaire de Théologie Catholique, 1:1274–1278, s.v. "Angelique" (salutation) by U. Berlière.

Enciclopedia Cattolica, 2:511–515, s.v. "Ave Maria" by Igino Cecchetti.

*Nuovo Dizionario di Mariologia, 1137–47. Ed. S. De Fiores and S. Meo. Milano: Edizioni Paoline, 1985. S.v. "Preghiera Mariana" by E. Lodi.

Theotokos: A Theological Encyclopedia of the Blessed Virgin Mary, 165–166, s.v. "Hail Mary" by Michael O'Carroll.

SELECTED BIBLIOGRAPHY OF BOOKS
IN ENGLISH ABOUT MARY

A comprehensive Marian bibliography would be enormous. I have therefore listed the books in English that I have used and found helpful in preparation for my writing on the Ave Maria. An asterisk signifies a book that I found particularly helpful. Many books about Mary prior to Vatican II remain valuable, but because of the contemporary scriptural critique I have been more selective. I have not listed some of the large Mariology studies, such as Matthias Scheeben, *Mariology* (2 vols.), or Juniper Carol, *Mariology* (3 vols.). These books have their place in a more comprehensive review of Marian studies than I have undertaken here. The post–Vatican II studies of Mary are not numerous, and I have included the most important ones available in English.

In an effort to find selections for a bibliography on the Ave Maria, I searched widely without encountering much writing by women on the subject of Mary of Nazareth. At first glance, this lack of material might seem due to the general lack of writing by women during the centuries when opportunity for education and publication greatly favored men. At second glance, however, it becomes clear that women writers were better represented on a topic such as the Eucharist than they were on the topic of Mary. Intermittent mention of Mary abounds in the theological literature by women, but substantial treatment is lacking. Catherine of Siena and Teresa of Avila, the two women doctors of the Church, have written nothing substantial about Mary that I could discover. There is no equivalent by a woman of the *Glories of Mary* by Alphonsus Liguori, or the *True Devotion to Mary* by Louis de Montfort. That women were in practice devoted to the Blessed Mother and were given to Marian prayer does not seem at issue. That they did not write about it remains a puzzle. Perhaps men were more fascinated with the mystery of Mary because more fascinated with the mystery of women. Accordingly, women themselves did not write as much about Mary because the mystery of the feminine was not outside their experience. In the index of authors in Hilda Graef's comprehensive two-volume *History of Doctrine and Devotion* I could find only a handful of female names in a list which counted hundreds of writers. Women writers on the topic of Mary since Vatican II have been somewhat more numerous. Anne Carr, Agnes Cunningham, Carol Frances Jegen, Elizabeth Johnson, Patricia Noone, and Rosemary Ruether come to mind in this country as leaders in the renewal of the doctrine of Mary.

Allchin, A. M. *The Joy of All Creation: An Anglican Meditation on the Place of Mary.* London: Darton, Longman and Todd, 1984. English poetry from Traherne to T. S. Eliot.

American Bishops. "Behold Your Mother: Woman of Faith." Pastoral Letter. Washington, D.C.: USCC, 1973.

Ashe, Geoffrey. *The Virgin.* London: Routledge and Kegan Paul, 1976.

Attwater, Donald. *A Dictionary of Mary.* New York: Kenedy, 1956.

Balthasar, Hans Urs von. *Mary for Today.* Trans. Robert Nowell. San Francisco: Ignatius Press, 1987.

Behringer, William. *Mary and the Beatitudes.* New York: Alba House, 1964.

*Benko, Stephen. *Protestants, Catholics, and Mary.* Valley Forge, Penn.: Judson Press, 1968.

*Boff, Leonardo. *The Maternal Face of God: The Feminine and its Religious Expressions.* Trans. Robert R. Barr and John W. Diercksmeier. San Francisco: Harper and Row, 1987.

Bouyer, Louis. *The Seat of Wisdom: An Essay on the Place of the Virgin Mary in Christian Theology.* Trans. A. V. Littledale. New York: Pantheon Books, 1962.

Branick, Vincent, editor. *Mary, the Spirit and the Church.* Ramsey, N.J.: Paulist, 1980.

*Braun, F. M. *Mother of God's People.* Trans. John Clark. New York: Alba House, 1967. Mariology in the Gospel of John.

*Brennan, Walter. *The Sacred Memory of Mary.* New York: Paulist, 1988.

Brookby, Peter, editor. *Virgin Wholly Marvelous: Praise of Our Lady by the Popes, Councils, Saints, and Doctors of the Church.* Cambridge: Ravengate, 1981.

*Brown, Raymond. *The Birth of the Messiah: A Commentary on the Infancy Narratives in Matthew and Luke.* New York: Doubleday, 1977.

*Brown, Raymond, K. P. Donfried, J. A. Fitzmyer, and J. Reumann. *Mary in the New Testament: A Collaborative Assessment by Protestant and Roman Catholic Scholars.* Philadelphia: Fortress Press, 1978.

Bruns, J. Edgar. *God as Woman, Woman as God.* New York: Paulist, 1973.

*Buby, Bertrand. *Mary, the Faithful Disciple.* New York: Paulist Press, 1985.

Caretto, Carlo. *Blessed Are You Who Believed.* Trans. Barbara Wall. Maryknoll, N.Y.: Orbis Books, 1983.

Carroll, Eamon R. *Understanding the Mother of Jesus.* Wilmington, Del.: Michael Glazier, 1979.

Carroll, Michael P. *The Cult of the Virgin Mary: Psychological Origins.* Princeton: Princeton University Press, 1986.

Congar, Yves. *Christ, Our Lady, and the Church: A Study in Eirenic Theology.* Trans. Henry St. John. Westminster, Md.: Newman, 1957.

*Cunningham, Agnes. *The Significance of Mary.* Chicago: Thomas More Press, 1988.

Cunningham, Lawrence. *Mother of God.* San Francisco: Harper and Row, 1982.

*Daniel-Rops, Henri. *The Book of Mary.* Trans. Alistair Guinan. New York: Hawthorn, 1960. Historical Review with apocryphal texts included.

Donnelly, Doris, editor. *Mary, Woman of Nazareth: Biblical and Theological Perspectives.* New York: Paulist, 1989.

de Satge, John. *Down to Earth, The New Protestant Vision of the Virgin Mary,* Wilmington, N.C.: Consortium Books, 1976.

Deiss, Lucien. *Mary, Daughter of Sion.* Trans. Barbara Blair. Collegeville, Minn.: Liturgical Press, 1972.

Feuillet, Andre. *Jesus and His Mother According to the Lucan Infancy Narratives, and According to St. John: The Role of the Virgin Mary in Salvation History and the Place of Woman in the Church.* Trans. Leonard Maluf. Still River, Mass.: St. Bede's Publications, 1984.

Flanagan, Donal. *The Theology of Mary.* Dublin: Mercier Press, 1976.

Galot, Jean. *Mary in the Gospel.* Trans. Maria Constance. Westminster, Md.: Newman, 1965.

Gebara, Ivon, and Maria Bingemer. *Mary, Mother of God, Mother of the Poor.* Maryknoll, N.Y.: Orbis, 1989.

Graef, Hilda. *The Devotion to Our Lady.* New York: Hawthorne, 1963.

*Graef, Hilda. *Mary: A History of Docrine and Devotion.* 2 vols. New York: Sheed and Ward, 1963.

*Grassi, Joseph. *Mary, Mother and Disciple: From Scriptures to the Council of Ephesus.* Wilmington, Del.: Glazier, 1988.

Greeley, Andrew. *The Mary Myth: On the Femininity of God.* New York: Seabury Press, 1977.

Guitton, Jean. *The Virgin Mary.* Trans. A. Gordon Smith. New York: Kenedy, 1952.

*Houselander, Caryll. *The Reed of God.* New York: Sheed and Ward, 1944. A classic meditation.

Jegen, Carol Frances. *Mary According to Women.* Kansas City, Mo.: Leaven Press, 1985.

Jelly, Frederick. *Madonna: Mary in the Catholic Tradition.* Huntington, Ind.: Our Sunday Visitor, 1986.

John Paul II. *Mary: God's Yes to Man: Encyclical Letter, Mother of the Redeemer (Redemptoris Mater).* San Francisco: Ignatius Press, 1988.

Johnson, Ann. *Miryam of Judah: Witness in Truth and Tradition.* Notre Dame, Ind.: Ave Maria Press, 1987.

Johnson, Ann. *Miryam of Nazareth: Woman of Strength and Wisdom.* Notre Dame, Ind.: Ave Maria Press, 1984.

*Kenny, S.J., John Peter. *The Meaning of Mary for Modern Man.* Melbourne: Spectrum, 1980.

*Kung, Hans, and Jurgen Moltmann, editors. *Mary in the Churches.* Trans. Marcus Lefebure. New York: Seabury Press, 1983. Scholarly, challenging essays on the frontier of Mariology.

Laurentin, Rene. *The Question of Mary.* Trans. I. G. Pidoux. New York: Holt, Rinehart and Winston, 1965.

Lentfoehr, Sister Therese, editor. *I Sing of a Maiden: The Mary Book of Verse.* New York: Macmillan, 1947.

Maestri, William F. *Mary, Model of Justice.* New York: Alba House, 1987.

Malone, Mary T. *Who Is My Mother? Rediscovering the Mother of Jesus.* Dubuque: Wm. C. Brown, 1984.

Maloney, George. *Mary, the Womb of God.* Denville, N.J.: Dimension Books, 1976. Contains eastern Mariology.

Mary and the Popes: Five Great Marian Letters. New York: America Press, 1954.

McHugh, John, *The Mother of Jesus in the New Testament.* Garden City, N.Y.: Doubleday, 1975.

McNamara, Kevin. *Mother of the Redeemer.* New York: Sheed and Ward, 1960.

Mascall, E. L., and H. S. Box, editors. *The Blessed Virgin Mary: Essays by Anglican Writers.* London: Darton, Longman, and Todd, 1963.

Maus, Cynthia. *The World's Great Madonnas.* New York: Harper, 1947.

Moloney, Francis. *Mary: Woman and Mother.* Collegeville, Minn.: Liturgical Press, 1988.

*Newman, John Henry. *The New Eve.* Westminster, Md.: Newman, 1952.

*Noone, Patricia. *Mary for Today.* Chicago: Thomas More Press, 1977.

O'Carroll, Michael. *Theotokos: A Theological Encyclopedia of the Blessed Virgin Mary.* Wilmington, Del.: Michael Glazier, 1982.

O'Meara, Thomas. *Mary in Protestant and Catholic Theology.* New York: Sheed and Ward, 1966.

*Palmer, Paul. *Mary in the Documents of the Church.* Westminster, Md.: Newman, 1952.

*Paul VI. *Marialis Cultus: Papal Exhortation.* Washington, D.C.: USCC, 1974.

Pelikan, Jaroslav, David Flusser, and Justin Lang. *Mary: Image of the Mother of Jesus in Jewish and Christian Perspective.* Philadelphia: Fortress Press, 1986.

Pennington, Basil. *Mary Today: The Challenging Woman.* Garden City, N.Y.: Doubleday, 1987.

Perrin, Joseph Marie. *Mary, Mother of Christ and of Christians.* Trans. Jean David Finley. New York: Alba House, 1978.

Rahner, Hugo. *Our Lady and the Church.* Trans. Sebastian Bullough. London: Darton, Longman, and Todd, 1961.

Rahner, Karl. *Mary, Mother of the Lord: Theological Meditations.* Trans. W. J. O'Hara. New York: Herder and Herder, 1963.

Ratzinger, Joseph. *Daughter of Zion: Meditations on the Church's Marian Belief.* Trans. John M. McDermott. San Francisco: Ignatius Press, 1983.

Rinaldi, Bonaventura, O.F.M. *Mary of Nazareth: Myth or History?* Trans. Mary F. Ingoldsby. Westminster, Md.: Newman, 1966.

Ruether, Rosemary. *Mary, The Feminine Face of the Church.* Philadelphia: Westminster Press, 1977.

Schillebeeckx, Edward, O.P. *Mary, Mother of the Redemption.* London: Sheed and Ward, 1964.

*Schillebeeckx, Edward, and Caterina Halkes. *Mary: Yesterday, Today, Tomorrow.* New York: Crossroad, 1993.

Semmelroth, Otto. *Mary, Archetype of the Church.* Trans. Maria von Eroes and John Devlin. New York: Sheed and Ward, 1963.

Sheed, Francis J., editor. *The Mary Book.* New York: Sheed and Ward, 1950.

Stacpoole, Alberic, editor. *Mary's Place in Christian Dialogue.* Wilton, Conn.: Morehouse-Barlow, 1983.

Suenens, Leon Joseph. *Mary, the Mother of God.* Translated by a nun of Stanbrook Abbey. New York: Hawthorn Books, 1959.

*Tambasco, Anthony. *What Are They Saying About Mary?* New York: Paulist, 1984.

*Thurian, Max. *Mary, Mother of the Lord, Figure of the Church.* Trans. Neville B. Cryer. London: Faith Press, 1963.

Vollert, Cyril. *A Theology of Mary.* New York: Herder and Herder, 1965.

Warner, Marina. *Alone of All Her Sex: The Myth and the Cult of the Virgin Mary.* New York: Knopf, 1976.